AF663881

Interest Rates, Prices, and the Economy

Jerry Mushin

Victoria University of Wellington,
New Zealand

SCIENTIFIC PUBLISHERS (INDIA)

P.O. BOX 91 JODHPUR (RAJ.)

Published by:
Tanay Sharma
Scientific Publishers (India)
5-A, New Pali Road, P.O. Box 91
Jodhpur - 342 001 (India)

Tel.: +91-291-2433323
Fax: + 91-291-2613449

E-mail: info@scientificpub.com
www.scientificpub.com

© Mushin, J., 2009

ISBN: 978-81-7233-576-2

Lasertype set: Rajesh Ojha
Printed in India

Preface

This book is intended to support an introductory undergraduate course in macroeconomics. It is aimed not only at students whose major subject is economics but also at other students who want to acquire some theoretical background to current economic issues. It is a revised and updated version, intended for the Indian market, of *Output and the Role of Money* (World Scientific Publishing Company, New York, London, and Singapore, 2002), which was aimed at the United States market, and which was based on *Income, Interest Rates and Prices* (Dunmore Press Ltd, Palmerston North, New Zealand, 1994, 1996, 1999). *Chan Chu He Huo Bi Jue Se Hong Guan Jing Ji Xue Xian Dai Guan Dian* (Hua Xia Chu Ban She, Beijing, China, 2004) is a Chinese translation of *Output and the Role of Money*.

No previous study of macroeconomics is assumed, though successful completion of an introductory course in microeconomics would be an advantage. Advanced mathematical skills are not needed, and calculus is not used.

Although this book refers to recent economic experience in India and in other countries, it is a textbook of macroeconomic theory and not a description of recent events. Use of it should therefore be supplemented with a study of applied material.

Acknowledgements

I am grateful to my colleagues who commented on earlier drafts of this book and its predecessors, especially Geoffrey Bertram, Penelope de Boer, Matthew Goodson, and Ganesh Nana, although they are not, of course, responsible for its remaining deficiencies. A special debt is to my students at Victoria University of Wellington, and at universities in the UK, who have asked penetrating questions on my lectures and have not been satisfied unless they received detailed and lucid answers. I also thank my wife Claudia and our son Stephen for their encouragement.

Contents

1

The Nature of Macroeconomic Issues

Macroeconomics is the study of the behaviour of the whole of an economic system, while microeconomics concentrates on its component parts. Microeconomists are concerned with the behaviour of individual households, firms, and industries, and with the output levels and prices of individual commodities. Macroeconomists analyse aggregates; they measure and attempt to understand fluctuations in the level of output and prices in the economy as a whole. Recent experience in India, and in other individual countries, is compared with experience in earlier years and in other comparable economies.

Macroeconomics is not, however, just about the recording of facts. If the determinants of fluctuations in aggregate variables can be understood, then it might be that they can be predicted, and also that governments who wish to influence the outcome can be offered useful policy advice.

The content of macroeconomics does not refer only to the level of aggregate output and the general level of prices. Other important variables include the volumes of imports and exports (and the prices of these), the amount and nature of taxation and of government spending, the unemployment rate, the rate of growth of the capital stock, the level of interest rates, the quantity of money in circulation, and the rates of exchange for the Indian rupee. All of these are influenced by decision-makers in both the government sector and the private sector.

Macroeconomic data enable trends in the whole of the economy to be observed, and in this sense provide more information than data relating to individual firms and households. Where some parts of the economy show non-typical behaviour, this is generally concealed by aggregate data. For example, fluctuations in the output figures of companies showing an unusually rapid growth rate will to some degree cancel with fluctuations in output of those companies showing a slower than average growth rate. By this means, issues concerning only a part of the economy do not constitute a distraction when considering the overall economic situation. In some cases, however, an industrial sector, or even a single firm, might be large enough to have a significant influence on the trend of aggregate data.

However, macroeconomic data, despite providing a global view of economic trends, have the disadvantage of a lower level of accuracy compared to data relating to individual firms and households. Combining sets of figures, each of which might be inaccurate, might lead to the compounding of errors.

Aggregate data might also, by concealing some of the detail of economic fluctuations, give a misleading impression of stability; for example, a stable figure for aggregate output can occur at a time when a large number of individual firms are showing significant rates of expansion or contraction. Average figures might also be deceptive; an increase in the amount of wealth per person, for example, does not necessarily mean that most people are getting richer. It might mean that a small number of rich people are getting richer faster than a larger number of poor people are getting poorer. It might even be true to state that the average amount of wealth per person is rising when the number of rich people is decreasing and the number of poor people is increasing.

Much of macroeconomic theory refers to equilibrium levels of important variables (including output, prices, interest rates). This is a critical concept. An equilibrium point is the point towards which the system is spontaneously moving. Movement towards the equilibrium might not be at a constant speed and it might not be by the shortest route. The equilibrium point might be overshot, and the error automatically corrected (though possibly after a delay). The definition of an equilibrium does not imply that this point is necessarily desirable. It also does not imply that the equilibrium point will be achieved quickly. Further, the position of the equilibrium point is likely to change, as circumstances change, and it might never be reached.

It is essential to understand the determinants of macroeconomic equilibria in order to be able to understand government policy designed to influence the aggregate economy. The government does not directly determine the macroeconomic outcome, but it can influence the equilibrium value of key variables, and the system will then spontaneously move towards this point. For example, the government is not in a position to specify the value of total output in the private sector, but it can stimulate increased production by paying more generous sums to unemployed and retired people, who will then be able to buy a greater quantity of goods and services, and firms will respond to this by increasing their output. It is the role of the macroeconomist to understand the precise relationship between the increase in government payments and the increase in output that follows.

Although there is general agreement on a large body of theory, disagreement among its practitioners is a feature of macroeconomics. Controversies are largely centred on policy objectives, the order in which they should be targeted, and the most effective means of reaching them. There are some economists who believe that the highest priority should be attached to reducing the rate of increase in the price level, and that once a fairly stable price level has been achieved the conditions will be right for other policy objectives, such as low unemployment, to be reached easily. Other economists believe that the social effects of a high level of unemployment make increased employment the most important objective. There are also controversies relating to the type of policy instrument chosen. Some economists favour changes in tax rates and in the amount of government spending, while others favour policies that affect the level of interest rates or of exchange rates. There are economists who advocate direct controls on, for example, the quantity of imports, the price of particular commodities, or increases in wage rates, while others believe that important gains in efficiency will result from severe reductions in the economic role of the government.

The choice of policy objectives is complicated by the fact that each aspect of the macroeconomy is related to many of the others. Reducing the severity of one problem will often lead to the worsening of another. For example, the restriction of imports in an attempt to stimulate increased purchases of Indian goods and hence decrease unemployment might lead to increases in the price level and, possibly, to retaliation from foreign governments.

Even when economists agree about policy objectives and the way to achieve them, they might disagree about the timing of the likely effects of a particular policy measure. Macroeconomists are interested not only in the events that are likely to occur in response to decisions, but also in how soon and in what order such events will be observed.

Analysis of macroeconomic policy is made more difficult by the interaction of politics and economics. Economic decisions might be made for political reasons and *vice versa*. Governments approaching an election might be tempted to devise a policy for short-term rather than long-term economic benefit. Further, as the political culture evolves, policies that were once popular might cease to be acceptable, even if they were clearly efficient. The extent of government intervention in the economies of many western European countries that was practised in the 1960s and 1970s, for example, is probably no longer generally acceptable even to most of the voters who support the objectives of this type of policy.

Measurement of Aggregate Output

A large part of macroeconomic theory deals with the analysis of changes in the level of total output in the economy, and of output in major sectors of the economy. In order to test the validity of theories, and to observe the effects of changing circumstances (including changes of government policy), information on developments in the economy is needed.

Output, as an economic concept, includes both goods and services. However, measurement of aggregate output ignores activity that is not paid for in money. This is not a moral judgement; it does not imply that people who care for their children, grow their own vegetables, or maintain their own cars are doing something that is without value to themselves and to the whole community. It merely implies that the amount and value of such activity is difficult to record, and probably does not vary much from one year to the next. The calculation of aggregate output also ignores, because of lack of information, illegal activity; this also is not a moral judgement. Finally, output is valued according to its current price. This again is not a moral judgement; a statistician who records the pay of a successful entertainer at a very much higher level than that of a nurse is doing no more than recording the actual outcome of the economic system.

The calculation of aggregate output ignores transfer payments. These are payments that are not made in return for work done. Purchases of second-hand goods, and also gifts, inheritances, and gambling winnings are examples of transfer payments and so are not included in calculations of aggregate output. Also ignored are transfer payments by the government, as no work is done in return for them; these include social security payments.

Table 1 illustrates the relationships between the some of the macroeconomic aggregates for which Indian data are available.

TABLE 1. GDP in India, 2006–07

		Rs. Crore
Private final consumption (*C*)		2312105
Gross fixed capital formation		1346501
Change in stocks	96103	
Gross private domestic investment (*I*)		1442604
Valuables (net acquisition)		49709
Exports of goods and services (*X*)	915674	
Imports of goods and services (*Z*)	–1040797	
Net exports of goods and services		–125123
Government final consumption expenditure (*G*)		427007
Discrepancy	39508	
Gross Domestic Product		**4145810**

Source: Ministry of Statistics and Programme Implementation, India
The financial year in India begins on 1 April.

Since all output is paid for, its value can be recorded either by measuring the sum paid by the buyer or by measuring the sum received by the seller. If the collection of data has been both accurate and complete, then these two figures will be identical.

Table 1 shows Indian data based on the expenditure calculation. To avoid multiple counting of the same output, only purchases of final output are recorded; all payments for intermediate goods (including raw materials, components, fuel) are ignored. For example, the total includes what customers paid for their purchases of jam, but not the value of the sugar and of the fruit and of the glass jars and of the paper labels bought by the jam manufacturer. The final price paid for jam includes the value of its ingredients.

The alternative way to calculate total output avoiding multiple counting is to measure the value added of each company. A business buys inputs that have been produced by other businesses, and then processes them, and sells the processed output at a price that is high enough to meet production costs and generate some profit. For example, a jam producer buys sugar, fruit, and other inputs from other firms, and then sells the jam to provide sufficient sales revenue to pay for inputs from other firms and for wages, rent, interest, and an acceptable amount of profit. The difference between what the jam firm pays for its inputs and what it receives in revenue, its value added, may be regarded as a measure of its production activity. The total of all firms' value added measures aggregate output.

Expenditure on final output is categorised according to the nature of the final customer. The first item in the table is private final consumption. This means purchases by people in India of goods and services for immediate use; it includes, for example, payments for food, clothing, fuel, entertainment, rent, and hairdressing. This is a large part of the total; a very significant part of economic activity in India is directed, ultimately, towards the production of goods and services for consumption in India.

The second item in the list is gross private domestic investment. This means payment for work to be done now from which the benefit is likely to be received in the longer term. Investment may also be defined as increases in the stock of capital in the economy, or as increases in the capacity of the economy to produce output. It principally means the construction of new buildings and new machinery. This is called gross fixed capital formation (or fixed investment). Investment also includes the net increase in the physical amount of stocks (or inventories) held by businesses; this includes stocks of raw materials and fuel (awaiting use), work in progress, and stocks of finished goods (awaiting sale). The third category of investment, for which separate data are not available, is investment in human capital, which means expenditure on education and training. Investment expenditure may be also divided into capital deepening (increasing the amount of capital per worker) and capital widening (providing capital for additional workers following an increase in the population or in the labour participation rate). Capital deepening increases technical efficiency but capital widening does not.

Investment expenditure does not include purchases of second-hand equipment. This is neither a part of current output nor does it represent an increase in the amount of output that the economy as a whole can produce. Measurement of aggregate output is not concerned with changes in the ownership of existing assets.

The level of investment is of importance because it indicates the potential for long-term growth in the level of output. If investment is low, then increased output in future years will be difficult or impossible.

The third item is net acquisition of valuables. This includes gold, gems, precious stones, jewellery, and some part of silver. This expenditure should perhaps be included in the total of investment because it represents expenditure on production of goods that will be of long-term benefit to the buyer. This category does not appear in the national accounts data of the UK, the United States, New Zealand, and other countries.

The fourth item is net exports. This is the difference between exports (the value of goods and services produced in India and sold in other countries) and imports (the value of goods and services produced in other countries and sold in India). A positive figure indicates that the value of exports is greater than the value of imports, and *vice versa*. The sum of money paid for exports must be included in the total value of output because it represents payments for work done in India. Payments for imports represent work done in other countries, so must not be included. Such payments are subtracted from the total because they have already been included in the figures for consumption, investment, valuables, and government spending, all of which include payments for a substantial amount of intermediate goods (raw materials, components, machinery, fuel, etc.) and services that were purchased from other countries.

The next item is government spending on consumption. This refers to payments by national, state, and local government in India. The figure comprises payments by government bodies for goods and services (education, police, roads, water supply, sewage disposal, armed forces, etc.) but, since the object of this exercise is to compute the value of output in the current year, it does not include government transfer payments (including social security payments). It is therefore not the same as total government spending in a budgetary sense.

The total of the figures is Gross Domestic Product (GDP). This is a measure of the value of goods and services produced within the boundaries of India in a twelve-month period. An alternative measure of aggregate output is Gross National Product (GNP). This includes the factor income (wages, rent, interest, profit) accruing to the residents of India from economic activity in other countries. Factor income that is generated in India but paid to people in other countries is subtracted.

GDP and GNP are measures of the amount of output produced in a country in a year. Unfortunately, the capital stock is slowly deteriorating, and so some of this year's production must be used to repair or replace existing equipment (including buildings) and therefore is not available for disposal. Gross output is converted to net output by subtracting the value of capital consumption, which is the amount of equipment that has fallen out of use during the year. It is impossible to calculate the value of capital consumption directly, so depreciation is used as a proxy. Depreciation is a figure calculated (using various formulae) by accountants, and is a measure of the decline in the value of capital assets. Subtraction of depreciation from GNP gives Net National Product (NNP).

When macroeconomists refer to income they mean National Income, which is a measure of the value of the total output of goods and services that is produced in the economy. National Income is the total income (wages, rent, interest, profit) received by the producers of goods and services. If the data have been collected accurately, National Income will be equal to Net National Product, which is a measure of the amount of resources that are available for disposal without reducing the existing stock of assets. The value of the discrepancy that is included in Table 1 is the difference between these two measured figures. The size of this discrepancy is of no importance. It is not an indication of the degree of accuracy in the data; it is just the difference between one inaccurate figure and another inaccurate figure. A small discrepancy merely indicates that both figures are equally inaccurate.

Data are also available that categorise GDP not according to the final customers of the output, but in two other ways. The value of aggregate output may be analysed according to who has benefited from the productive process. The principal distinction is between those who are employed and those who receive profit. Employees' income includes payments both to manual and to managerial and professional workers, and also to self-employed people. Profit is paid to the owners of businesses. Finally, aggregate output may be allocated to industrial groups. This identifies the relative importance in the economy of farming, manufacturing, transport, education, health care, financial services, etc. in the economy.

Aggregate output is measured by several methods for two reasons. First, economists are interested not only in the total value of output, but also in how it is distributed among types of buyer and types of industry and in how its benefit is shared between labour and the owners of businesses. Second, the additional calculations also provide further estimates of what is probably a very inaccurate total.

It is not easy to estimate the accuracy of the published figures relating to aggregate output. The definitions chosen include only those goods and services that are paid for, and exclude illegal activity. The problem is, however, not purely a matter of definition. The data are calculated from information provided by companies and by individuals, and it is likely that not all of this information is accurate. Some is used in tax calculations, and tax-payers might have an incentive to conceal some of their income. There might also be genuine errors. In addition, it might be difficult to allocate production to the correct year.

At each stage of the calculation, errors are likely to be increased. For example, depreciation (an inaccurate figure) is subtracted from Gross National Product (another inaccurate figure) to calculate Net National Product (which is therefore an even more inaccurate figure).

The uncertain level of accuracy of GDP data does not make their production useless. It is better to have inaccurate figures than no figures at all. In addition, the figures, which are in millions of crores of rupees, are so large as to be difficult to understand, and what really matter are comparisons with earlier years. Such comparisons can be made even if the figures are not accurate, provided that the percentage error in each year's figures is approximately the same, which is probably a reasonable assumption.

A further complication is that the unit of measurement, the Indian rupee, does not have a constant value. As the general level of prices rises, a larger number of rupees is needed to buy the same quantity of output. During a period of rising prices, therefore, increases in GDP are not a useful measure of increases in output unless an allowance has been made for changes in the price level. In order to make valid comparisons between aggregate output levels in different years, data at current prices (nominal GDP) need to be converted to data at constant prices (real GDP). This calculation involves the making of an estimate of what each year's output would have cost had prices not changed from those that applied in some earlier reference year. This conversion injects an additional inaccuracy into the figures.

Figure 1 shows the importance of using real GDP data in preference to nominal GDP data. The trend of real GDP shows that the rate of increase in Indian output measured by the nominal GDP data from 1987 to 2007 is distorted by changes in the price level. Increases in GDP are much less impressive once the effects of changes in the price level have been removed. Although this is not shown in Table 1, it is possible, during a period of rising prices, that nominal GDP increases while real GDP decreases.

Macroeconomic Models

Economists present their theoretical ideas in the form of models. A model is a simplified description of an aspect of the real world, and is usually expressed in an algebraic or diagrammatic form. Reality is often too complex to be readily understandable, but a model based on strong assumptions about certain aspects of economic behaviour enables the analysis of other aspects to become manageable. As these assumptions are relaxed, the model becomes more complex but more closely related to the real world.

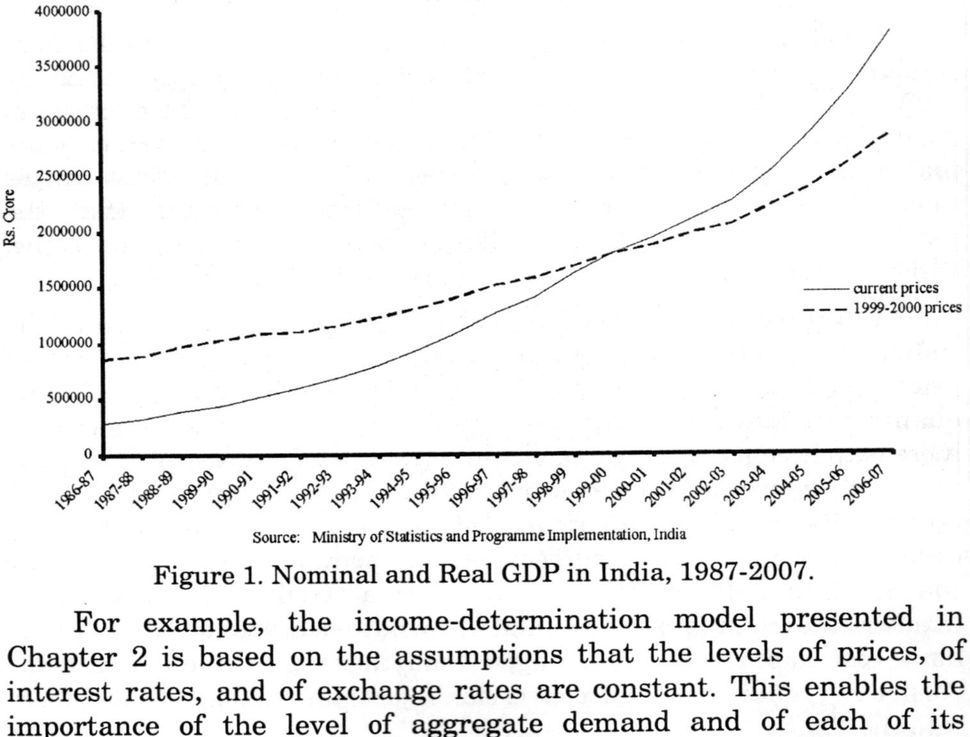

Source: Ministry of Statistics and Programme Implementation, India

Figure 1. Nominal and Real GDP in India, 1987-2007.

For example, the income-determination model presented in Chapter 2 is based on the assumptions that the levels of prices, of interest rates, and of exchange rates are constant. This enables the importance of the level of aggregate demand and of each of its components to be demonstrated. The model is then enhanced by the addition of a variable level of interest rates in Chapter 3, a variable price level in Chapter 8, and a variable exchange rate in Chapters 11 and 12.

A successful model is one that assists in the understanding and prediction of economic behaviour. In all cases the assumptions of a model are important; a theory is only as valid as the premises upon which it is based.

2

Determinants and Significance of Aggregate Demand

The theory of income determination is derived from the work of John Maynard Keynes (1883-1946) whose principal book is *The General Theory of Employment, Interest, and Money* (1936). This approach concentrates on the importance of the level of aggregate demand, which is the quantity of newly produced goods and services that individuals and corporate bodies wish to buy, and are able to pay for, at current prices. Firms respond to changes in the level of aggregate demand; the greater the quantity that people try to buy the greater will be the quantity that producers aim to produce. In order to understand fluctuations in the level of output, therefore, it is necessary to understand changes in the level of aggregate demand. At this stage, prices, interest rates, and exchange rates are assumed to be constant.

Aggregate demand, which government statisticians record as total final expenditure, is partly determined by the level of income. An increase in income means that people can afford to buy more goods and services. The precise nature of this relationship varies between sectors of the economy. A change in aggregate demand will lead to a change in output (and, therefore, income) which will lead to a further change in demand, and then to a further change in output, and so on. This extended process means that a change in the level of aggregate demand in the economy will have a final effect that is very much greater than the initial disturbance. This is called the multiplier process.

A convenient model to illustrate this is the circular flow of income, which is shown in a simplified form in Figure 2. This shows flows of money between the major sectors in the economy. Flows within each sector are ignored; this includes purchases of intermediate goods by one firm from another.

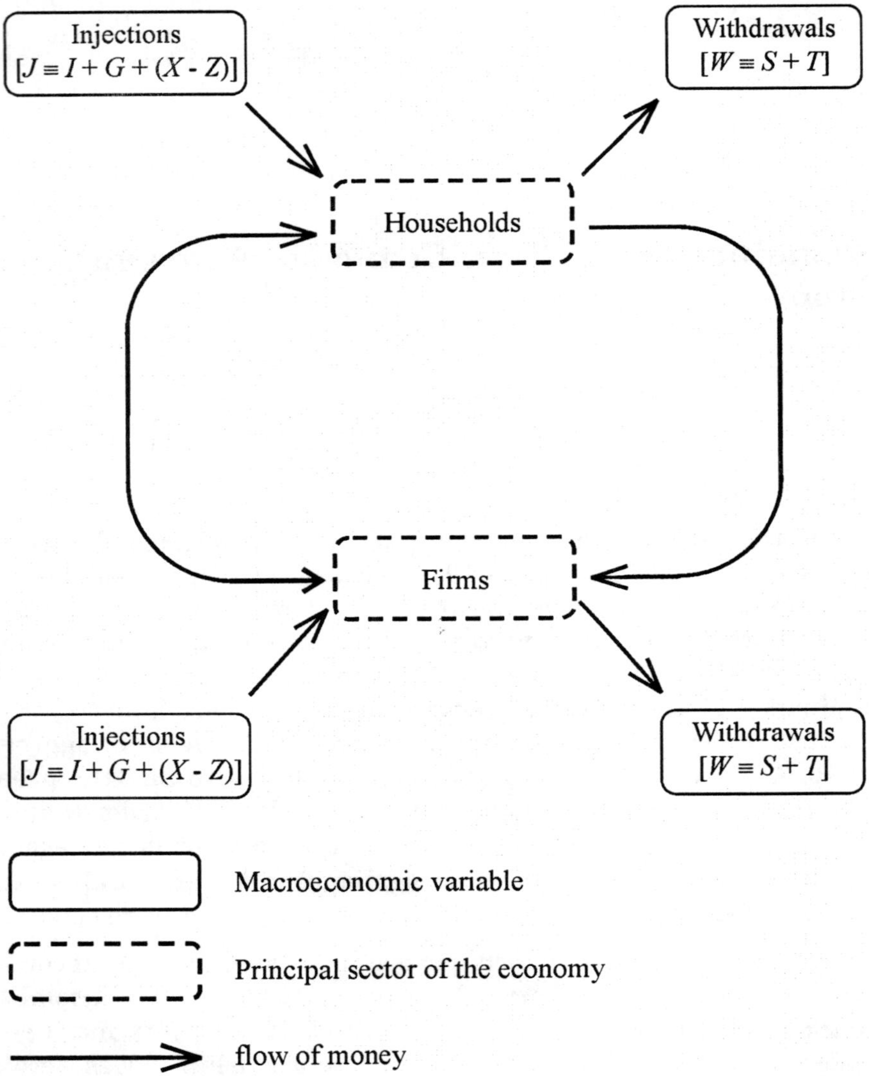

Figure. 2. The Circular Flow of Income

The main flows are between households and firms. These may be regarded as the two principal sectors in this model. Households buy newly produced goods and services from firms, and receive from firms payments for factor services. Factor payments comprise wages, salaries, and professional fees (for labour), rent (for the use of land), interest (for the use of capital), and profit (to the owners of businesses). The immediate receivers of rent, interest, and profit may be companies, but the ultimate owners of all firms are households, so this is the sector to which such payments finally accrue.

Money flows from households to firms, and back to firms, and then back to households, and so on. If households receive more from firms, they can pay more to firms; and if firms receive more from households, they can pay more to households. This means that a firm that sells more goods than it expected is likely to increase production, which means that a greater sum will be paid as wages to its employees, which enables them to buy a greater quantity of goods from firms, which will encourage firms to increase the level of output further. The reverse is also true; if a firm finds that its sales are decreasing, it will probably decrease production, thus decreasing wage payments, which will decrease the amount that its employees can spend on output, which will lead to a further cut in production, and so on. Purchases of output by households using current receipts from firms are called consumption.

Components of Income and Expenditure

It might be that not all of the money that households receive from firms is returned to firms, and that not all of the money that firms receive from households is returned to households. That part of money flows that one of these sectors receives from the other but does not pay back to the other in the current period is called withdrawals. The two categories of withdrawals are savings and taxation.

Savings refers to deferred consumption. It is that part of income that could have been spent but, in order to enable spending to occur in some future period, was not. Both companies and individuals save; company savings may be called retained profits. Savings might be negative; this implies the running down of existing assets. When this happens spending is greater than current income.

Taxation means compulsory payments to the government. It does not refer to purchases of services from the government. There are two broad types of taxation: direct taxes, which are levied on personal incomes and on company profits, and indirect taxes (also known as sales taxes), which are levied on expenditure. Taxation might be negative; this occurs when people receive government transfer payments (social security payments) or firms receive subsidies. In this analysis, tax revenue refers to net tax revenue, which means payments of tax to the government minus subsidies and government transfer payments.

Because savings and taxation might be negative, the total of withdrawals might be negative (although this is unlikely).

There are, therefore, two ways in which income (Y) may be disposed of: some is spent on consumption (C) and some is withdrawn (W). Withdrawals comprise savings (S) and net taxation (T).

$$Y \equiv C + W$$

$$Y \equiv C + (S + T)$$

The levels of both of the categories of withdrawals are related to the current level of income. When their income is high, households and firms can afford to save, and are required to pay more tax, and *vice versa*. When their income is low, they are more likely to draw on their existing savings (negative savings), and to receive government transfer payments (negative taxation). The level of income is, however, not the only determinant of the amount of withdrawals.

Just as not all of the money received by one of the two principal sectors is necessarily returned to the other, it might be that the sum that one sector pays to the other is greater than its receipts in the current period from the other. Payments of money from one sector to the other that are not financed by receipts from the other are called injections (J). The three categories of injections are investment (I), net exports (exports (X) minus imports (Z)), and government spending (G). The definitions of these correspond to the definitions used in the calculation of GDP (see Chapter 1). It is important to note that government spending refers to government purchases of goods and services, and that investment refers to the creation of additional capacity to produce output. Net exports will be negative if the value of imports exceeds the value of exports in the current period, but the other two parts of injections necessarily have positive values. Investment expenditure is financed partly by savings and partly by net capital inflows from other countries. International transfer payments and flows of property income are not shown on the circular flow diagram (Figure 2).

There are therefore two ways in which aggregate demand, which may also be called planned expenditure (E_P), can be paid for. It might be consumption expenditure (C) which is the spending of current income, or it might be injections (J). Injections comprise investment (I), government spending (G), and net exports ($X - Z$).

$$E_P \equiv C + J$$

$$E_P \equiv C + (I + G + (X - Z))$$

The ultimate determinant of the level of income (Y), which measures output, is aggregate demand (E_P). Firms will increase production if their customers wish to buy more output. The components of aggregate demand are consumption, investment, government spending, and net exports.

The four lines of algebra above are definitions; they must necessarily be true because of the way in which the symbols are defined. For this reason a three-bar identity sign (≡) is used. Of greater interest than definitions is a set of behavioural equations that show how each part of aggregate demand is likely to respond to a change in circumstances. The influence of the level of income is of particular interest; those parts of planned expenditure that change in response to income changes are described as induced, and those that are independent of the level of income are described as autonomous.

Consumption expenditure has both autonomous and induced components. It is likely to show a strong positive relationship with income, but there are also other significant influences. It is not, however, the value of total income that influences consumption expenditure, but disposable income (Y_d), which is defined as income after net taxation (T). A simple form of this relationship is shown in Figure 3. This diagram, which is an example of a consumption function, shows the effect on C (the dependent variable) of a change in Y_d (the independent variable).

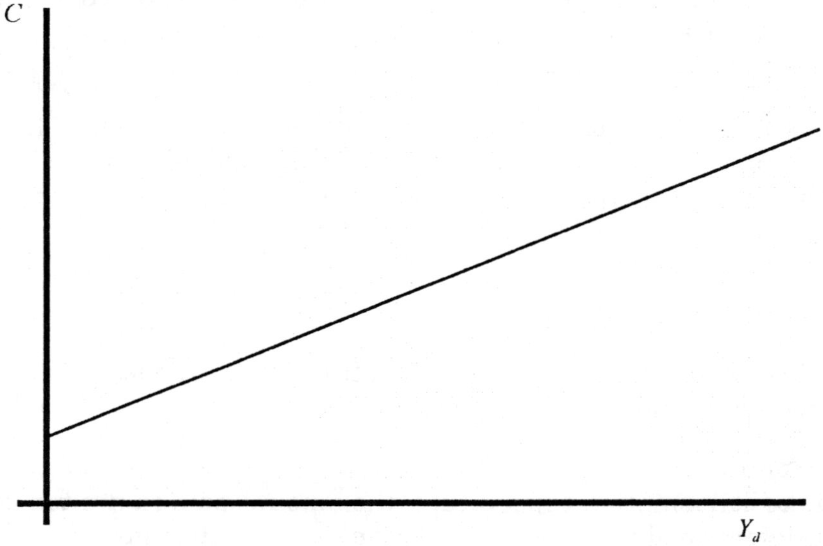

Figure 3. Consumption Expenditure

The equation of the graph shown in Figure 3 is:

$$C = a + b(Y_d)$$

The part of C that is not influenced by the level of disposable income is shown by a, the intercept on the vertical axis, and the part that is induced by the level of disposable income is shown by $b(Y_d)$. The value of the gradient (or slope) of the function is b. The gradient of a consumption function is known as the marginal propensity to consume (MPC); this measures the proportion of an increase in disposable income that is spent on consumption, and similarly for a decrease.

$$MPC \equiv \frac{\Delta C}{\Delta Y_d} = b$$

The value of b shows how people change their consumption expenditure following a change in disposable income. For example, if the value of b is 0.8, then an increase in disposable income of Rs. 1000 leads to an increase in consumption spending of Rs. 800. The value of a depends on other determinants of consumption behaviour. The level of confidence in the future is probably an important determinant of a. For example, people who are worried about becoming unemployed are likely to increase their rate of saving, which means that they will decrease their consumption spending. A change in the level of confidence changes the value of a and thus leads to a parallel shift of the consumption function.

The proportion of total disposable income spent on consumption is known as the average propensity to consume (APC).

$$\text{APC} \equiv C / Y_d$$

A straight-line consumption function implies a constant MPC and a declining APC as disposable income rises, and *vice versa*. This is probably a reasonable assumption for small changes in aggregate income.

The definition of disposable income is:

$$Y_d \equiv Y - T$$

This definition might be substituted into the behavioural equation for consumption expenditure:

$$C = a + b(Y - T)$$

Like consumption expenditure, the amount paid in net tax is also partly determined by the current level of income. In general, increased income will lead to an increased payment of tax. It will also lead to a decreased amount of government transfers (for example, social security payments). Net taxation (T), therefore, is likely to be a positive function of income.

Figure 4 shows a tax function.

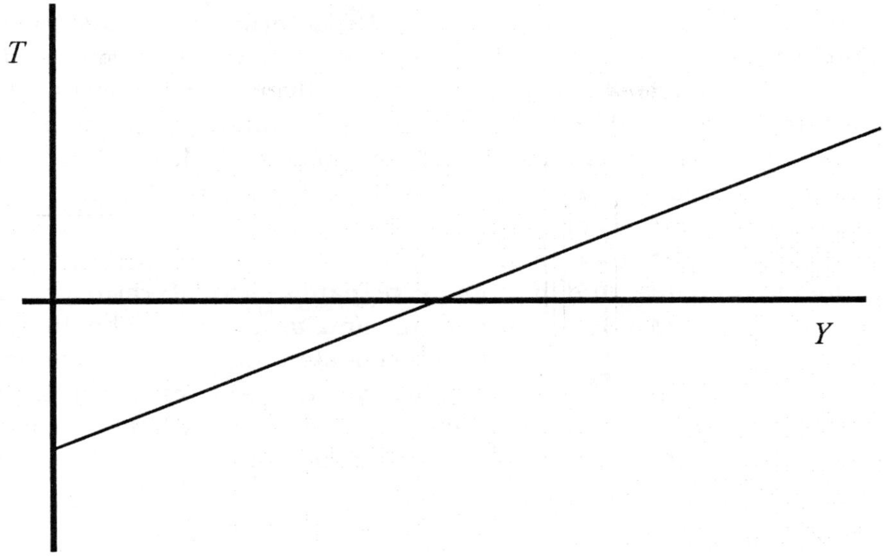

Figure 4. Net Tax Revenue

The equation of the straight-line graph shown in Figure 4 is:

$$T = v + tY$$

The autonomous element of T is shown by the vertical intercept (v) and the induced element is shown by tY. The effect on net tax revenue of a change in income (Y) is shown by the gradient (t). A linear (straight-line) relationship is probably reasonable for small changes of income. The value of T will be negative if subsidies and government transfer payments are greater than tax revenue; this might occur at very low levels of income. The values of v and t are determined by political decisions concerning tax rules and by the responses of the private sector to these. Changes in tax rules will change the value of either or both of t and v; the tax function will show a parallel shift and/or a change of gradient.

The behavioural equation for net tax revenue may be substituted into the equation for consumption expenditure:

$$C = (a - bv) + b(1 - t)Y$$

This shows that, assuming consumption expenditure to be a linear function of disposable income (Y_d), and net tax revenue to be a linear function of income (Y), it follows that consumption expenditure is a linear function of income. The autonomous element of consumption is $(a - bv)$ and the induced element is $b(1 - t)Y$. The model therefore allows for the influence of net taxation decisions on aggregate consumption spending.

Investment expenditure also is partly determined by the level of income. A time of high output is likely to be a time when firms need to purchase additional equipment or train additional employees. It is also a time when they can afford to do so. Equally, when the output level is low, many businesses are producing at less than their maximum production level, so have no incentive to spend on investment projects. There will also be an autonomous element of investment. For example, high interest rates might discourage some investment spending and a high anticipated rate of return might encourage some investment spending, and *vice versa*. The level of business confidence is probably of considerable importance as a determinant of investment expenditure. If decision makers feel optimistic about economic prospects, then they are likely to invest, and *vice versa*, regardless of the current levels of output and interest rates.

Figure 5 shows an investment function.

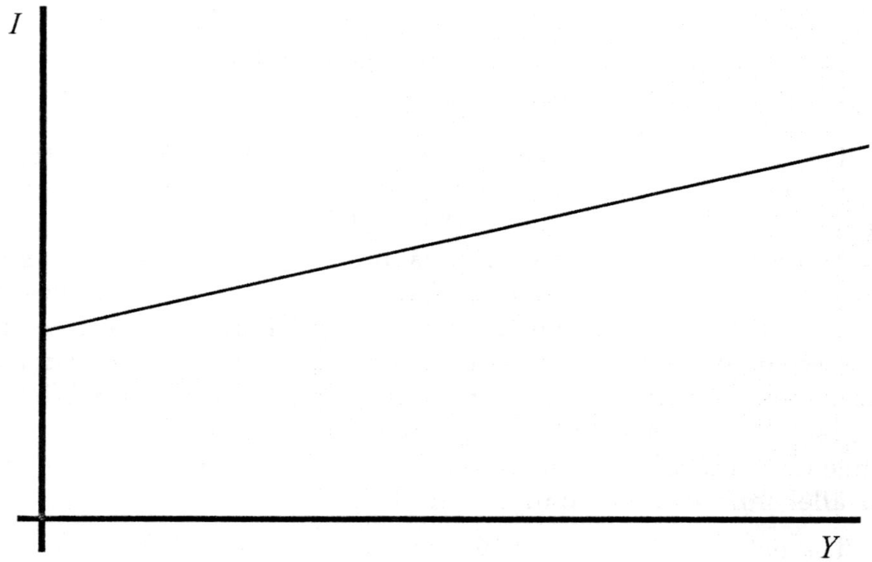

Figure 5. Investment Expenditure.

The equation of the straight-line graph shown in Figure 5 is:

$$I = h + jY$$

The autonomous part of I is shown by the intercept on the vertical axis (h) and the induced element is shown by jY. The effect on investment expenditure of a change in income (Y) is shown by the gradient (j). A linear relationship is probably reasonable for small changes of income. The autonomous element of investment expenditure is influenced by, for example, the level of interest rates, the expected rate of return and the level of business confidence; a change in any of these would cause a parallel shift of the line. A change in the way that firms alter their investment plans following a change in income is shown by a change in the gradient of the line.

Government spending (*G*) is treated as being purely autonomous; it is not determined by the current level of income. It is influenced very largely by political decisions, which might be related to the current government's ideology, or to commitments that arise from earlier decisions, or to the response to current economic, political, and other events (including elections and natural disasters).

Figure 6 shows a government spending function.

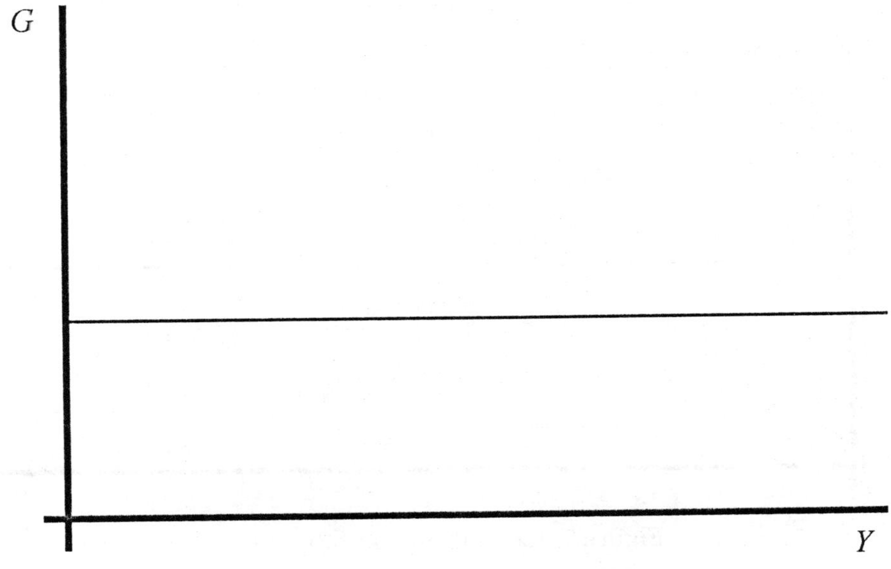

Figure 6. Government Expenditure

The equation of the graph shown in Figure 6 is:

$$G = G^*$$

The asterisk does not imply that the value of *G* is fixed, just that it is autonomous (not influenced by the current level of income (*Y*)). If any of the determinants of *G* change, then the line will shift to a new position, but it will still be parallel to the horizontal axis.

Like government spending, expenditure on exports (*X*) is also regarded as being purely autonomous; it is not determined by the current level of income in the Indian economy. It will be influenced by the quality and price of Indian goods and services, especially in relation to those that can be obtained from other countries. It will also be influenced by foreign income levels. If other countries have increases in their income they will be able to afford to buy more Indian goods.

Political decisions might also be relevant. In order to protect their own economies, some countries (including Japan) impose restrictions on purchases of Indian exports. For political reasons, some governments have forbidden exports to specific countries. For example, this applied to United States exports to Iraq after its invasion of Kuwait in 1990.

Figure 7 shows an export expenditure function.

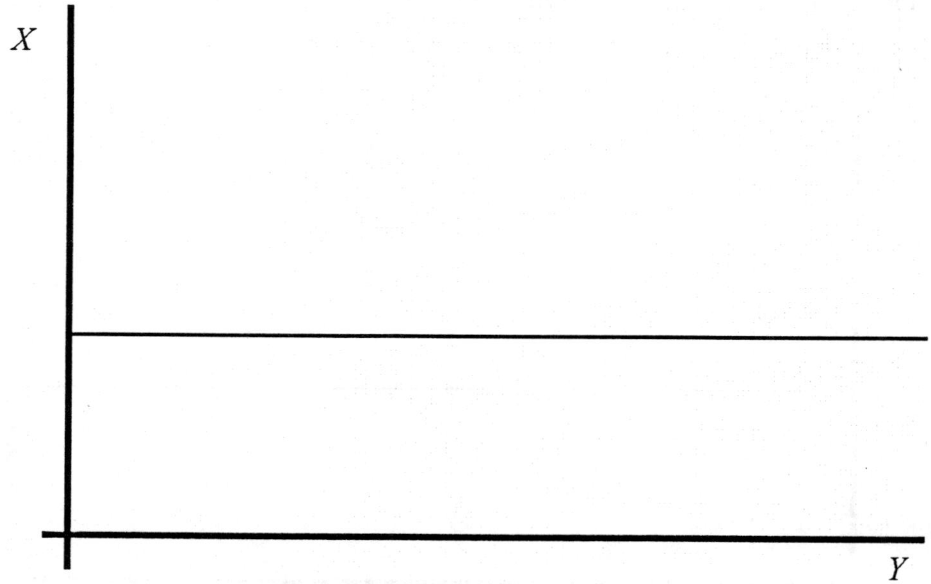

Figure 7. Expenditure on Exports.

The equation of the graph shown in Figure 7 is:

$$X = X^*$$

This does not imply that the value of X is fixed, just that, being autonomous, it is not influenced by the current level of income in India (Y). Changes in any of the determinants of X cause a parallel shift of the line.

The value of imports (Z) has both autonomous and induced elements. It shows a positive relationship with income (Y). A high level of income in India means that people can afford to buy more imported goods and services. In addition, when output increases there is an increased need for imported intermediate goods (raw materials, fuel, components). There are, however, influences on the value of imports other than current income. In particular, governments might impose tariffs or quotas on purchases of goods from other countries. The prices of imported goods, especially relative to the prices of comparable goods produced locally, are also likely to have a significant influence on Z.

Figure 8 shows an imports function.

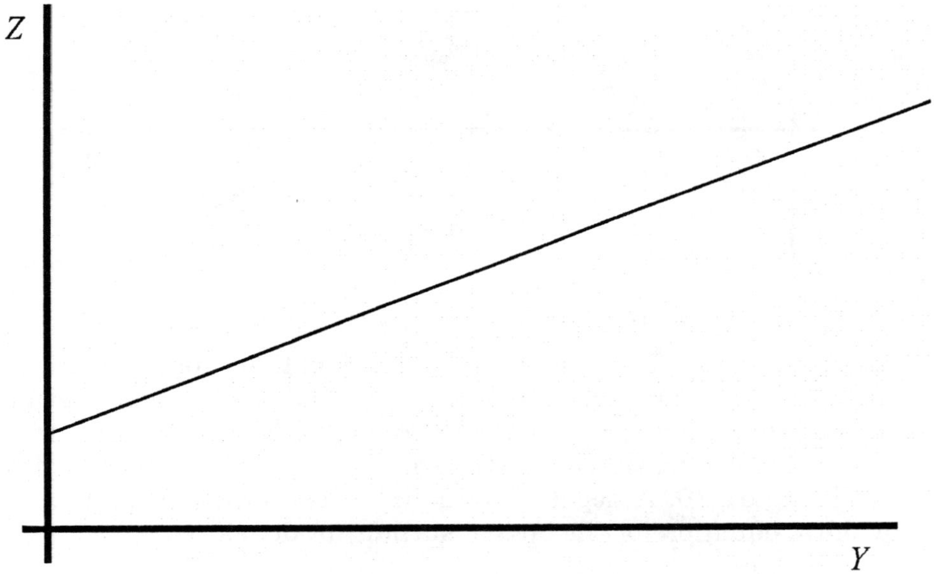

Figure 8. Expenditure on Imports.

The equation of the straight-line graph shown in Figure 8 is:

$$Z = n + mY$$

The autonomous part of Z is shown by the intercept on the vertical axis (n) and the induced element is shown by mY. The effect on the value of imports of a change in income (Y) is shown by the gradient (m). A linear relationship can be assumed for small changes in income. Changes in the autonomous element of spending on imports cause a parallel shift of the function. A change in the gradient is caused by change in the way the value of imports responds to a change in income.

It follows from the behavioural equations for the value of exports and of imports that the value of net exports ($X - Z$) will show a negative relationship with current income. This is shown in Figure 9. The behavioural equation for net exports is:

$$(X - Z) = X^* - (n + mY)$$
$$= (X^* - n) - mY$$

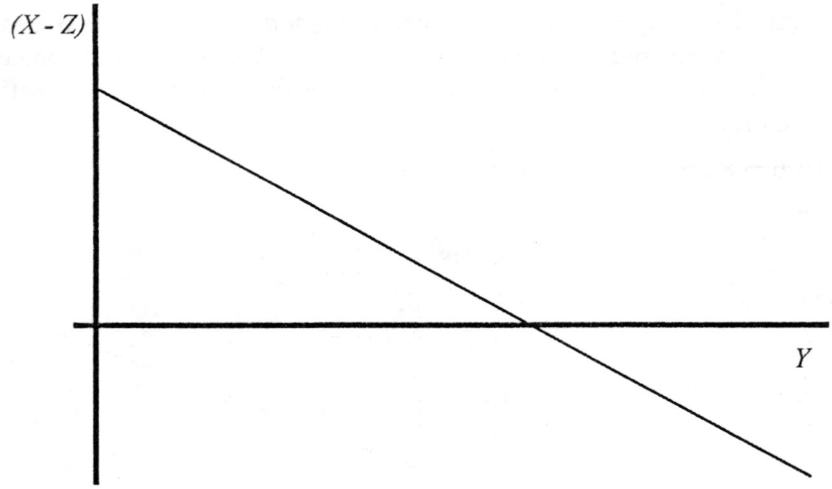

Figure 9. Expenditure on Net Exports.

It also follows from the behavioural equations for the value of government spending and of net taxation that the budget surplus, which is the difference between net taxation and government spending $(T - G)$ will show a positive relationship with current income. This is shown in Figure 10. A negative value indicates a budget deficit. The behavioural equation for the budget surplus (or deficit) is:

$$(T - G) = (v + tY) - G^*$$
$$= (v - G^*) + tY$$

The macroeconomic consequences of an unbalanced government budget are explained in Chapter 6.

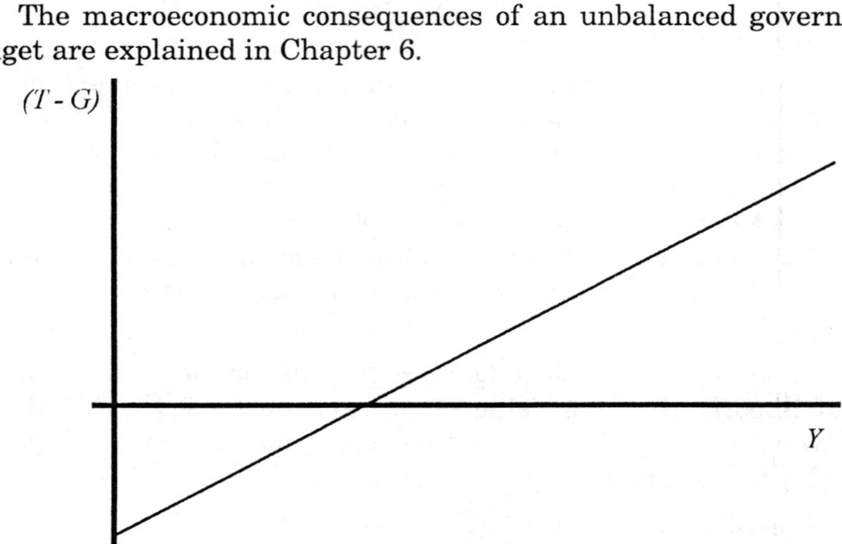

Figure 10. Budget Surplus or Deficit.

Aggregate demand (E_P) comprises the total of consumption, investment, government spending, and net exports, and so the sum of the behavioural equations of each of these will give a behavioural equation for aggregate demand.

$$E_P \equiv C + (I + G + (X - Z))$$

$$E_P = [(a - bv) + b(1 - t)Y] + [h + jY] + G^* + (X^* - [n + mY])$$

This may be rearranged to show clearly the autonomous and induced elements of aggregate demand.

$$E_P = [(a - bv) + h + G^* + X^* - n] + [b(1 - t) + j - m]Y$$

This shows that aggregate demand (E_P) can be regarded as a linear function of current income (Y). The autonomous part of aggregate demand is shown by $[(a - bv) + h + G^* + X^* - n]$, and the gradient of the function (known as the marginal propensity to spend (MPE)) is shown by $[b(1 - t) + j - m]$. Figure 11 shows E_P as a function of Y.

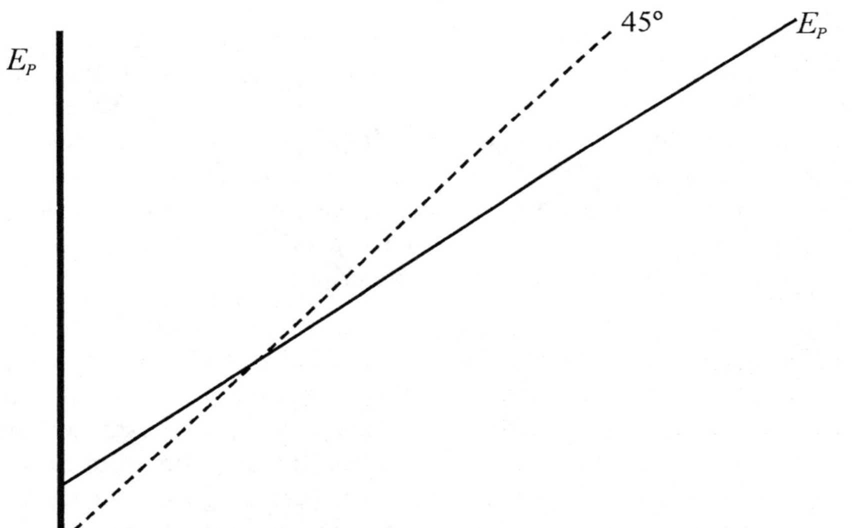

Figure 11. Aggregate Demand.

The Equilibrium Process

Superimposed on the planned expenditure function in Figure 11 is a line at 45° to each of the axes. This is the locus of points which have the same perpendicular distance from each axis; it shows those points where planned expenditure (E_P) (aggregate demand) is equal to income (Y) (aggregate supply). The 45° line crosses the E_P function at one point only. It is likely, therefore, that aggregate output during a particular period of time will not equal the quantity of newly produced goods and services that individuals and corporate bodies wish to buy, and can pay for, at current prices.

If planned expenditure (E_P) does not equal output (Y) then the output level will change.

If planned expenditure exceeds output, then firms will find that their stocks run down; they are able to sell more than the amount of current production, and therefore sell some of their accumulated stocks from earlier periods' production. This is not a stable situation; it will encourage firms to increase their output levels to match the level of demand.

The reverse will happen if output exceeds planned expenditure. In this case, part of current output will remain unsold, and the stock level will rise. This is also an unstable situation; it will encourage firms to decrease their output levels.

In both cases, the level of output (shown on the horizontal axis of Figure 11) will tend to move towards the point where it equals planned expenditure. The stimulus for firms to change their output levels is any unplanned change in the level of stocks of finished goods awaiting sale or of intermediate goods awaiting use. If firms succeed in selling the precise quantity of output that has been produced, then there is no incentive to increase or to decrease the level of output. This is called the equilibrium level of income (Y_e).

In the case of firms producing to order rather than for stock (for example, ship-building), changes in the length of the order book are the stimulus to change the level of current output. In the case of firms providing a service (for example, hairdressers, dentists, chimney-sweeps), changes in the length of the queue are the stimulus. The distinguishing feature of services (in contrast to goods) is that they cannot be stored, so that production occurs simultaneously with delivery to customers. Both for goods produced to order and for services, an imbalance between output (Y) and *ex-ante* demand (E_P) cannot cause an unplanned change in the level of stocks.

The definition of an equilibrium point is that it is the point towards which the system is spontaneously moving. It is not implied that the equilibrium point is necessarily desirable; it is merely a point of stability.

Although the economy will be moving towards the equilibrium level of income, it will rarely be at this position. Firms know whether to increase or decrease their output levels according to whether their unplanned stock levels are falling or rising, but they do not know precisely by how much to change output. Each firm cannot predict what the other firms will do, and so might make too tentative a change and need a further change in the next period. Alternatively, a firm might make too dramatic a change and overshoot the equilibrium point, and then subsequently have to change output in the opposite direction.

In addition, the position of the equilibrium point is likely to be changing. As circumstances change, the autonomous component of planned expenditure might change; this causes a parallel shift in the E_P function. People might also change the nature of their response to changes in income; this changes the gradient of the E_P function. In either case, the position of Y_e will change, and the economy will begin to move towards the new equilibrium point. Table 2 summarises the possible determinants of upward (parallel) and clockwise shifts of the E_P line. The directions of changes in the values of the parameters in the equation of the E_P line are shown. Downward and anti-clockwise shifts are caused by changes of the same parameters in the opposite direction. A change in the value of b (MPC) leads to both a parallel shift and a change of gradient.

TABLE 2. Causes of E_P shifts

Upward:	$a\uparrow$	$b\downarrow$	$v\downarrow$	$h\uparrow$	$G^*\uparrow$	$X^*\uparrow$	$n\downarrow$
Clockwise:	$b\downarrow$	$t\uparrow$	$j\downarrow$	$m\uparrow$			

The equilibrium level of income is the point that the economy is moving towards. This movement might not occur at a fast or at a steady pace, and might not be by the shortest route. The position of the equilibrium point might have changed before it has been reached; the economy is chasing a moving target.

Other macroeconomic equilibrium processes, including the level of interest rates (see Chapter 5) and the level of prices (see Chapter 8) show the same characteristics. The equilibrium value of a macro-economic variable is not necessarily a desirable situation, is likely to occur very rarely, and frequently changes.

Planned expenditure is also known as *ex-ante* expenditure. The equilibrium point occurs where actual output is equal to *ex-ante* expenditure. At this point businesses have produced exactly the quantity of output that their customers wish to buy; consumers' behaviour has been correctly forecasted.

All output must be paid for. This includes output that firms have failed to sell and have added to their (unplanned) stocks. It is therefore true that, even when planned expenditure does not equal the value of output, actual expenditure must still be equal to output. If there is an unplanned increase in the stock level, for example, the additional stocks must be financed by the firm. The employees will receive their wages even if the level of customers' demand has been over-estimated and some goods have not been sold. Actual expenditure, including "purchases" by firms of their own unsold output, is known as *ex-post* expenditure.

It is only when the economy has reached equilibrium that *ex-ante* (planned) expenditure is equal to output, but it is a truism (necessarily true) that *ex-post* (actual) expenditure is always equal to output.

In this definition of the income equilibrium process, it is assumed that firms do not change their output prices when the level of planned expenditure (E_P) is not equal to the level of output (Y). In Chapter 8, this assumption is relaxed, recognising that firms might change either their prices or their production levels or both if the equilibrium point has not yet been reached. If planned expenditure exceeds output (E_P is greater than Y), causing an unplanned decrease in the level of stocks or (in firms producing to order) an increase in the length of the order book or (in firms providing a service) an increase in the length of the queue, firms might decide to increase their prices or to increase their output levels or might choose a combination of these two, and *vice versa*.

Figure 12 shows an alternative presentation of the same theory. Consumption (C) is shown as a positive function of income (Y). From this is derived the withdrawals (W) function. Withdrawals comprise savings (S) and net taxation (T), and are the part of income not spent on consumption. At the point where the consumption function crosses the 45° line, consumption is equal to income, so withdrawals must be equal to zero. At the point where the consumption function touches the vertical axis, consumption is purely autonomous ($a - bv$); since income is equal to zero at this point, the consumption must be financed from negative withdrawals. Therefore, when income is zero, the value of withdrawals is negative by the same amount as autonomous consumption is positive. Of course, it is not possible for a country to have zero income, and this part of the graph may be regarded as a mathematical extrapolation. It is, however, possible for an individual to have zero income, and this may be regarded as a useful analogy. In this case, consumption would be paid for using existing assets (negative *S*) or government transfer payments such as social security payments (negative *T*).

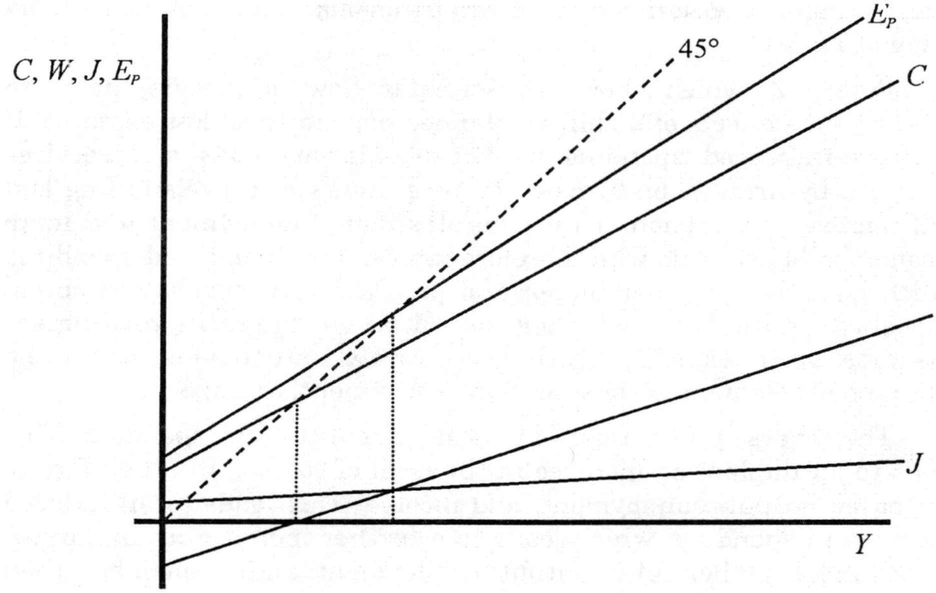

Figure 12. Aggregate Demand and Equilibrium Income.

The gradients of the consumption and withdrawals functions sum to 100%. Additional income is either spent on consumption or it is withdrawn from the circular flow in savings and taxation; the proportion that is spent on consumption (the gradient of the *C* function) plus the proportion that is not spent on consumption (the gradient of the *W* function) must therefore total to 100%. If, for example, 80% of an increase in income is spent on consumption, it follows that 20% of it is not spent on consumption.

The value of injections (*J*) (which consist of investment (*I*), government spending (*G*), and net exports (*X* – *Z*)) is also shown as a positive function of income (*Y*). The planned expenditure (E_P) function is derived by the vertical summation of the consumption and the injections functions. The equilibrium level of income (Y_e) is at the intersection of the planned expenditure function and the 45° line.

This diagram also shows that Y_e can be derived as the point when withdrawals (*W*) are equal to *ex-ante* (planned) injections (*J*). Expenditure on unplanned stockbuilding is included in *ex-post* investment (and injections) but not in *ex-ante* investment (and injections).

There are likely to be frequent shifts in the position of the planned expenditure function. Parallel shifts are caused by changes in the autonomous element of planned expenditure, and changes of gradient by changes in the way in which people respond to changes in their income. Any shift of the E_P function leads to a change in the value of Y_e.

Figure 2, which shows the circular flow of income, helps to illustrate the effects of a shift in planned expenditure. For example, if there is increased spending by households on goods and services produced by firms, then firms will notice their stock levels falling and will increase production. This generates more employment and more income for households who therefore increase their induced spending, which leads to a further increase of production by firms, and so on. The effect is the same whether the initial change is in government spending or in exports, which are entirely autonomous, or in the autonomous element of consumption, investment, or imports.

The reverse effect occurs following a reduction in spending. This leads to an unplanned increase in the level of stocks, and therefore to decreased output, employment, and income. This leads to an induced decrease in spending, which leads to a further increase in unplanned stocks and a further cut in output, employment, and income, and then further cuts in induced spending, and so on.

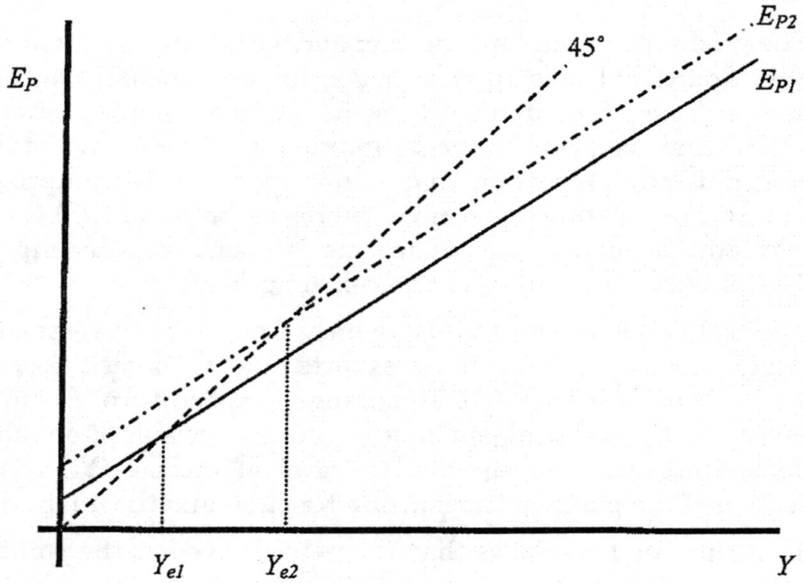

Figure 13. The Multiplier Effect

Figure 13 shows the effect of an increase in autonomous planned expenditure. The increase in equilibrium income ($Y_{e2} - Y_{e1}$) is very much greater than the increase in autonomous expenditure ($E_{P2} - E_{P1}$).

The same effect may be demonstrated with a simple numerical exercise. Assume that the gradient of the planned expenditure function (MPE) is 0.75 (which implies that 75% of an increase in income is spent), and that government spending on road maintenance is increased by Rs. 10 crore. All of this sum becomes income. Much of it will be paid as wages to employees, much of the rest will become profit to construction companies or to the suppliers of their inputs, and some will be paid as rent to such firms' landlords or as interest to banks. The recipients of this additional income will spend 75% of it, which is an increase in demand for output, and which will therefore lead to an expansion of output and employment and hence to an equal increase in income. Those receiving additional income will spend 75% of it, leading to a further increase in income, and so on.

TABLE 3. The Multiplier Process : Numerical Illustration

Time	Increase in income	Increase in spending
1	10.00	7.50
2	7.50	5.63
3	5.63	4.22
4	4.22	3.16
5	3.16	2.37
6	2.37	1.78
7	1.78	1.33
8	1.33	1.00
9	1.00	0.75
10	0.75	0.56
11	0.56	.
12	.	.
13	.	.
	40.00	

Assumed :

Change in autonomous planned expenditure = Rs. 10 crore

Marginal propensity to spend (MPE) = 0.75

The final increase in income is Rs. 40 crore. Since the initial change in expenditure was Rs. 10 crore, the value of the multiplier is 4.

Table 3 shows the numerical exercise in more detail. Of the additional Rs. 10 crore income received in the first period, Rs. 7.5 crore (75%) is spent, and becomes income in the second period. Of this, Rs. 5.63 crore (75%) is spent, and becomes income in the third period. This leads to spending of Rs. 4.22 crore (75%), and to spending of Rs. 3.16 crore in the fourth period, and so on. The final effect of this infinite process is a total increase of income of Rs. 40 crore.

This is known as the multiplier process. The ratio of the change in equilibrium income (Y_e) to the change in autonomous spending (A) that caused it is called the multiplier, and is usually represented by K. Its value depends on the gradient of the planned expenditure function, and is likely to lie in the range 2.5 to 5.0. In Table 3, the value of the multiplier is 4. The smaller the amount of withdrawals (W) from each increment to income (Y), the greater will be the next addition to expenditure (E_P) and thus the next addition to income, and so the greater will be the value of K.

$$K \equiv \frac{\Delta Y_e}{\Delta A} \equiv \frac{1}{(1-\text{MPE})}$$

This conclusion can be derived algebraically.

The components of planned expenditure are consumption, investment, government spending, and net exports.

$$E_P \equiv C + (I + G + (X - Z))$$

At the equilibrium point, income is equal to planned expenditure.

$$Y_e = C + (I + G + (X - Z))$$

This equation can be expressed in a behavioural form, in which the autonomous and induced parts are identified, and rearranged to identify the multiplier.

$$Y_e = [(a - bv) + h + G^* + X^* - n] + [b(1 - t) + j - m]Y_e$$

$$Y_e - [b(1 - t) + j - m]Y_e = [(a - bv) + h + G^* + X^* - n]$$

$$Y_e\{1 - [b(1 - t) + j - m]\} = [(a - bv) + h + G^* + X^* - n]$$

$$Y_e = [(a - bv) + h + G^* + X^* - n] \,/\, \{1 - [b(1 - t) + j - m]\}$$

$$Y_e = AK$$

$$\Delta Y_e = K\,\Delta A$$

$$K \equiv \frac{\Delta Y_e}{\Delta A} = \frac{1}{\{1-[b(1-t)+j-m]\}} = \frac{1}{(1-\text{MPE})}$$

If the gradient of the planned expenditure function is known, and this implies that the gradient of each of its components is known, then the value of the multiplier can be calculated. This value may be used to predict the effects on equilibrium income of a change in autonomous planned expenditure. This includes changes in investment, government spending, and net exports, which are important components of planned expenditure and thus of income. It also includes changes in net tax rates, which affect disposable income and therefore consumption expenditure and, through the multiplier effect, the level of income.

Full-Employment Income

The equilibrium level of output in the economy is not regarded as being necessarily the desirable level of output. Identification of the desirable level is a matter of judgement, and will be related to political and economic ideology. Economists considering themselves to hold Keynesian views usually concentrate on the importance of achieving low unemployment; according to this approach, the desirable level of income is one that is consistent with full employment.

Full employment implies that maximum output, consistent with long-term efficiency, has been achieved with the existing resources. In practical terms, the concept of full employment is more difficult to define. It does not mean that everyone is working; many people are not part of the labour force because they are too old or too young, or choose not to be employed, and others are not able to participate in the labour force because they are ill, in prison, or unable to learn new skills. The attainment of the full-employment level of output also implies that people are working a reasonable number of hours per week; part-time workers who prefer full-time employment are not fully employed. However, the number of hours per week that is regarded as reasonable depends on social norms, which may, of course, change. During the twentieth century, the length of the normal working week in industrial countries has fallen very significantly. The concept of full employment also implies that people are doing work that is appropriate to their skills; employees who are over- or under-qualified for their work are not operating at maximum efficiency.

Full employment is sometimes defined as a situation when the number of unemployed people equals the number of unfilled vacancies. This is, however, misleading, as labour is not homogeneous, and the abilities of the unemployed might not match the abilities required for the available vacancies.

The level of income (Y) that corresponds to full employment may be regarded as fixed in the short term. In the longer term, it is certainly not fixed. For example, the population might rise, skills might improve, the labour force participation rate might increase, or better equipment might be installed, and any of these would lead to a higher level of output resulting from full employment.

Full employment is not impossible. Unemployment was very low in many industrialised countries in the 1950s. An extreme case is New Zealand where, in 1950–54, the weekly average of the number of registered unemployed people was eleven, which, relative to the size of the labour force, is not significantly different from zero.

If the equilibrium level of income (Y_e) is less than the full-employment level (Y_{FE}), then the quantity of new goods and services that people wish to buy is less than can be produced, and less than maximum output has been achieved. This leads to unemployment; in severe cases, as happened during the 1930s in many countries, it may be called a depression. If the equilibrium level of income is greater than the full-employment level, then the quantity of new goods and services that people wish to buy is more than can be produced, and some of these demands cannot be satisfied. This is likely to lead to rising prices, which is a situation known as inflation.

Fiscal Policy

Keynesian economists believe that governments should respond to inflation (caused by excess demand) and to unemployment (caused by inadequate demand) by manipulating the level of aggregate demand. One means of doing this is fiscal policy.

Fiscal policy means changes in government spending and/or changes in net taxation that are designed to influence the level of aggregate demand. Aggregate demand (E_P) might be decreased, during a period of inflation, by increasing net taxation (T) (to decrease disposable income (Y_d) and so decrease consumption (C)), or by decreasing government spending (G). During a period of unemployment, it might be increased by decreasing net taxation (to increase disposable income and thus increase consumption) or by increasing government spending. The size of the effect on equilibrium income depends on the value of the multiplier (K).

A loose (or expansionary) fiscal policy is one that is designed to increase aggregate demand during a depression, and a tight (or contractionary) fiscal policy is intended to decrease aggregate demand during a period of inflation.

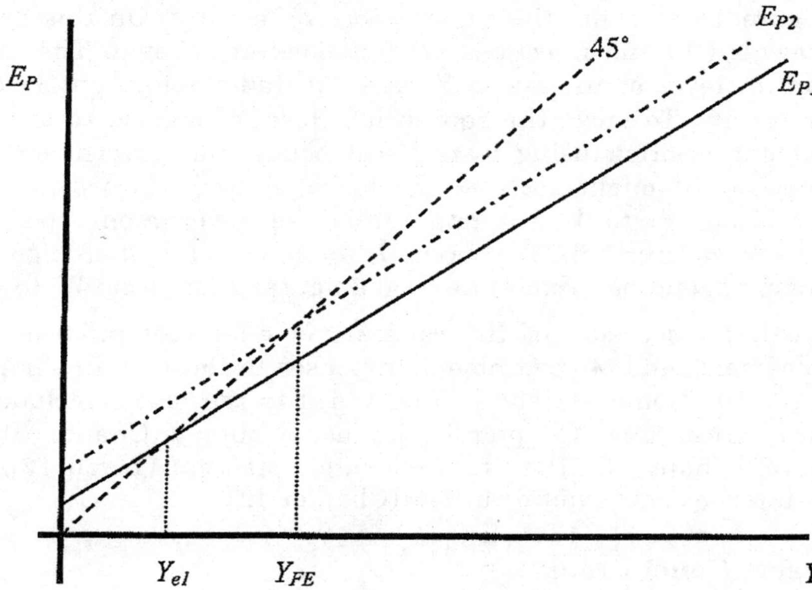

Figure 14. Loose Fiscal Policy.

Figure 14 illustrates the use of loose fiscal policy during a depression. The initial planned expenditure function is E_{P1} and the initial equilibrium level of income is Y_{e1}. The full-employment level of income is Y_{FE}. Following an increase in government spending, or a cut in net tax, the function shifts to E_{P2} which causes a multiplied increase of output to Y_{FE}. During a period of inflation, Y_{FE} is less than Y_e, and a tight fiscal policy shifts the E_P function downwards. In both cases, the intention is to move Y_e so that it is coincident with Y_{FE}, and the level of output will then move towards the new equilibrium.

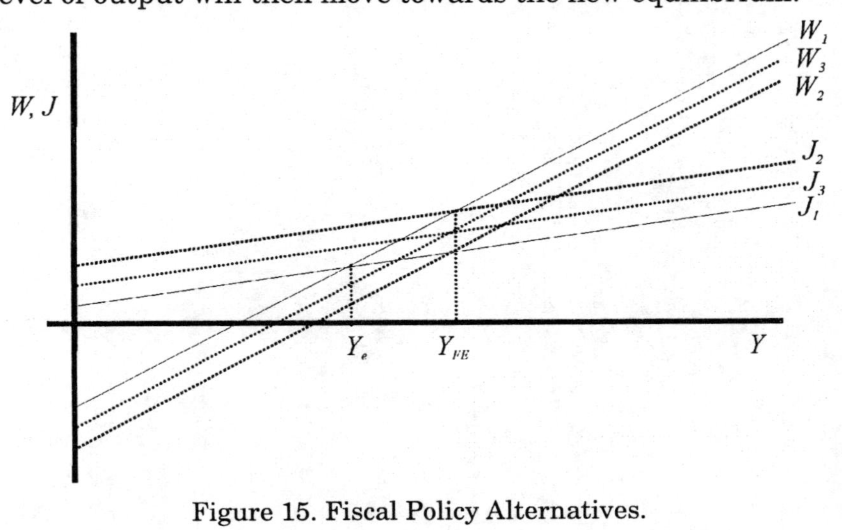

Figure 15. Fiscal Policy Alternatives.

Figure 15 presents the same theory differently. On this graph, withdrawals (W) and injections (J) functions are shown. The initial equilibrium level of income is Y_e and the full-employment level of income is Y_{FE}. To move the equilibrium level of income to the full-employment position using loose fiscal policy, the government has three options. It might decrease net taxes, shifting the withdrawals function from W_1 to W_2, it might increase government spending, shifting the injections function from J_1 to J_2, or it might change both government spending (from J_1 to J_3) and net taxation (from W_1 to W_3).

Further discussion of the causes and effects of inflation and unemployment, and of government responses to these, is in Chapters 9 and 10. Additional variables to be added to the model include the level of interest rates (Chapter 3), the money supply (Chapter 5), the price level (Chapter 8), the exchange rate (Chapters 11 and 12), and the net international capital outflow (Chapter 12).

Keynesian Conclusions

The conclusion of the Keynesian model of income determination is that the determinant of the equilibrium level of income (Y_e) is the level of planned expenditure (E_P). Movement towards the equilibrium might take considerable time. The current level of income is a major determinant of the amount of planned expenditure; in this presentation of the model, other determinants are regarded as autonomous. Full employment might not occur spontaneously, but fiscal policy can be used to manipulate the level of aggregate demand (E_P) if the equilibrium level of income (Y_e) is not equal to the full-employment level of income (Y_{FE}).

3

The *IS* Line: Income, Interest Rates, and the Goods Market

In the presentation of the Keynesian model of income determination described in Chapter 2, the level of income (Y) is the sole independent variable for each of the parts of planned expenditure (E_P). The influence of other variables is incorporated in the autonomous element of each of the behavioural equations.

The equation for investment spending is:

$$I = h + jY$$

The value of the autonomous parameter h incorporates the effects on investment spending of variables other than current income (Y). These include the levels of interest rates and of business confidence. High interest rates might discourage some businesses from embarking on investment projects, and *vice versa*, and a general mood of optimism or pessimism might be powerful enough to overrule every other influence on investment spending.

The influence of the general level of interest rates (r), which is incorporated in the autonomous element h, may be identified separately:

$$I = (g - fr) + jY$$

In this equation, g is the new autonomous term; it shows the influence on investment spending of all variables other than income (Y) and interest rates (r). The value of r is calculated as a weighted average of interest rates. The part of investment spending that is induced by interest rates is $-fr$. The coefficient $-f$ shows the effect on investment of a change in interest rates.

Figure 16 shows the negative effect of the level of interest rates (r) on investment (I). The gradient is f and the intercept on the vertical axis is $(g + jY)$. A straight-line function is probably reasonable for small changes in the level of interest rates.

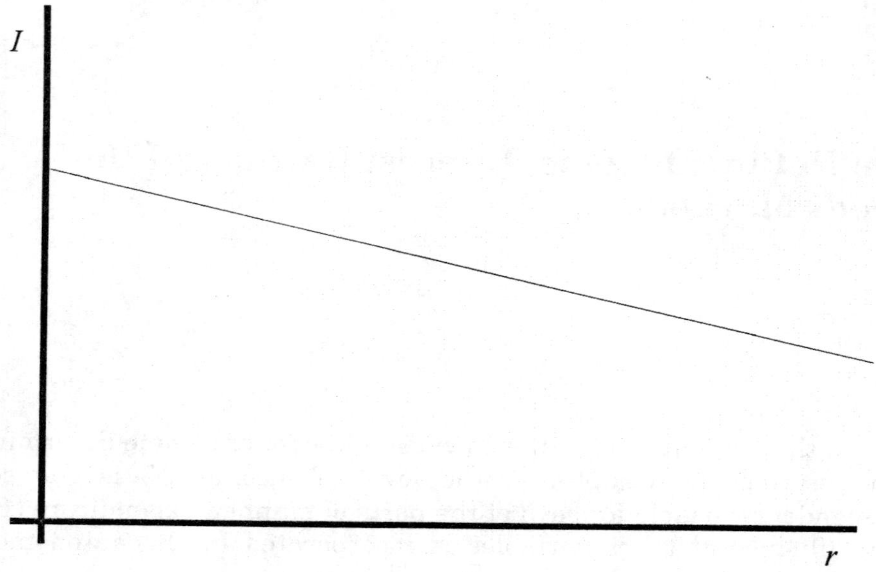

Figure 16. Investment Expenditure

At any moment there are many interest rates. Banks offer different rates on loans according to the perceived level of risk. Rates on deposits also vary, in this case according to the term, the amount deposited, and the type of services provided (including, for example, the use of cheques and cash-dispensing machines). The variable r, therefore, represents the general level of interest rates. The determinants of the level of interest rates are discussed in Chapter 5.

The behavioural equation for the equilibrium level of income, incorporating the effect of interest rates on investment spending, becomes:

$$Y_e = E_P = [(a - bv) + g + G^* + X^* - n] + [b(1 - t) + j - m]Y - fr$$

This equation has two independent variables; it refers to the effects on equilibrium income (Y_e) of the current level of income (Y) and of the general level of interest rates (r). The effects of other variables, which are assumed to be constant, are shown by the autonomous term $[(a - bv) + g + G^* + X^* - n]$.

The *IS* Line

Only certain combinations of Y and r permit income to reach an equilibrium level. A high level of interest rates (r) is likely to decrease investment (I) and therefore to decrease planned expenditure (E_P) and equilibrium income (Y_e), and *vice versa*. This is illustrated in Figure 17.

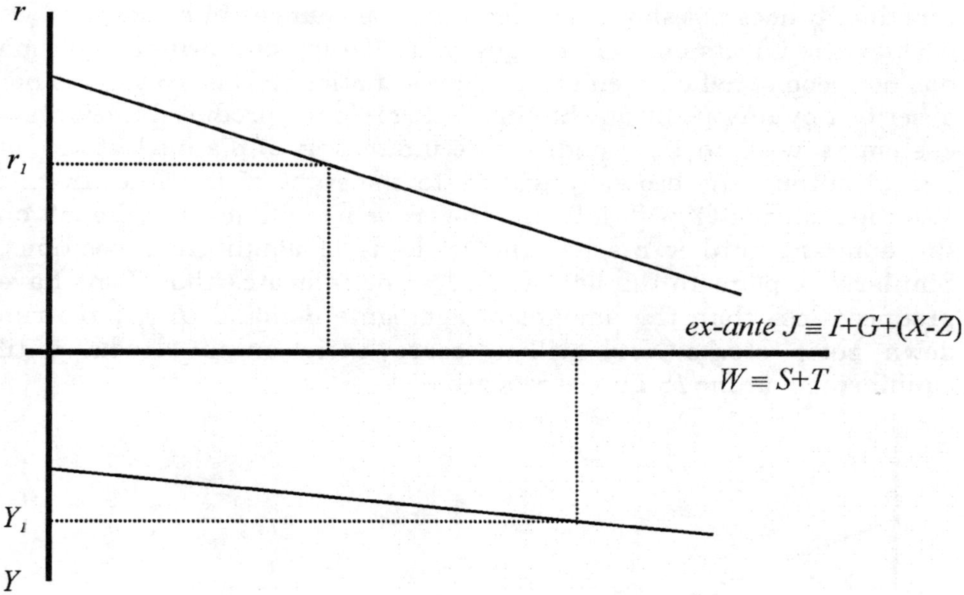

Figure 17. Equilibrium Output

The diagram shows the inverse effect of the level of interest rates on investment and hence on *ex-ante* injections (*J*) (which comprise investment (*I*), government spending (*G*) and net exports ($X - Z$)), and the positive effect of income on withdrawals (*W*) (which consist of savings (*S*) and net taxation (*T*)). Equilibrium income (Y_e) occurs when withdrawals are equal to *ex-ante* injections. These two variables are plotted on the same scale and placed on superimposed horizontal axes to make it easy to identify equilibrium combinations of *r* and *Y*. Figure 17 does not refer to the effects of *Y* on *I* and of *Y* on *Z*.

If income is at Y_1 and the level of interest rates is at r_1, equilibrium has not been achieved. It can be seen that *W* is greater than *ex-ante J*. In this situation, firms have over-estimated their sales; this leads to unplanned stockbuilding. Their response will be to cut output levels. Income will therefore fall, and will continue to fall until there is no unplanned stockbuilding, which will occur when *W* is equal to *ex-ante J*. At this point income reaches the equilibrium level Y_e. The reverse process will occur if the levels of *r* and *Y* are such that *W* is less than *ex-ante J*.

These relationships are summarised in Figure 18. This graph is the locus of combinations of levels of income and of interest rates that lead to equilibrium of output of new goods and services. When equilibrium has been reached, a high level of income will occur with a low level of interest rates and *vice versa*. The *IS* line is a locus, not a function. It does not show the effects on Y of changes in r and nor does it show the effects on r of changes in Y. If the equilibrium condition has not been satisfied then the present situation in the economy is not described by any point on the line. If firms have produced more than customers wish to buy, and are accumulating unplanned stocks of unsold output, the economy will be to the right of the line. In this situation, output (Y) will fall, and the economy will move to the left on the diagram until it reaches the *IS* locus of equilibrium positions. Similarly, a point to the left of the *IS* line indicates that firms have produced less than the amount of aggregate demand (E_P), have run down their stocks, and will increase their output levels until equilibrium, on the *IS* line, is reached.

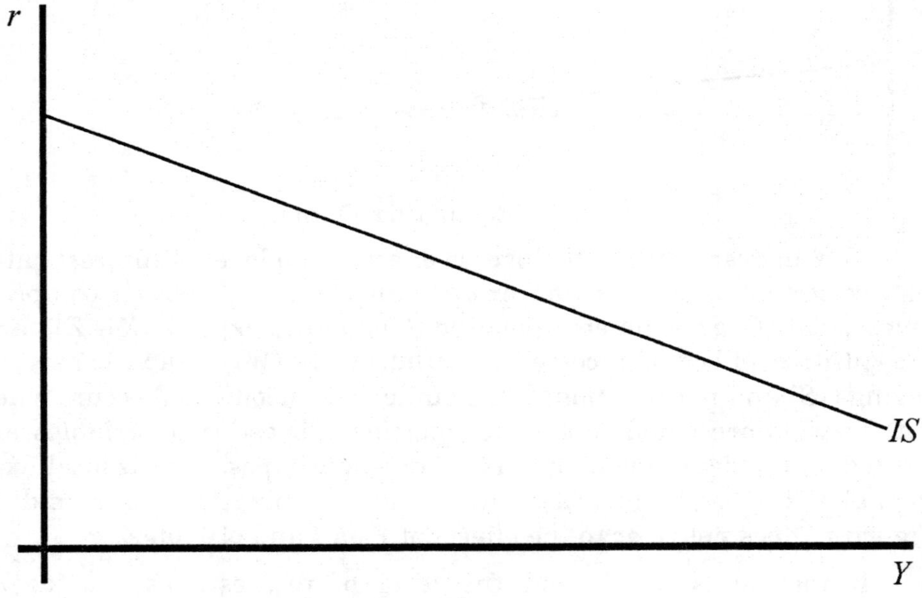

Figure 18. The *IS* Line

The *IS* line is derived from the behavioural equation for planned expenditure. It will be linear, as in Figure 18, if the functions on which it is based are linear. The *IS* line shows those points where Y_e is equal to E_P, so the equation of the line is derived from setting Y_e equal to the behavioural equation for E_P, and rearranging the algebra:

$$Y = \frac{[(a-bv)+g+G^*+X^*-n]-fr}{(1-[b(1-t)+j-m])}$$

Or:

$$r = \frac{[(a - bv) + g + G^* + X^* - n]}{f} - \frac{(1 - [b(1 - t) + j - m])Y}{f}$$

The *IS* line will shift to a new position if the value of any of the parameters in the E_P equation changes. There will be a parallel shift following a change in any of the autonomous elements of planned expenditure, and a change of gradient following a change in any of the induced elements. For example, Figure 19 shows the effect of an increase in exports (X^*), government spending (G^*), autonomous consumption ($a - bv$), or autonomous investment (g), or a decrease in autonomous imports (n). Each of these leads to an increase in equilibrium income for each level of interest rates. The line would shift in the opposite direction following a reduction in exports, government spending, or the autonomous elements of consumption, or investment, or an increase in autonomous imports.

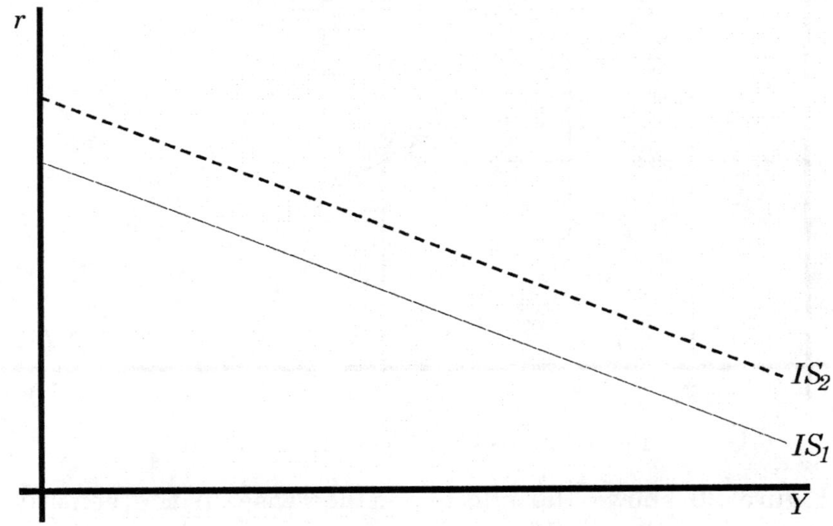

Figure 19. *IS* Line Shift

There will be a change of gradient of the *IS* line following a change in the way in which people respond to changes in the level of income or of interest rates. The gradient of the behavioural function of each part of expenditure measures its responsiveness (or sensitivity) to a change in the independent variable. For example, $b(1 - t)$ shows the sensitivity of consumption spending to a change in income, j measures the sensitivity of investment to a change in income, and f measures the sensitivity of investment to a change in interest rates.

Two of the parameters appear in both parts of the equation of the *IS* line. A change in the value of b or of f will therefore cause both a parallel shift and a change of gradient.

The possible determinants of upward (parallel) and clockwise shifts of the *IS* line are shown in Table 4. The directions of changes in the values of the parameters in the equation of the *IS* line are shown. Downward and anti-clockwise shifts are caused by changes of the same parameters in the opposite direction.

TABLE 4. Causes of *IS* Shifts

Upward:	$a\uparrow$	$b\downarrow$	$v\downarrow$	$g\uparrow$	$G^*\uparrow$	$X^*\uparrow$	$n\downarrow$	$f\downarrow$
Clockwise:	$b\downarrow$	$t\uparrow$	$j\downarrow$	$m\uparrow$	$f\downarrow$			

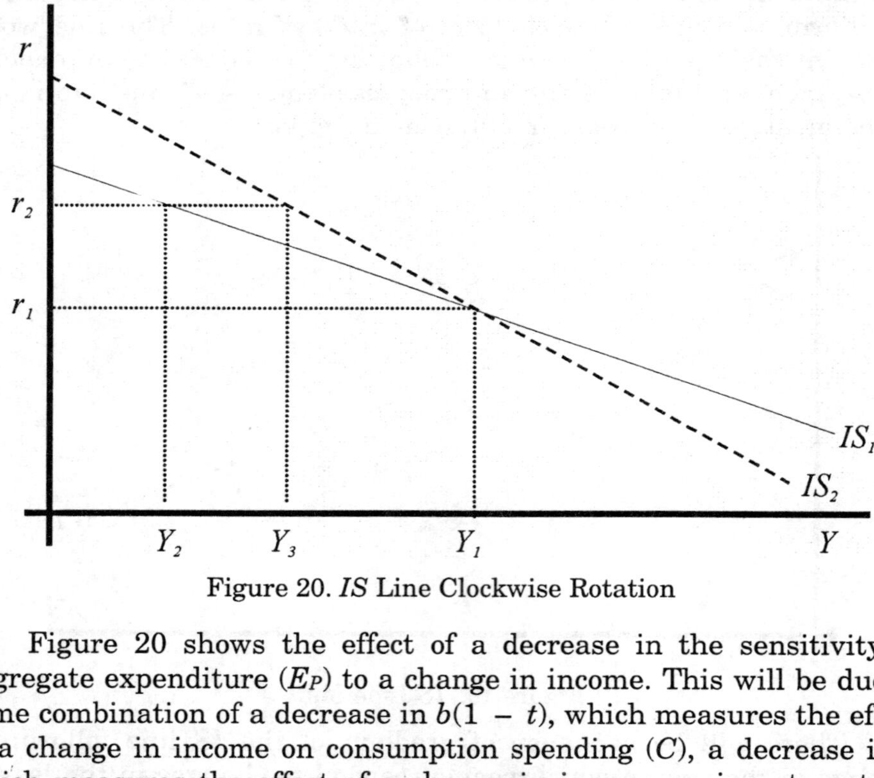

Figure 20. *IS* Line Clockwise Rotation

Figure 20 shows the effect of a decrease in the sensitivity of aggregate expenditure (E_P) to a change in income. This will be due to some combination of a decrease in $b(1 - t)$, which measures the effect of a change in income on consumption spending (C), a decrease in j, which measures the effect of a change in income on investment (I), and an increase in m, which measures the effect of a change in income on imports (Z). If the initial levels of income and interest rates are Y_1 and r_1, then the new *IS* line, after the clockwise rotation, shows that the effect of a change in the level of interest rates to r_2 is less than it was; the new equilibrium level of income is Y_3 instead of Y_2. A decreased sensitivity of expenditure to changes in income leads to a decreased value of the multiplier (K) (see Chapter 2), so a change in investment (I) following a change in the level of interest rates (r) will have a smaller effect on income (Y) than previously. Similarly, an increase in the sensitivity of expenditure (E_P) to a change in income (Y) leads to an increase in the value of the multiplier and causes a rotation of the *IS* line in the opposite direction.

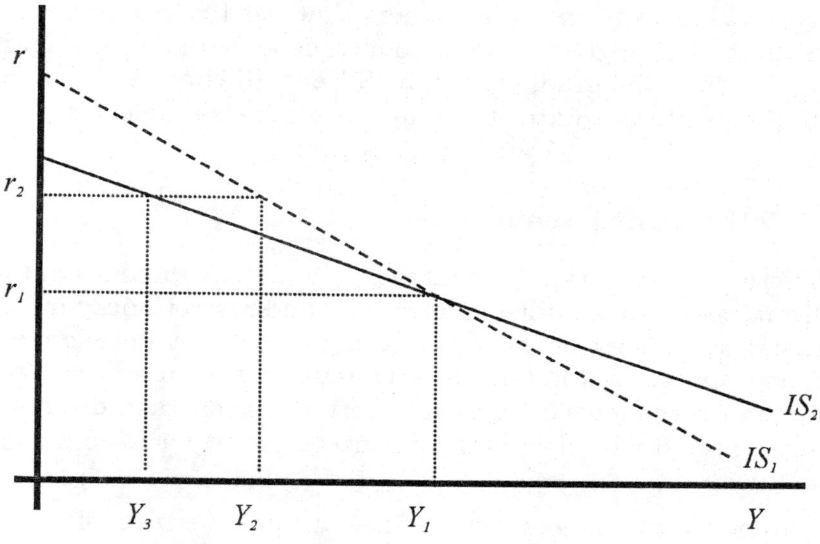

Figure 21. *IS* Line Anticlockwise Rotation

Figure 21 shows the effect on the *IS* line of an increase in the sensitivity of investment spending to a change in interest rates. If the initial levels of income and interest rates are Y_1 and r_1, then the new *IS* line, after the anti-clockwise rotation, shows that the effect of a change in interest rates to r_2 is greater than it was; the new equilibrium level of income is Y_3 instead of Y_2. This arises because the new sensitivity means that a change in the level of interest rates has a greater effect on investment spending, and hence a greater multiplied effect on income, than previously.

Events in other countries that influence economic conditions in India also cause shifts of the *IS* line. For example, a decreased demand for Indian manufactured exports, causing output to fall, shifts the line to the left. Equally, a change in the general level of confidence in the economy, which leads to increased consumption and investment spending, will shift the *IS* line to the right and might also cause a change in gradient.

Fiscal Policy

The *IS* line can be used to illustrate the effects of fiscal policy. A tight fiscal policy, involving increased taxation (net of government transfer payments) (T) or decreased government spending on goods and services (G), has the effect of shifting the line to the left; equilibrium income will be decreased for each level of interest rates. Similarly, a loose fiscal policy moves the *IS* line to the right. If, however, a change in tax rules means that net tax revenue responds differently to a change in income (known as a change in the marginal rate of tax) then the gradient of the *IS* line will change. An increased marginal rate of tax rotates the line in a clockwise direction, and *vice versa*.

Fiscal Policy Instruments

There are two types of fiscal policy instruments: automatic stabilisers (also called built-in stabilisers) and discretionary measures. Automatic stabilisers do not require a government decision to take effect, and operate automatically, as circumstances merit, to decrease fluctuations in the level of aggregate output. In contrast, discretionary measures need to be deliberately introduced on each occasion that they are used.

Automatic stabilisers are defined as any feature of the fiscal system that acts to decrease the value of the multiplier. The progressive system of income tax, in which tax-payers are required to pay an increasing proportion of their income in tax as their income rises, is an example of an automatic stabiliser. If income (Y) changes (in either direction), the effect of a progressive tax system is that disposable income (Y_d) will change by a significantly smaller amount; this decreases the effect on consumption (C) and on aggregate demand (E_P). Similarly, the existence of social security payments decreases the effect on disposable income of increased (or decreased) unemployment.

The advantage of automatic stabilisation is that it comes into effect without delay. As soon as income falls or rises significantly, the system ensures that marginal rates of net tax change immediately in the direction that decreases the impact on output. Discretionary measures (for example, the building of a new road) might be subject to substantial administrative delay, but can be targeted to particular industries or regions. To have the intended effects, however, they depend on a high level of accuracy in economic forecasts. A policy that is introduced to counter the effects of predicted rising demand will have very undesirable effects if demand actually falls, and *vice versa*. Inadequate forecasting might mean that policy measures that are intended to decrease the problem of fluctuations in income actually have the effect of increasing the severity of fluctuations. Accurate forecasts are, of course, very difficult to achieve.

The boundary between the two types of fiscal policy is not always clear. In the year in which they are introduced or amended, automatic stabilisers are effectively discretionary measures.

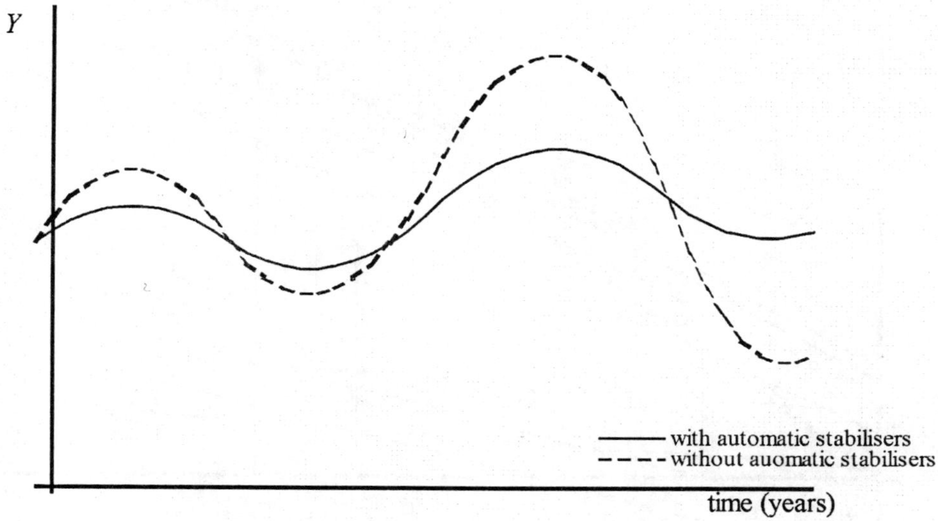

Figure 22. Effects of Automatic Stabilisers.

Figure 22 shows the effect of automatic stabilisers on the level of income. This type of fiscal policy decreases the amplitude (severity) of the economic cycle without changing its frequency (the timing of peaks and troughs). Graphs of macroeconomic data are, however, unlikely to be as smooth as those shown in Figure 22.

Balanced Budget Multiplier

The macroeconomic effects of fiscal policy depend partly on how it is financed. The effects of a loose fiscal policy will be decreased if it is financed by increased net taxation. The expansionary effects of an increase in government spending will be partly offset by the contractionary effects of higher net tax rates. The effects will not, however, be completely neutralised, even if the increase in government spending is totally financed by increased tax revenue. The reason for this is that, although people decrease their consumption when required to pay higher taxes, some of the additional tax payment comes from a decreased rate of savings as tax-payers try to minimise the effects on their consumption. There is, therefore, a net increase in demand following an increase in government spending which is fully financed by increased net taxation. This net increase in demand is then subject to the usual multiplier process.

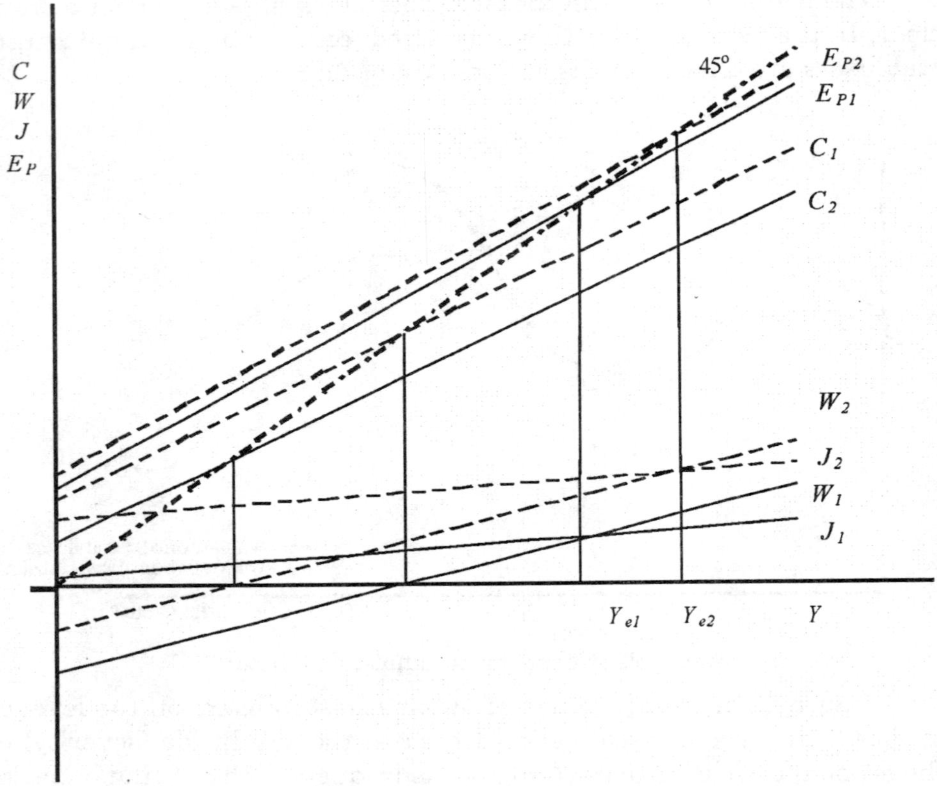

Figure 23. Balanced Budget Multiplier.

This series of events, known as the balanced budget multiplier process, is described in Figure 23. The initial equilibrium is at the intersection of aggregate demand (E_{P1}) (the sum of consumption (C_1) and injections (J_1)), and the 45° line. It is also at the intersection of withdrawals (W_1) (which comprise savings (S) and net taxation (T)) and *ex-ante* injections (J_1) (which comprise investment (I), government spending (G), and net exports ($X - Z$)). The increase in net taxation (ΔT), which is equal to the increase in government spending (ΔG) decreases consumption spending by a smaller amount (ΔC). The consumption function shifts from the line identified as C_1 to the line identified as C_2; this shift might also involve a change of gradient. Following the increase in government spending, the aggregate demand function shifts from the E_{P1} line to the E_{P2} line (which shows the value of [E_{P1} – ΔC + ΔG]). The new equilibrium is at Y_{e2}, where this function crosses the 45° line.

The same conclusion is reached if the effects on withdrawals and injections are examined. The increase in government spending (ΔG)

shifts the injections function from the J_1 line to the J_2 line. The equal increase in net taxation (ΔT) leads to decreased savings (ΔS) so the withdrawals function moves from W_1 to W_2 (which shows the value of [$W - \Delta S + \Delta T$]). The new equilibrium is where the new injections function intersects the new withdrawals function.

The same approach leads to the conclusion that a reduction in government spending will be contractionary even if it is accompanied by an equal cut in net taxation, as people are unlikely to spend the whole of a tax reduction on consumption, and some will be saved. The balanced budget multiplier theorem means that it is not necessary for the government budget to be in deficit for a loose fiscal policy to be effective, nor for the government budget to be in surplus for a tight fiscal policy to be effective. The value of the multiplier (K) will, however, be very much greater if there is no change in net taxation. In this situation, increased government spending is financed by borrowing, and decreased government spending leads to a decrease in government debts.

Fiscal policy that is combined with changes in net taxation to maintain a balanced government budget has a decreased effect on the level of income (Y), and so shifts the *IS* line by a smaller amount.

If changes in government spending are financed by changes in the money supply, this shifts the *LM* line, which is introduced in Chapter 5.

The *IS* diagram is further developed in Chapters 6 and 12. The significance of the *IS* line is that it enables the level of interest rates, an additional independent variable, to be incorporated into the Keynesian income-expenditure model.

The Size of the Budget Deficit or Surplus

Fiscal policy changes are sometimes introduced with the intention of reducing the government budget deficit ($T - G$). However, neither decreased government spending nor increases in net taxation can be relied upon to decrease the deficit.

Figure 24 shows a government spending (G_1) function and a net taxation (T) function. The initial equilibrium is at Y_{e1}, and the budget deficit is the distance from **A** to **B**. A reduction in government spending would shift the function from G_1 to G_2. The effect on the budget deficit depends on the value of the multiplier. If the multiplier is small, and the equilibrium moves from Y_{e1} to Y_{e2}, then the deficit has been decreased to the distance from **C** to **D**, but if the multiplier has a larger value, so that the equilibrium level of income falls to Y_{e3}, then, because of decreased net tax revenue at a lower level of income, the size of the budget deficit has increased to the distance from **E** to **F**.

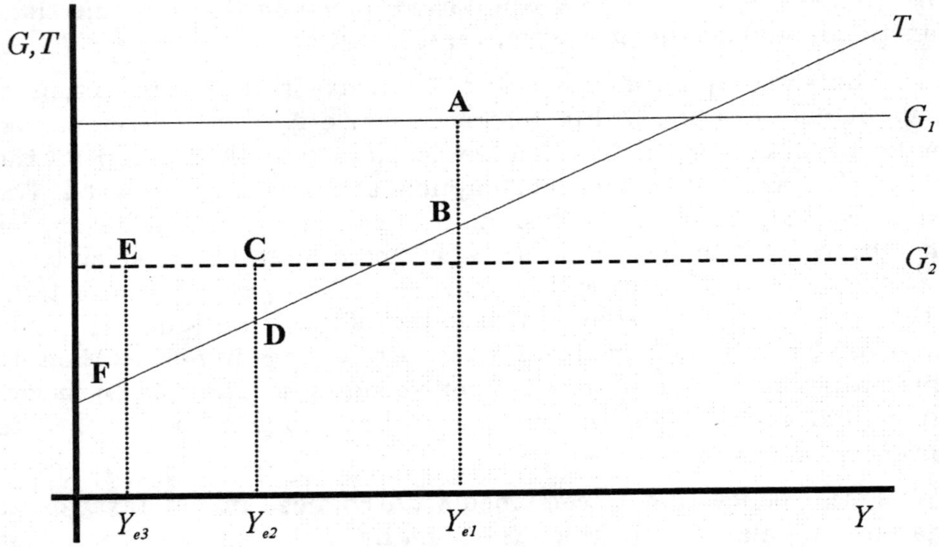

Figure 24. Budget Deficit.

Measurement of the Severity of Fiscal Policy

It is useful to have a measure of the severity of fiscal policy so that different circumstances can be compared. However, such a measure is difficult to devise. In particular, the size of the budget deficit is not an adequate indicator, since the effect of a tight fiscal policy on the budget deficit depends on the value of the multiplier.

One possibility is to use the full-employment budget surplus. This is an estimate of the value of the budget surplus ($T - G$) that would occur under current fiscal policy if full employment had been achieved. This requires making an estimate of the value of income that corresponds to full employment, estimating the equation of the current net tax function, and estimating the current annual value of government spending. The first two of these three cannot be done with accuracy.

4

The Money Supply and its Determinants

Many economic variables are measured in money terms. The figures for GDP, for example, are quoted in millions of crores of rupees. The Indian rupee is a convenient unit for the measurement of value, and enables statisticians to total the value of the production of a very wide range of different items. It is, of course, possible to use any commodity as a unit of account. The value of aggregate output could be expressed in terms of any commodity that is of importance in the economy. It could be calculated, for example, in terms of cotton-kilogram or apple-kilogram value units.

Money is not, however, merely a unit of account; it is also the usual medium of exchange. When goods and services are bought and sold, it is generally in exchange for money. Barter, the exchange of goods or services for other goods or services, is possible but, in industrial economies, occurs in only a very small proportion of transactions. In almost all cases, firms sell their output to their customers for money, pay the suppliers of their raw materials and fuel in money, pay their employees in money, pay their taxes or receive subsidies in money, and distribute profit to their share-holders in money.

The third function of money is its role as a store of wealth, although other assets, including both physical goods (such as houses, jewellery) and financial securities (such as company shares) might also have this function. The existence of an adequate store of wealth enables part of income to be saved and thus part of consumption spending to be postponed. However, money forms an adequate store of wealth only if the price level is stable; if prices are rising, a particular sum of money buys a smaller and smaller quantity of goods as time passes.

Since there are alternatives to money for its unit of account and store of value functions, it is the medium of exchange function that is of particular interest.

The existence of money means that the three problems of barter can be avoided. It is a problem of barter that some goods are not easily divisible. If a healthy live sheep is worth twenty chickens, for example, it is impossible for the owner of such a sheep to buy a single chicken unless the sheep can be sold for a sum of money and one twentieth of that sum used to pay for the chicken.

The second problem of barter trading is the need for double coincidence of wants. In a money system, where goods are exchanged for money, it is necessary for the seller of an item to find someone who wants to buy that item. This is called single coincidence. The seller can then choose how to spend the money received from the buyer. In a barter system, however, the seller not only needs to find a buyer for the goods offered but, simultaneously, the buyer needs to be someone who has acceptable goods available in exchange. If the seller of a sheep wants twenty chickens for it, it is not enough to find someone who wants a sheep, it must be the same person who wishes to dispose of twenty chickens. If the prospective buyer of the sheep offers other goods, which the owner of the sheep does not wish to acquire, then trade will be impossible.

The third problem of a barter system is that many goods are not durable, which means that spending cannot be delayed and so wealth cannot be accumulated. The owner of chickens, for example, receives income each day in the form of eggs. These are likely to deteriorate and so must be spent quickly before their value becomes zero. It is likely that the goods received in exchange are also perishable (fruit, milk, meat, perhaps) and so must also be used without delay.

Barter is therefore an inefficient means of trading. The widespread use of money widens the choices available to both buyers and sellers. In particular, it gives them control over the timing of purchases, and so permits producers to save some of their income. This enables people to protect themselves from some of the consequences of difficult times (such as severe winters). It also enables them to acquire larger amounts of wealth and therefore to buy larger items. When wealth is in the form of money, or in a form that can easily be exchanged for money, the process of borrowing and lending becomes very much easier. This means that modest amounts of wealth held by each of a large number of individuals may be borrowed by an entrepreneur and used to create production methods that are efficient and on a large scale. This includes investment in training and in specialised equipment.

By encouraging trade, the use of money encourages the specialisation of labour. If it is easy to sell their output, people will be encouraged to concentrate their efforts on producing what they are best at, and this is likely to lead to increased total production. Further, the use of money facilitates saving, so that hardship is decreased in times of crisis. Finally, it encourages the accumulation of wealth and its lending, and thus the accumulation of physical and human capital, which leads to increased output and efficiency.

The Nature of Money

The form taken by money varies between countries and at different times in history, but the economic significance is the same provided that it is generally accepted in settlement of debts. The economic function of money does not depend on whether it is an item with some other use (for example, salt, iron), a naturally occurring object in strictly limited supply (for example, a precise type of shell), or tokens that have been manufactured specifically for use as money (for example, coins). If something functions as money then, in the eyes of academic economists, it is money.

The supply of early types of money was often subject to random fluctuations and could not be controlled by governments. As circumstances demanded, commodities used as money were sometimes absorbed into other uses, and the amount available frequently varied with climatic change or with new mineral discoveries. These had economic effects. If the money supply falls, there might not be a sufficient quantity in circulation to enable the economy to operate smoothly, and increases in the money supply might lead to increases in the general level of prices.

Later in history, money issued by the authority of governments became important, and some governments abused this power by paying their debts with newly-issued currency. This type of action also had the economic effect of raising the price level.

The quantity of money circulating in an economy is therefore likely to be of economic significance.

Modern Money

Today's money in India and other countries is of two types. The first type comprises notes and coins, which are also known as cash.

These are issued by the government. They have value because they are legal tender, which means that sellers must, as a legal requirement, accept notes and coins in payment. There is no economic distinction, in the twenty-first century, between notes and coins, though the historical origins are different. Early coins represented a guaranteed weight of precious metal (for example, gold, silver), and the original bank-notes were receipts which entitled the holder to claim the specified amount of precious metal (or coins) from safe keeping. Today, however, both notes and coins are tokens, without intrinsic value, which are issued by the government for monetary use, and which the government requires people to accept. The non-money uses of notes and coins, for example as ornaments or collectors' pieces, can be regarded as negligible.

The second type of money in current use is bank deposits. A very large proportion of payments, especially of larger sums of money, is not made with notes and coins, but by means of cheques. A cheque is a request to a bank to transfer ownership of a bank deposit. Cheques themselves are not money; a cheque may be returned by the bank on which it is drawn if there are insufficient funds in the account to which it refers. Bank deposits are not legal tender; there is no requirement to accept payment in other than notes and coins. They are, however, regarded by academic economists as money because they are generally accepted in payment of debts. Other means of transferring bank deposits are standing orders, direct debits, electronic funds transfer, and credit cards. The precise method is not critical; what is important is that it is bank deposits that are being used in payment.

Bank deposits are an intangible form of money; they have no physical existence. They are liabilities of the banks since they represent sums that banks owe to their depositors. Bank deposits are ledger entries, or the equivalent in a modern computerised system, which can be transferred between customers or exchanged, at the request of the depositor, for cash.

Measures of the money supply do not refer solely to the number of notes and coins in the system. Notes and coins are, of course, money, but a large proportion of the money supply is in the form of bank deposits.

TABLE 5 Money Supply in India, 31 March 2008

	Rs. crore
Notes and coins (outside the banks)	567746
Demand deposits	575894
M1	1143640
Other deposits in banks and the post office	2884518
M4	4028158

Source: Reserve Bank of India

Table 5 shows a summary of recent money-supply data published by the Reserve Bank of India. The figure for cash in circulation is the value of notes and coins on issue by the Reserve Bank of India minus the amount held by banks as till money. Banks' holdings of notes and coins are subtracted to avoid double counting. An individual who deposits cash at a bank, and acquires a bank deposit in exchange, does not obtain additional spending power and so does not increase the money supply. It would, therefore, be misleading to include both the value of the cash (held by the bank) and the value of the deposit in the total value of the money supply.

There is some disagreement about exactly which bank deposits should be included in measures of the money supply. There is no dispute that bank deposits should be regarded as money, as a very large proportion of payments are made by the transfer of bank deposits from one holder to another, and therefore all measures of the money supply include the value of demand deposits. Not all economists, however, approve of the inclusion in the total of other types of bank deposit. The most widely quoted measures of the money supply in India are *M1* and *M4*. Both of these include the value of cash in circulation (outside the banks) and the value of cheque accounts and other demand deposits. *M4* also includes other bank deposits.

The definitions of *M1* and of *M4* that are used in India are:

$M1 \equiv$ Notes and coins (outside the banks) + demand deposits

$M4 \equiv M1$ + other deposits in banks and the post office

Money should not be confused with wealth, which includes not only money (those assets that are generally accepted in payment) but also all other assets. Such other assets include houses, land, company shares, and gold. Wealth also includes assets that might be difficult or impossible to sell, such as pension rights, copyright, and patent rights.

Wealth ≡ Money + other assets

Measurement of the money supply is complicated by the problem of selecting the most appropriate definition. The accuracy of the figures is also unclear. It can be assumed that the banks and the Reserve Bank of India keep accurate records, so the figures are certainly accurate in the crude sense. It is unclear, however, how much of the cash and deposits in existence are in use as money. Some notes and coins have been permanently lost, or are held by collectors, or have been made into jewellery, or have been retained as souvenirs by foreign visitors, and so are no longer in circulation as money. Some bank deposits have been forgotten, and so are also no longer functioning as money. A further complication arises because of unused overdraft facilities, which represent spending power for bank customers but are not included in money-supply data until they are used (and the amount that is spent is held as cash or added to the payees' bank accounts).

As Table 5 shows, notes and coins form a small part of the Indian money supply, and the amount of bank deposits, whichever definition is chosen, greatly exceeds the amount of cash.

The Creation of Bank Deposits

An understanding of the nature of bank operations is necessary for the understanding of the process of the creation of bank deposits. Banks accept deposits and promise to repay them if requested. Customers benefit from the convenience of using cheque and other payments systems, from the knowledge that their money is secure from theft, and, in many cases, by receiving interest. Customers, especially those with small balances or making large numbers of payments, might also be charged fees. Banks use the money deposited with them to lend to borrowers. They charge interest, and use this money to pay their expenses and leave an amount of profit which is acceptable to their share-holders.

There is an apparent inconsistency here. Banks promise to keep their depositors' money in safe custody, but then lend it to borrowers who are not necessarily trustworthy. The important concept that is essential to the operation of banks is confidence. Depositors need to be confident that banks will repay their savings if they ask for them but, equally, banks need to be confident that, at a particular time, only a very small proportion of their depositors will do so. They need to be able to assume that most people will keep most of their money in banks most of the time. Banks therefore hold a small proportion of their total deposits in reserve to enable them to make repayments to depositors, and lend the rest. A further type of confidence is needed here; banks need to be confident that borrowers will repay loans in full, with interest, and on the due date.

If any one of these three types of confidence were to collapse then the banking system would be unable to function.

When a bank lends money to a borrower, that money will almost certainly be spent. Since most people keep most of their money in banks most of the time, the person to whom it is paid will probably deposit the money (or most of it) in a bank account. This creates a bank deposit that did not already exist. The bank's response to this will be to place a small amount of the deposit in reserve and, in order to make profits, to lend the rest. The money that is lent will (almost certainly) be spent and will (probably) be deposited in a bank, whereupon most will be lent again, and then spent, and then re-deposited. This is an infinite process, though each loan is smaller than the previous one. The important point is that each time that money is deposited in a bank it creates a new deposit, without destroying those that already exist, and since the money supply includes bank deposits, it creates an addition to the money supply. This explains why the total value of bank deposits is very much greater than the value of cash in circulation.

The numerical example in Table 6 shows the process of bank deposit creation. The illustration is presented in the form of a series of balance sheets, each of which describes the position of a bank at a particular time. A bank's assets are the things in its possession that have a money value. Assets may be physical (for example, buildings, computers) or they may be financial. Financial assets include loans, which are sums of money that banks are confident that they will receive at a specified date in the future. A bank's liabilities are the sums that it owes. These include deposits, which must ultimately be repaid to the depositors (if they request this).

For simplicity, the numerical illustration assumes that banks keep 10% of their assets in reserve. It is also assumed that there is excess demand for loans, so that the bank is always able to find acceptable borrowers for all the money that it wishes to lend. Finally, it is assumed that all of the money that is lent is ultimately re-deposited in a bank account, so that the maximum amount is available for banks to lend. The second and third of these assumptions mean that the creation of the bank deposits is maximised from each initial deposit of cash.

TABLE 6. Bank Deposit Creation

Rs.	Liabilities				Assets
Stage 1	Deposit	*(1)*	1000	1000	Cash
Stage 2	Deposit	*(1)*	1000	100	Reserve
				900	Loan *(2)*
			1000	1000	
Stage 3	Deposits	*(1)*	1000	100	Reserve
		(3)	900	900	Loan *(2)*
				900	Cash
			1900	1900	
Stage 4	Deposits	*(1)*	1000	100	Reserve
		(3)	900	900	Loan *(2)*
				90	Reserve
				810	Loan *(4)*
			1900	1900	
Stage 5	Deposits	*(1)*	1000	100	Reserve
		(3)	900	900	Loan *(2)*
		(5)	810	90	Reserve
				810	Loan *(4)*
				810	Cash
			2710	2710	
Final Result	Deposits		10000	1000	Reserve
				9000	Loans
			10000	10000	

Assumed : 10% Reserve ratio
Excess demand for loans, therefore no excess reserves
All loans are re-deposited

It is assumed that there is only one bank in the system. Alternatively, the balance sheets in Table 6 can be regarded as describing the whole of the banking system.

It is assumed that *Customer 1* deposits Rs. 1000 in notes and coins. The bank now has an asset in the form of cash. The deposit is a liability; it is the sum owed to the customer. This is the situation described as *Stage 1*.

In order to generate profits, and because it is confident that *Customer 1* is very unlikely to seek immediate repayment of the whole of the deposit, the bank lends most of it. It is operating a reserve ratio of 10%, so it lends Rs. 900 to *Customer 2*. This is *Stage 2*. The bank regards the loan as an asset because it is confident of receiving that sum in the future.

Customer 2 spends the loan and pays it to *Customer 3*, who deposits it in a bank account. This is described as *Stage 3*. The deposit of Rs. 1000 in the name of *Customer 1* is still intact, since it has not been withdrawn, but there is now an additional deposit of Rs. 900 in the name of *Customer 3*. The bank now has liabilities of Rs. 1900; it owes Rs. 1000 to *Customer 1* and Rs. 900 to *Customer 3*. The cash deposited by *Customer 3* is a new asset for the bank. The loan in the name of *Customer 2* has not yet been repaid and remains one of the assets of the bank. This is *Stage 3*. The total value of bank deposits, which are the major part of the money supply, has, through the operation of the banking system, now risen to Rs. 1900.

Having received a deposit of Rs. 900, the bank places Rs. 90 (10%) in reserve and lends Rs. 810 to *Customer 4*. This is shown as Stage 4.

Customer 4 pays the loan to *Customer 5* who deposits it in the bank. This generates an additional bank deposit, bringing the total to Rs. 2710, and an additional asset in the form of cash. This is *Stage 5*.

This is an infinite process which is mathematically similar to the multiplier process described in Chapter 2. The *Final Result* shows that an initial deposit of Rs. 1000 could lead to bank deposits of Rs. 10000 if the reserve ratio is 10%. This conclusion depends on the assumptions that all money lent is deposited and that 90% of all money deposited is lent. It is likely that neither of these assumptions is valid. It is probable that banks are unable to find acceptable borrowers for all of the money they wish to lend, or that not all of the money that is lent by banks returns to the banks.

The numerical example shows the significance of the banks' reserve ratio in the determination of the money supply. Had the reserve ratio in this exercise been 5%, the initial deposit of Rs. 1000 would have led to a loan of Rs. 950 (95% of Rs. 1000), and then a loan of Rs. 902.5 (95% of Rs. 950), and so on. The final result would have been total deposits of Rs. 20000.

The money multiplier (MM) (also called the bank credit multiplier) measures the effect on the money supply of a new deposit of cash. It is defined as the ratio of the value of additional deposits to the amount of the initial deposit of cash. The value of MM in Table 6 is ten; had the reserve ratio been 5%, the value of MM would have been twenty. The maximum value of MM is the reciprocal of the reserve ratio (RR). In practice, however, it will be less than this as it is likely that less than all of the money that is lent by banks is re-deposited and that the amount that banks actually lend is frequently less than the maximum that they are in a position to lend.

$$MM \equiv \frac{\text{New deposits}}{\text{New cash}} \leq \frac{1}{RR}$$

Although the banking system as a whole creates money by creating bank deposits, its power is not unlimited. Banks' lending is constrained by the willingness of their customers to deposit their money and the willingness of another set of customers to borrow. It is also constrained by the reserve ratio, which might be imposed by the government.

The operation of the banking system leads to the creation of deposits whose value greatly exceeds the amount of cash that has been deposited, but each individual bank cannot lend more than most of the money that has been deposited with it. In Table 6, an initial deposit of Rs. 1000 leads to total deposits of Rs. 10000, but in each time period only 90% of the latest round of deposits can be lent. A bank can decrease its cash to one tenth of its deposits, but it cannot increase its deposits to ten times its cash. Only the banking system as a whole can do that.

The operation of banking system is, of course, grossly simplified by the numerical example shown in Table 6. When deciding the form in which to hold their assets, banks can choose between assets of varying risk, term, liquidity, and return. It is in the interests of their share-holders to aim for high return (profitability), but such assets might bear a high risk of default, and will probably not be liquid. An asset is liquid if it can be sold quickly and without making a loss. It is important, in order to maintain the confidence of depositors, that banks have a sufficient amount of liquid assets so that any unusually high requests for repayment of deposits can be met.

Liquid assets generally offer a low return and *vice versa*, so that there is an inconsistency between banks' need to satisfy their depositors (with sufficient liquidity) and their need to satisfy their shareholders (with sufficient profits). To remain in operation, however, banks need to satisfy both of these needs. A further constraint on the operation of banks is their need to satisfy the requirements of the regulatory authority (which, in India, is the Reserve Bank of India). In some cases, precise reserve ratios are imposed; in others there is a more general requirement to operate in a prudential manner.

One of the reasons why people keep their money in bank accounts is the convenience of making payments by cheque, by credit card, and other simple and secure means. The existence of an efficient payments system decreases the need for large holdings of cash. A cheque is a request by a depositor to transfer a bank deposit to another depositor. If a cheque is paid into another account at the bank on which it is drawn, that bank experiences neither a change in total assets nor a change in total liabilities. It merely changes two book entries so that the amount in the drawer's account is decreased by the amount of the cheque, and the amount in the payee's account is increased by the same amount.

In a system comprising more than one bank, however, many cheques are paid into a bank other than the one on which they are drawn; the writer of a cheque is likely to have an account at a different bank to the recipient of the cheque. In this case, the receiving bank acquires both an additional asset and an additional liability, each equal to the amount of the cheque, and the paying bank's assets and liabilities each fall by the same sum. A bank which receives a cheque drawn on another bank credits its customer's account and thus acquires a liability, as it must pay the amount to the depositor on request. It can then claim this sum from the bank on which the cheque is drawn; this represents an additional asset to the receiving bank. The paying bank's assets fall by the amount of the cheque because it has to pay this sum to the receiving bank. Its liabilities fall when this sum is deducted from the account of the person who signed the cheque.

Every time that a cheque drawn on an account at one bank is paid into an account at another bank, therefore, a debt between the two banks is created. The paying bank has to pay the amount of the cheque to the receiving bank. Of course, with very many cheques being used each day, banks do not settle each of these debts individually. At the end of each business day, each bank calculates the total sum that it is owed by each of the other banks. The amount owed in the opposite direction is subtracted to give the net debt between each pair of banks. This is the amount to be settled.

In order to settle the debts between the banks that arise because of payments by cheque (and by other non-cash means), the banks use their Reserve Bank of India accounts. Although the Reserve Bank of India is principally the body that runs the monetary system on behalf of the government, it also has some banking functions. These include acting as the banks' bank. Debts between banks are paid by transferring sums from one bank's account to another bank's account, which decreases the assets of one bank and increases the assets of the other.

The banks' accounts at the Reserve Bank of India are also used when funds are transferred between a bank (or one of its customers) and the government. The government's principal bank accounts, into which its receipts from the private sector are paid and from which its payments to the private sector are drawn, are held at the Reserve Bank of India. For example, tax-payers send their cheques to their tax office, which pays them into its account at the Reserve Bank of India, which collects payment by deducting the appropriate sums from the accounts of the tax-payers' banks. This decreases the amount of banks' deposits at the Reserve Bank of India and, therefore, the amount of reserves held by the banks. The process occurs in reverse when the government pays money to the private sector. Sums paid, for example to road-building contractors or to the holders of government bonds, are drawn from the government's accounts at the Reserve Bank of India. Such cheques are deposited by their recipients in banks, who deposit them in their accounts at the Reserve Bank of India. This increases the value of banks' deposits and, hence, of banks' reserves.

Monetary Policy

Government action that is intended to affect the growth of the money supply is called monetary policy. Any government that wishes to pursue an active monetary policy will devise a system of controls that are designed to influence the supply of, and/or demand for, bank loans. Controlling the amount of bank lending controls the creation of bank deposits which are the dominant part of the money supply.

Notes and coins in circulation form a small proportion of the money supply. In March 2008, for example, as shown in Table 5, the proportion of *M4* in India was 14.1%. This figure varies substantially between countries. For example, the equivalent figure for New Zealand, where the banking system is used for a very large proportion of small transactions, is 1.5% [Source: Reserve Bank of New Zealand]. Controlling the quantity of cash in the system is not part of monetary policy. Notes and coins are issued passively by the Reserve Bank of India in whatever quantities and in whatever combination of denominations that the economic system requires in order to operate smoothly. If people draw larger than usual amounts of cash from their bank accounts, as generally happens each year at the start of the holiday season, the banks might find that they hold an inadequate amount, and so will draw additional notes and coins from their accounts at the Reserve Bank of India. If the Reserve Bank of India does not have enough notes and coins in stock, it will manufacture more. If the banks find that they receive more cash than they wish to hold, they will deposit the excess amount at the Reserve Bank of India, where it will either be stored for future re-use or destroyed. Notes and coins that are damaged or of obsolete design are withdrawn from circulation, and replaced, by the same mechanism.

Although the issue and withdrawal of notes and coins is not part of monetary policy, it is nevertheless an important function of the Reserve Bank of India. A very large proportion of smaller payments are made in cash and an adequate supply of it is essential for the economy to operate efficiently. Notes and coins are issued in whatever quantity of each denomination is necessary to satisfy demand. Failure to do this is likely to lead to a reduction of economic activity, the appearance of unofficial money, and the occurrence of barter. These effects were observed, for example, during the shortage of coins in Italy in the 1970s.

A policy that is intended to decrease the money supply is called a tight (or contractionary) monetary policy, and the reverse is called a loose (or expansionary) monetary policy. Monetary policy in India is administered by the Reserve Bank of India, which is the central bank of India. Monetary-policy decisions in India have used four types of instrument: open market operations, reserve requirements, interest-rate controls and directives.

Open Market Operations

Open market operations are important in Indian monetary policy. The undertaking of open market operations by the Reserve Bank of India means the selling or buying of securities by (or on behalf of) the government to or from the private sector. When the government sells securities, it receives money in exchange, which is therefore withdrawn from circulation. Similarly, when the government buys securities, it issues new money to pay for them. Sales of securities by the government constitute tight monetary policy, and government purchases of bonds constitute loose monetary policy. The process is, however, complicated by the multiplier process that is illustrated in Table 7, which shows the balance sheet of a banking system.

TABLE 7 Open Market Operations

Rs. crore	Liabilities		Assets	
Stage 1	Deposits	10000	1000	Reserve
			9000	Loans
		10000	10000	
Stage 2	Deposits	9998	998	Reserve
			9000	Loans
		9998	9998	
Stage 3	Deposits	9980	998	Reserve
			8982	Loans
		9980	9980	

Assumed : 10% Reserve ratio
Excess demand for loans, therefore no excess reserves
All loans are re-deposited
Government sales of securities are worth Rs. 2 crore

It is assumed that banks keep to a minimum 10% reserve ratio, that the availability of acceptable reserve assets is controlled by the government, and that the banks face an excess demand for loans. *Stage 1* shows the initial situation in which the banks' reserve comprises 10% of their total assets.

Stage 2 shows the immediate effect of a tight monetary policy involving the sale by the government of securities worth Rs. 2 crore. The buyers of these securities send their cheques to the Reserve Bank of India, which collects payment for each cheque by deducting the appropriate amount from the appropriate bank's account. This decreases the assets of the banks. Of greater significance is that it decreases their reserves, which include their deposits at the Reserve Bank of India. Each cheque is then sent to the bank on which it is drawn, which deducts the amount from the drawer's account. This decreases the liabilities of the banks by the same amount, which, in this case, is Rs. 2 crore. At this stage, banks' other assets are not affected, and so the reserve ratio falls below the target level, in this case to 9.98%.

Stage 3 shows how banks react to bring their reserve ratio back to the desired percentage. If it is assumed that banks cannot obtain additional reserve assets, then they must decrease their other assets. If their reserve is Rs. 998 crore, then, for a reserve ratio of 10%, the banks' maximum total assets are Rs. 9980 crore, and their maximum non-reserve assets are Rs. 8982 crore. They must therefore decrease other assets by Rs. 18 crore to Rs. 8982 crore. The principal assets in this category are loans outstanding. It is generally not possible to recall existing loans in advance of the agreed date for repayment. It is, however, possible to decrease the amount of loans outstanding by receiving repayments of existing loans and not re-lending the money. Instalments on existing loans, which decrease the amounts outstanding and so decrease the assets of a bank, are likely to be paid by deducting sums from bank deposits, which decrease the liabilities of a bank by the same amount. A customer who wishes to decrease a loan might write a cheque in favour of the bank. This decreases both the amount owed to the bank (which is one of the bank's assets) and the sum in the depositor's account (which is owed to the depositor, and so is one of the bank's liabilities).

Open market operations have a multiplied effect on the money supply. *Stage 3* shows that, if banks aim for a 10% reserve ratio and the supply of reserve assets is restricted, a sale of Rs. 2 crore worth of securities by the government will lead to a reduction in the amount of bank deposits, and hence the money supply, of Rs. 20 crore. In this situation, the value of the money multiplier is ten. This illustrates the importance of the money multiplier; it describes the effect of monetary policy on the money supply.

If a bank is unable to find acceptable borrowers for all the money that it wishes to lend, its reserve ratio will be greater than its target reserve ratio. In this situation, tight monetary policy will have a decreased effect. When the Reserve Bank of India sells securities, the banks' reserve ratios will fall, but the reduction in assets (loans outstanding) that is necessary to adjust the reserve ratio to its target value will be less than would be expected from the amount of the open market sale. This decreases the value of the money multiplier. The extreme (and implausible) case, when the money multiplier has a value of one and tight monetary policy has no multiplied effect on the money supply, occurs when the banks' reserve ratios are so high that they remain above their target reserve ratios after the Reserve Bank of India has sold securities to the private sector. Similarly, loose monetary policy will have no multiplied effect if the banks cannot find sufficient additional acceptable borrowers when their reserve ratios increase above their target ratios as a result of open market purchases of securities by the Reserve Bank of India.

In the banking system described by Table 7, the banks are at their desired reserve ratio of 10% and so an open market sale of securities for Rs. 2 crore leads to a reduction in the money supply of Rs. 20 crore and the money multiplier has a value of ten. If, however, the banks were aiming for a reserve ratio of 8%, then a reserve ratio of 10%, as in Table 7, would indicate an insufficient demand for loans. This means that the banks would have preferred to lend to their customers a part of the assets now held in their reserves. In this case, the sale of securities for Rs. 2 crore by the Reserve Bank of India does not lead to a multiplied decrease in the volume of bank deposits. The reduction of the banks' reserves from Rs. 1000 crore to Rs. 998 crore decreases their reserve ratio from 10% to 9.982% (calculated by dividing Rs. 998 crore by Rs. 9998 crore) which remains above their target ratio (of 8%) and therefore does not require a further adjustment. In this situation, the value of the money multiplier (MM) is one; the decrease in the money supply is equal to the value of the securities sold by the Reserve Bank of India.

A tight monetary policy will, if the banking system is at its target reserve ratio, force the money supply to contract. In contrast, a loose monetary policy merely permits an expansion of the money supply, and the amount of the increase in the money supply depends on the willingness of bank customers to borrow additional funds. This illustrates that monetary policy decisions and the banks' reserve ratios are not the only influences on the growth of the money supply. Other determinants include the demand for loans and the willingness of individuals and businesses to hold their money in the form of bank deposits.

Reserve Requirements

Many countries' governments have imposed minimum reserve ratios on banks, thus restricting the amount that banks can lend. It might also be required that banks' reserves are held in the form of certain defined securities whose supply is directly controlled. Restricting the availability of these securities also decreases the amount that banks can lend, and *vice versa*.

Reserve requirements are now a less significant part of monetary policy implementation in India than they were in the 1960s and 1970s.

Interest-Rate Controls

Many governments directly control the interest rates that are paid by banks to their depositors and charged by banks to their borrowers. In India, these controls have been simplified since the 1990s. However, controls remain on savings deposit rates (and on Reserve Bank of India deposit rates). In addition, the banks set their lending rates with reference to the Benchmark Prime Lending Rate (BPLR), which is specified by the Reserve Bank of India. Changes in these interest rates, which are determined administratively, are part of monetary policy and are intended to influence the general level of interest rates in the Indian economy.

An increase in interest rates is part of a tight monetary policy and *vice versa*. An increase in the level of interest rates decreases the value of securities [see Chapter 5] and therefore decreases the value of banks' reserves and decreases the availability of loans, and *vice versa*. Increases in interest rates might also decrease the demand for loans, and *vice versa*.

Directives

Directives are specific instructions about their lending to the banks. In the 1960s, for example, banks in India were required to seek permission for any loan above Rs. 1 crore.

5

The *LM* Line: Income, Interest Rates, and the Money Market

Interest is the price that has to be paid if a sum of money is held. If the money has been borrowed, then interest is paid to the lender. If the money is owned by the holder and has not been borrowed, an interest cost is still incurred; in this case it is the income which could have been received but has been foregone by not lending the money to someone else. Interest, which is received by the owners of capital, is a component of income (Y), which is a major determinant of the level of aggregate demand (E_P), which determines the level of equilibrium income (Y_e) in the following time period. The level of interest rates is also an influence on the level of investment spending (I), a part of aggregate demand which is of particular importance. Investment spending tends to fluctuate more than other elements of expenditure; it also enables production capacity to grow.

In the Keynesian theory of interest-rate determination, also called the theory of liquidity preference, the level of interest rates (r) depends on the level of money demand (M_D), the amount of money that people choose to hold, and the money supply (M_S), the amount of money that is in the system. Both of these concepts are measured at a point in time. This is in contrast to the concepts of aggregate demand (E_P) and aggregate supply (Y), used in Chapters 1 and 2, which are measured over a period of time. The value of planned expenditure (E_P), which measures aggregate demand, describes the quantity of output that people wish to buy per week or per year, not the amount they own at a point in time. Similarly, income (Y), which measures aggregate supply, refers to output during a time period and not to the value of stocks awaiting sale.

Money Demand

There are three components of money demand (M_D). The first is the demand for transactions balances (M_D^T), which means money held in order to make payments. Transactions balances are needed because the timing of receipts rarely exactly matches the timing of payments. For example, a person receiving wages weekly or monthly might need to pay bus fares twice a day and electricity bills every month. Transactions balances are held by firms and other bodies for the same reasons as they are held by individuals.

A major determinant of the level of transactions balances is the level of income. The relationship is positive; an increase in income enables people to increase expenditure and they need, therefore, to hold a greater amount of money in order to be able to make payments at the due time. When a company increases its output, of which income (Y) is an aggregate measure, it needs to hold an increased transactions balance to pay for its additional labour, materials, components, fuel, and other costs, and *vice versa*. The relationship between income and transactions demand for money is shown in Figure 25.

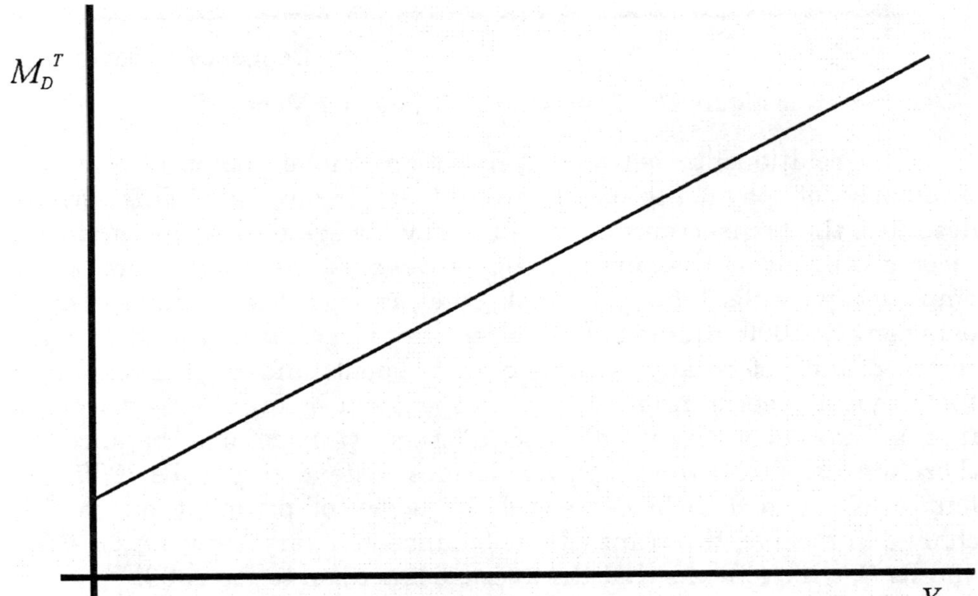

Figure 25. Transactions Demand for Money

Income is not the only determinant of the demand for transactions balances. There is also an inverse relationship with the frequency of payments (FP). For a particular amount of annual expenditure, frequent payments imply that each payment is small, and small transactions balances are necessary to make small payments. Similarly less frequent payments imply larger individual payments, so larger sums must be held. This is shown in Figure 26.

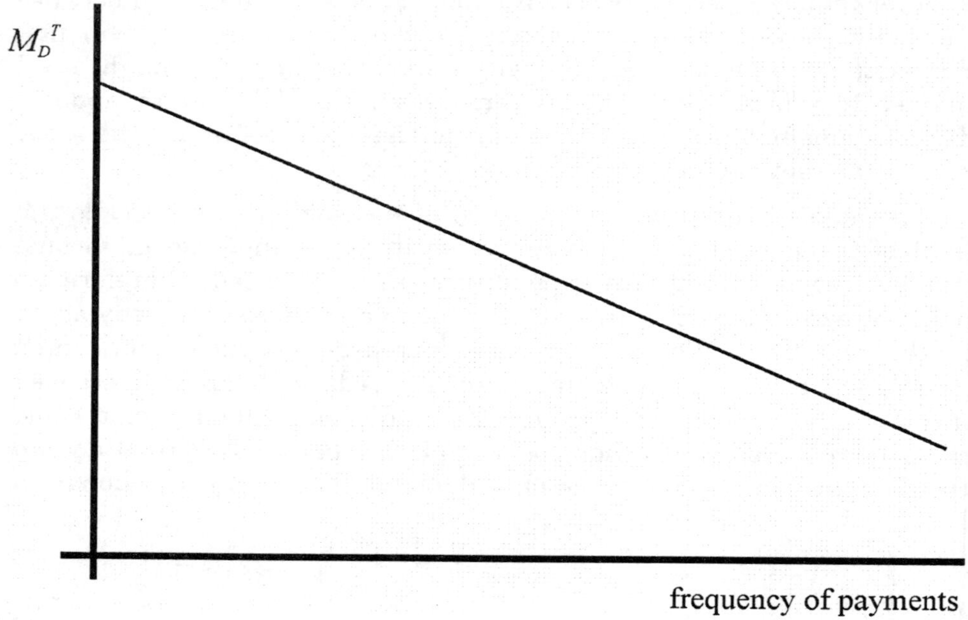

Figure 26. Transactions Demand for Money

The relationship between transactions money demand and the frequency of payments is illustrated in Figure 27. This graph describes the transactions balance held by a wage-earner, all of whose income is spent by the next date when wage payments are due. If the employer pays Rs. 1000 per week, the transactions balance varies between Rs. 1000 (immediately after the wage payment has been received and before any of the money is spent) and Rs. 0 (after all of the previous week's income has been spent but before the next week's income has been received); the average transactions balance is therefore Rs. 500. If the employer decides instead to pay Rs. 4000 per four weeks, which is a decreased frequency of payment but not a change in income, the transactions balance will vary between Rs. 4000 and Rs. 0, which means that the average has risen to Rs. 2000.

The inverse relationship between demand for transactions balances ($M_D{}^T$) and the frequency of payments (FP) does not just refer to payments by employers to employees. It refers to any kind of payments, for example fuel bills, rent, loan repayments, income tax.

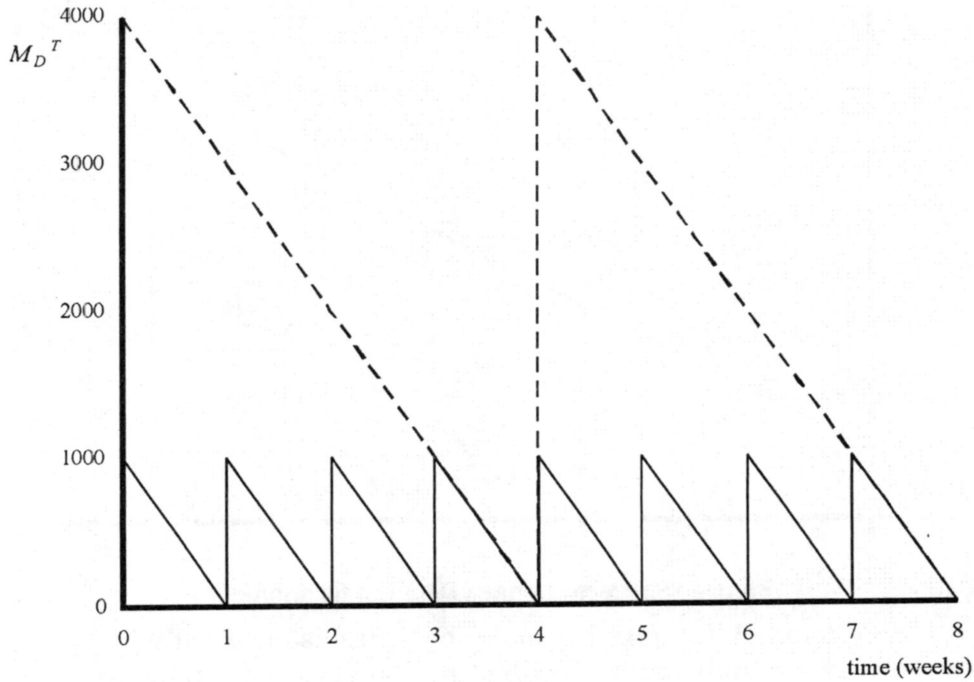

Figure 27. Transactions Demand for Money.

Money demand for transactions purposes is therefore a function both of the frequency of payments and of the level of income:

$$M_D{}^T = f(Y, \text{FP})$$

The second element of money demand is the demand for precautionary balances ($M_D{}^P$). This means money held in case of disaster. Both individuals and corporate bodies frequently hold money which will be spent only if some damaging circumstance arises. For individuals this might be unemployment or severe illness; for companies it might be a sudden rise in input prices or fall in demand for output.

The demand for precautionary balances is principally determined by the level of income. The relationship is positive; a high level of income means that people can afford to hold a large amount of money for precautionary reasons, but if income is low this might be difficult or impossible. When a company increases its output, of which income (Y) is an aggregate measure, it receives an increased amount of money from its customers, and is therefore probably able to hold an increased precautionary balance, and *vice versa*. The relationship between income and precautionary demand for money is shown in Figure 28.

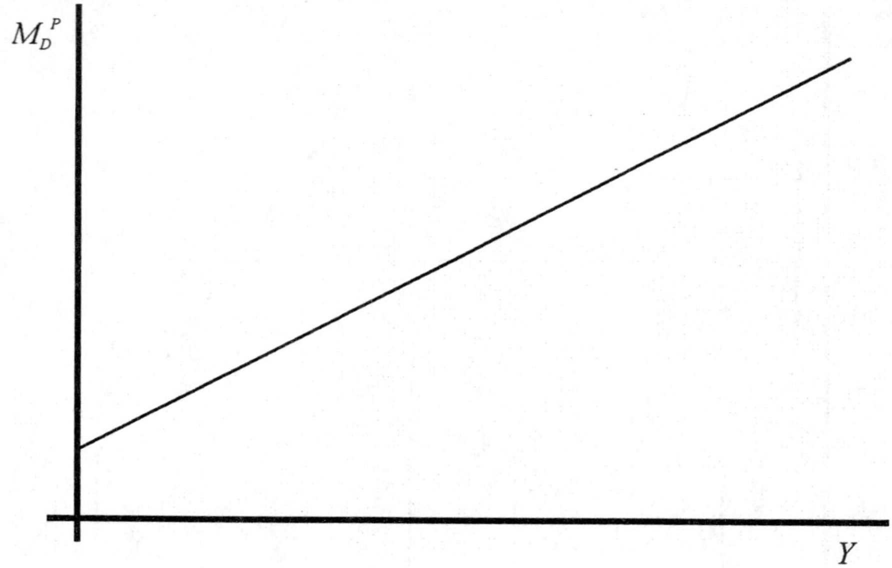

Figure 28. Precautionary Demand for Money

The demand for precautionary balances is also influenced by variables other than the level of income. The level of confidence is of importance; people who are frightened of losing their jobs are more likely to hold precautionary balances than those who are in employment that is perceived to be secure. The availability of services and transfer payments provided by the government is also relevant. For example, the availability of social security payments and other government transfers decreases the financial burdens associated with illness, unemployment, and other personal crises.

In addition, demand for precautionary balances will be influenced by the availability of financial assets that are perceived to be secure. If institutions providing insurance, pension schemes, and unit trusts, for example, are regarded as trustworthy and secure, there will be an incentive to use these services in preference to holding money balances for precautionary reasons.

Money demand for precautionary purposes is therefore a function of the level of income and of various other circumstances such as confidence and the availability of welfare services and secure financial assets:

$$M_D{}^P = f(Y, \ldots.)$$

The total of transactions and precautionary balances is sometimes called active balances. The third category of money demand is the demand for speculative balances ($M_D{}^S$) (also known as idle balances). Unlike transactions and precautionary balances, speculative balances are sums of money which are not held in order to make purchases. The difference between the other two is that transactions balances will be spent, while precautionary balances have a condition attached to their use, and they will be spent only if a specified type of hardship occurs.

Speculative balances are held as an alternative to other forms of wealth, and money is selected in preference to other assets if this is perceived to be in the holder's financial interest. The decision to hold speculative balances is, therefore, a profit-maximising decision. In Keynesian monetary theory, however, it is assumed that the holding of money does not generate income; this is one of the distinguishing features of money in comparison to other assets of which ownership might generate income in the form of profit or rent. This assumption is no longer always correct; some banks now pay interest on cheque accounts. In Keynesian theory, however, since it is assumed that money does not yield profit, the speculative motive for holding money can be more explicitly described as the desire to avoid making the losses that would result from holding some other asset that is likely to fall in value. This refers to both financial assets (for example, company shares) and physical assets (for example, houses).

In the absence of statutory controls, fluctuations in the price of a particular asset are caused by variations in its demand (the quantity that people wish to buy) and its supply (the quantity that people wish to sell). If demand exceeds supply, the price will rise, and *vice versa*. In many cases, such changes are related to the particular asset and are therefore a microeconomic rather than macroeconomic change. It is, however, of macroeconomic significance when many of the assets that can be held as an alternative to money show price movements that are in the same direction and of very similar magnitude. It frequently happens that the average price of company shares, for example, changes significantly. If it is generally predicted that the value of shares, or of other assets, is likely to rise, then this will stimulate demand for such assets; buyers will hope to purchase them when the price is low and then to make a profit by selling them after the price has risen.

The demand for speculative balances is, therefore, related to the price level of other assets. This price level is principally determined by the level of interest rates. The general relationship between asset prices and interest rates is negative; high asset prices occur in times of low interest rates and *vice versa*. This applies equally to the prices of both physical assets and financial assets.

In the case of financial assets, the interest rate or yield is calculated as the ratio of the annual income to the price. For example, a bond which is worth Rs. 1000 and produces an annual income of Rs. 50 has a yield of 5%. The current price is, however, affected by changes in interest rates elsewhere in the market. If banks are paying 10% on term deposits, then an income of Rs. 50 per year can be derived from a deposit of Rs. 500, which is what the bond paying Rs. 50 per year is therefore worth.

In equilibrium, the yield on all assets of equal risk will be the same. If it is not, then people will buy or sell securities until it is. This is illustrated in Table 8. If the equilibrium rate is 12.5%, then the equilibrium price of a security paying Rs. 1000 per year is Rs. 8000. If such a security is on sale for Rs. 5000, then the holder is receiving a yield of 20%, which is very attractive because it is above the ruling rate in the market. Demand for this security will therefore rise, causing its price to rise and its yield to fall, and this process will continue until its price has risen to Rs. 8000 and its yield has fallen to 12.5%, which is the equilibrium rate. The same process happens in reverse if the price of a security is above the equilibrium level. If the equilibrium rate is 12.5%, a security paying Rs. 1000 per year which is priced at Rs. 10000 has a yield of 10%, which is below the ruling rate. Holders of this security are therefore likely to sell it in order to buy other assets with a higher yield. The price of this security will therefore fall, and will continue to fall until it has reached Rs. 8000, which is the price at which the yield is at the equilibrium level of 12.5%

TABLE 8 Security Prices and Yields

Price (Rs.)	Yield (% per year)	Interest (Rs. per year)
5000	20	1000
8000	12.5	1000
10000	10	1000
20000	5	1000
25000	4	1000

The annual payment on a financial security is determined by the precise nature of that security and can be regarded as autonomous. The price and the yield are inversely related to each other because of the way in which they are defined, and can be regarded as two ways of expressing the same variable.

The relationship is, therefore, that high interest rates will occur with low security prices, and *vice versa*, though it might take time to reach equilibrium, and the prices of particular securities might be influenced by other factors.

Prices of financial assets might be influenced by expectations of changes in interest rates. If it is anticipated that asset prices are going to rise, following an anticipated fall in interest rates, then demand for securities will rise, as people try to buy them at a low price in the hope of making a capital gain. This will cause prices to rise, which decreases the yield (expressed as a percentage).

The inverse relationship between asset prices and the level of yields (interest rates) applies as much to physical assets (for example, houses) as to financial assets, though, in this case, it might take longer for the equilibrium point to be reached. A landlord who sees substantial and persistent rises in the level of interest rates might be tempted to sell houses and buy other assets. If enough property-owners do this, the value of houses will fall and, if the amount of rents received does not change, the yields on the houses will rise. Similarly, low interest rates on financial assets might encourage people to buy houses, which will raise the price level of houses and lower their yields.

The same inverse relationship between prices and interest rates applies in the case of owner-occupied houses. If interest rates fall, then buyers of houses can afford to borrow more, and therefore to pay more for houses. This increases the demand, expressed in money terms, for houses, but does not, in the short term, lead to increases in the number available. The price of houses will therefore rise. The reverse happens when interest rates rise.

As explained earlier, the demand for speculative balances depends principally on the price level of assets other than money. Speculative balances are, of course, held as an alternative to non-money assets. If such an asset has a high price, which is thought likely to fall, then there is an incentive to sell that asset, while the price is high, to avoid making a capital loss. In this situation people are choosing to hold money for speculative purposes. They are likely to continue to hold this money until it is perceived that asset prices are low and likely to rise, when demand for speculative balances falls as people buy such assets (when they are cheap) in the hope of selling them later (when they have become expensive). Since there is an inverse relationship between the level of interest rates and the level of asset prices, it follows that demand for speculative balances will be high when interest rates are low (because asset prices are high) and will be low when interest rates are high (because asset prices are low).

$$M_D^S = f(r, ...)$$

The relationship between the level of interest rates (r) and the demand for speculative balances (M_D^S) is shown in Figure 29.

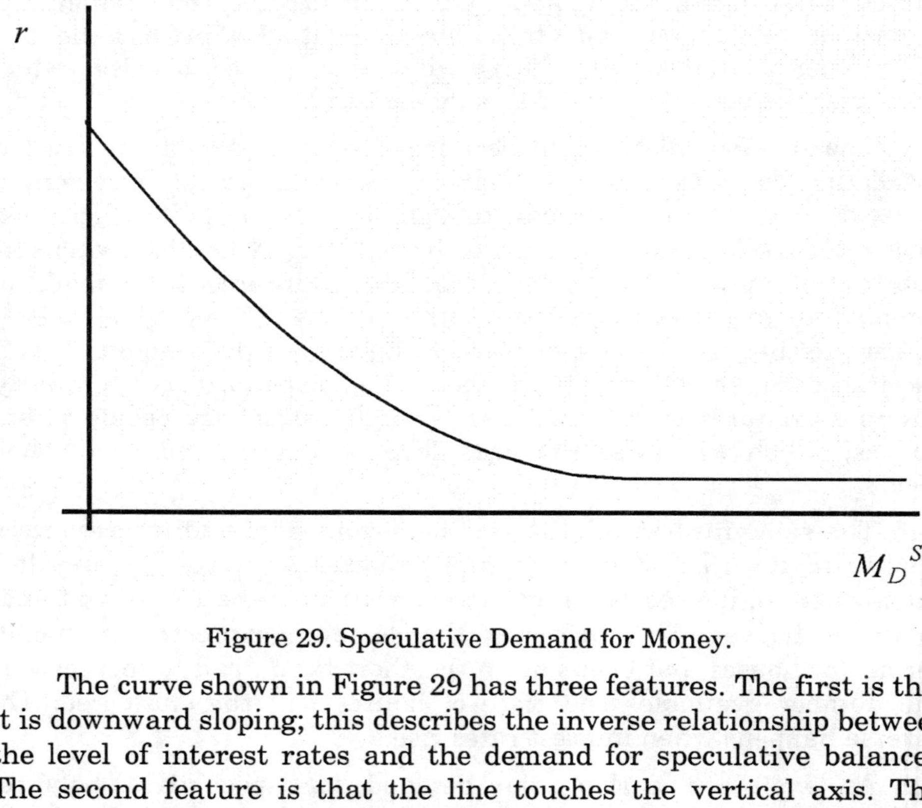

Figure 29. Speculative Demand for Money.

The curve shown in Figure 29 has three features. The first is that it is downward sloping; this describes the inverse relationship between the level of interest rates and the demand for speculative balances. The second feature is that the line touches the vertical axis. This implies that there is some level of interest rates which is so high that wealthy people feel that it is certain to fall, and therefore that asset prices are certain to rise, so they hold all their wealth in non-money form and none in money. The third feature of the line is that it becomes horizontal at low rates of interest. This implies that there is a minimum level of interest rates, which is greater than zero, at which demand for securities is zero and demand for money is, therefore, infinite. This is merely stating that there is a minimum return which is necessary in order to persuade people to forego the benefits of holding money when they buy securities.

Since the extreme parts of the $M_D{}^S$ function describe circumstances that are unlikely to occur, the graph is often simplified and drawn as a straight line, as shown in Figure 30.

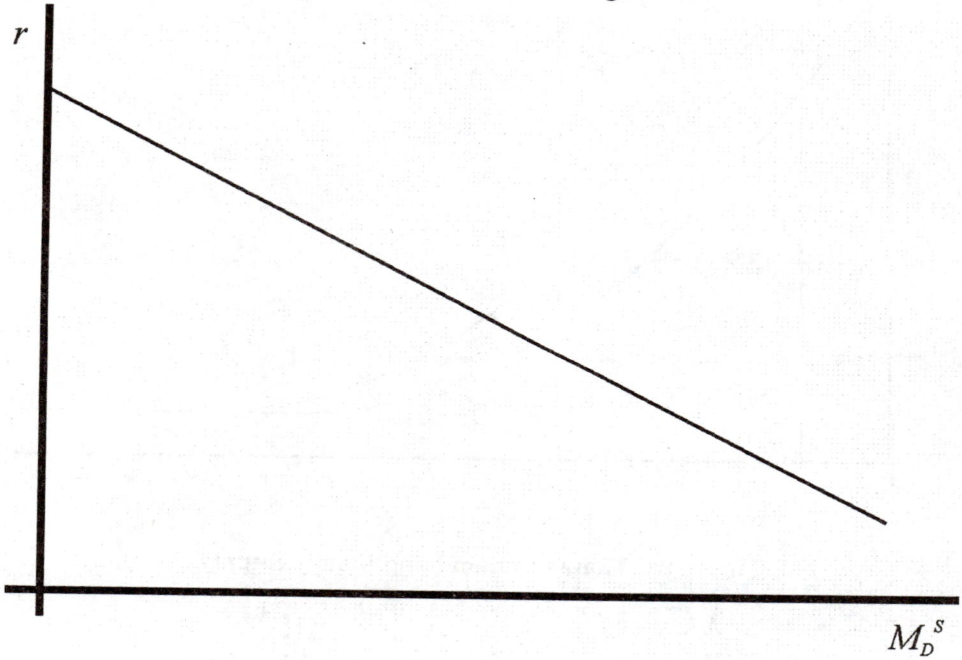

Figure 30. Speculative Demand for Money.

Total money demand (M_D) is the sum of demand for transactions, precautionary, and speculative balances.

$$M_D = M_D{}^T + M_D{}^P + M_D{}^S$$

The behavioural equation for total money demand is derived from the behavioural equation for each of its components, and shows that it is a function of both the level of interest rates (r) and the level of income (Y).

$$M_D = f(Y, r, ...)$$

Figures 31 and 32 show adaptations of Figures 29 (non-linear) and 30 (linear simplification) that illustrate the relationship between the level of interest rates (r) and total money demand (M_D). In both graphs a vertical line is used to indicate the demand for transactions ($M_D{}^T$) and precautionary ($M_D{}^P$) balances because neither of these are functions of the level of interest rates. Other independent variables, including the level of income (Y), are regarded as autonomous. A horizontal summation of the ($M_D{}^T$ + $M_D{}^P$) function and the $M_D{}^S$ function gives the M_D function.

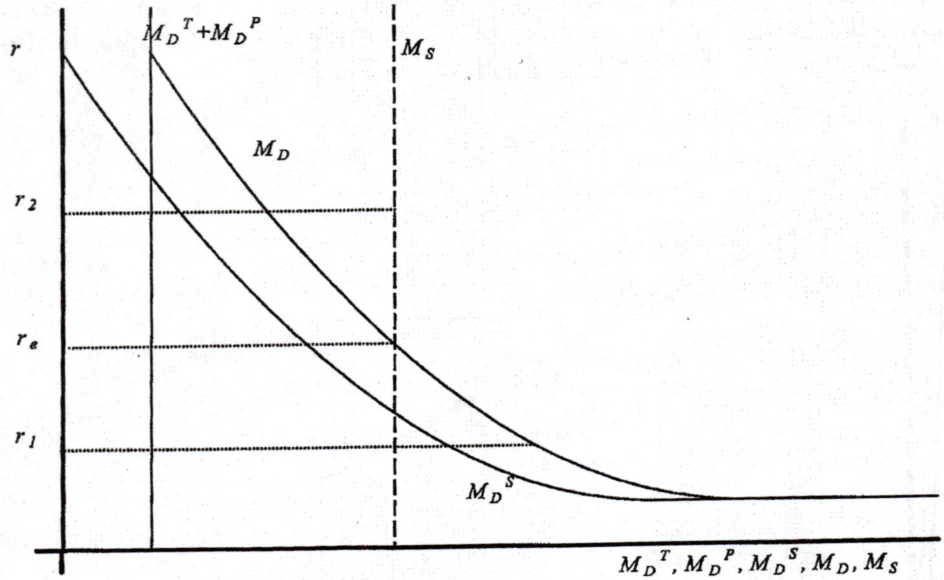

Figure 31. Money Demand and Money Supply.

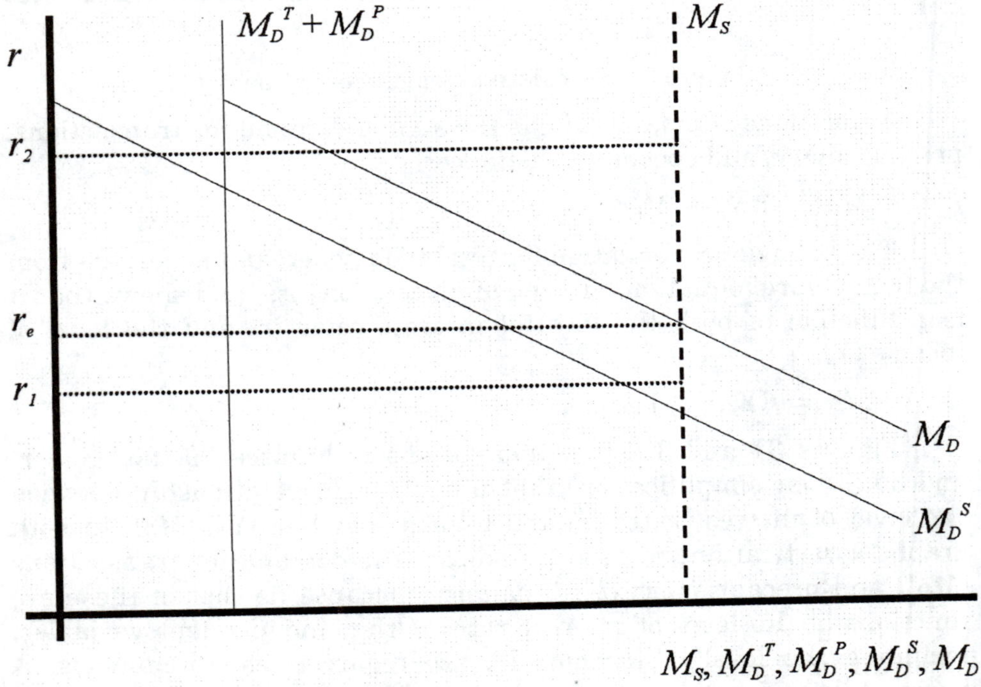

Figure 32. Money Demand and Money Supply.

Interest Rate Equilibrium

Also shown in both Figure 31 and in Figure 32 is a line representing the money supply (*Ms*), which comprises cash in circulation plus bank deposits. This line is vertical, but this does not mean that the money supply is fixed, just that it is not a function of interest rates. There are three determinants of the money supply. First, the money supply is principally a function of government policy; a loose monetary policy will tend to increase the money supply and a tight monetary policy will have the reverse effect. Second, the money supply is a function of the behaviour of banks; if banks choose to increase the amount they lend (and therefore to decrease their reserve ratio), the money supply will rise, and *vice versa*. Third, the money supply is influenced by the behaviour of the rest of the private sector. If people are willing to deposit their money in banks then the banks are in a position to lend and, when they do so, the money supply rises, but if people choose to keep their money in the form of cash, the banks are prevented from lending and bank deposit creation cannot occur. In addition, the non-bank private sector influences the rate of growth of the money supply through its demand for loans. If the demand for loans is low then money supply expansion is inhibited and *vice versa*. The *Ms* function shifts to the right if there is an increase in the money supply and *vice versa*.

One of the assumptions in Figures 31 and 32 is that prices are constant. However, if prices are increasing, there will be an increase in the amount of money that will be needed to buy a particular quantity of output, which is the same as saying that the real value of each rupee has decreased. If the nominal money supply (*Ms*) is constant, therefore, an increase in the price level leads to a reduction in its real value and shifts the money supply function to the left. The reverse occurs if there is a fall in prices. In this book, *Ms* and *MD* functions, and the *LM* locus which is derived from them, assume constant prices; *Ms* and *MD* therefore refer to the real value of the money supply and of money demand.

It is possible that the money supply is not independent of the level of interest rates. It may be, for example, that high interest rates encourage lending or discourage borrowing. This is ignored in Figures 31 and 32.

Figures 31 and 32 illustrate the Keynesian interest-rate equilibrium mechanism. If the level of interest rates is r_1, money demand (*MD*) is greater than money supply (*Ms*). In this situation, large organisations and wealthy people wish to hold more money than they are currently holding. They will therefore sell some assets to generate the additional money they wish to hold. If it happens in sufficient volume, this will cause the prices of these assets to fall, and their yields to rise. The level of interest rates r_1 is not, therefore, an equilibrium position.

If the level of interest rates is r_2, money demand (M_D) is less than money supply (M_S). This means that people are holding more money than they want. They will therefore exchange this surplus money for other assets. The increased demand for other assets will increase their prices and decrease their yields. If interest rates are at r_2, therefore, they will tend to fall.

The equilibrium level of interest rates is r_e. At this point M_D is equal to M_S. People are satisfied with their money holdings. They are neither trying to decrease nor trying to expand their money holdings, so they are neither buying nor selling assets, so the price of assets is neither rising nor falling, and so the level of interest rates is neither falling nor rising. This approach to interest-rate determination is called the theory of liquidity preference. If people prefer to hold their wealth in a more liquid form, then, by selling assets and causing prices to fall, they cause interest rates to rise; if, however, they prefer less liquidity, then, by buying assets, they cause prices to rise and interest rates to fall. Changes in the level of interest rates depend, therefore, on changes in the form in which people wish to hold their wealth.

The level of interest rates (r) is of macroeconomic significance because it is likely to influence investment expenditure (I) (see Chapter 2) and international flows of capital (see Chapters 11 and 12).

The prices of assets which are traded in financial markets fluctuate from day to day and even during a day's activity, and these fluctuations, which are explained by changes in the pressures of buying and selling, lead to equivalent fluctuations in the yield (interest rate) on securities. Changes in retail interest rates, for example on bank loans and on term deposits at banks, occur less frequently, but follow the same trend, as shown in Figure 33.

The wholesale (calculated from security prices) and retail levels of interest rates tend to converge. If the wholesale rate is above the retail rate there is an incentive for people to withdraw money from banks and buy financial assets. This will cause the price of securities to go up and their yield to go down; it might also lead to banks raising their rates to attract funds back again. The reverse is also true; if wholesale rates are lower than retail rates, people will sell securities (causing their prices to fall and their yields to rise) and place their money in banks (which are likely to react to this inflow of funds by reducing rates to encourage borrowers).

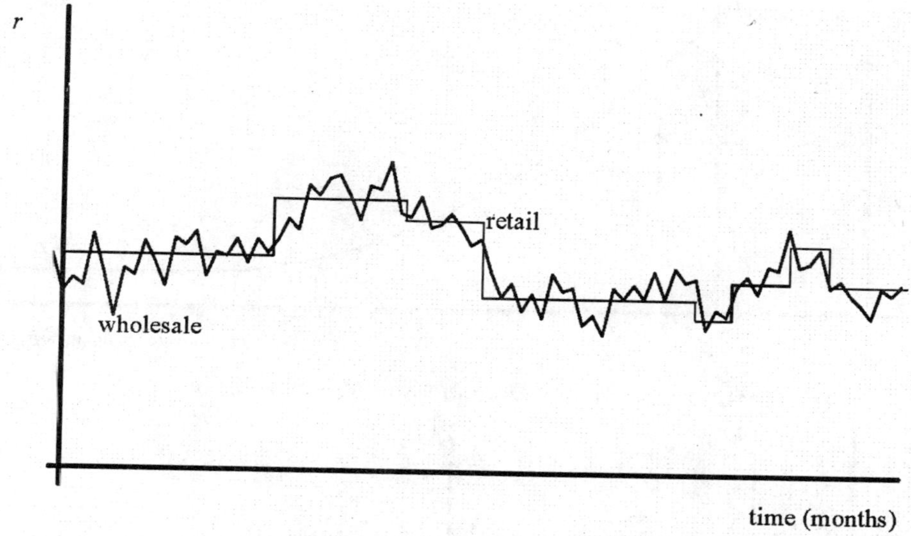

Figure 33. Retail and Wholesale Interest Rates.

The equilibrium level of rates of interest, at the intersection of the M_D and M_S functions, is not in a fixed position. It will shift if either of these functions shifts.

Monetary policy measures are designed to change the money supply, and therefore shift the M_S line. A loose monetary policy shifts the line to the right, and a tight monetary policy moves it to the left. The effects of a change in money supply, which might arise from causes other than monetary policy decisions, are shown in Figure 34, and in Figure 35, its simplified linear form. A shift of the M_S line could also be due to a change in the price level (which has an inversely proportional effect on the real value of the money supply).

If the money supply decreases, then, at the current equilibrium rate of interest, money supply will be less than money demand. Some people will find that they are holding less money than they wish to hold, and will therefore sell some assets. This will cause asset prices to fall and the level of interest rates to rise. The reverse happens when the money supply increases. This effect is shown both in Figure 34 and in Figure 35.

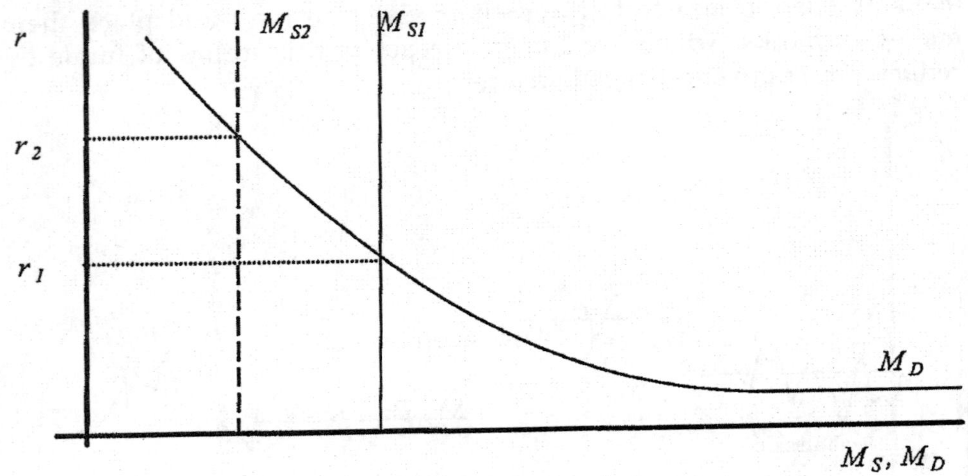

Figure 34. Money Demand and Money Supply.

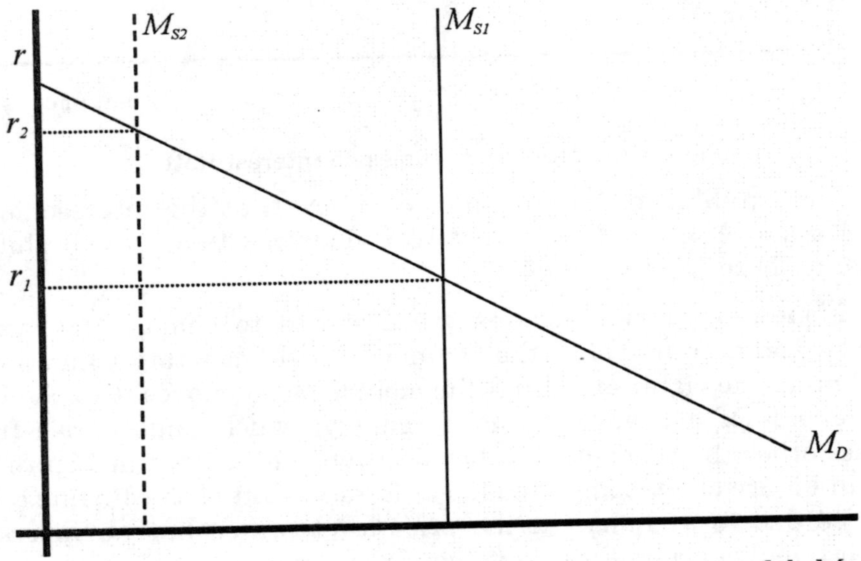

Figure 35. Money Demand and Money Supply.

The non-linear diagram shows, in addition, that if interest rates are at their minimum level, then increases in the money supply will have no effect. In this situation, called the liquidity trap, additional money supply is absorbed into speculative balances; there is no incentive to buy securities, as interest rates are not high enough, so asset prices cannot rise and the level of interest rates cannot fall. Speculative balances are held in the hope of avoiding the losses that would occur if interest rates were to rise and so assets were to become cheaper. When the level of interest rates (r) is at its minimum, and thus the M_D line is horizontal (because the $M_D{}^S$ line is horizontal), a change in the money supply (M_S) has no effect on r. In this situation, money demand is infinitely elastic. The liquidity trap phenomenon is not of current importance.

The equilibrium level of interest rates is also influenced by shifts in the M_D function. Figures 36 and 37 show the effects of an increase in the transactions demand for money ($M_D{}^T$); this could be due to a reduction of the frequency of payments (by, for example, the payment of employees monthly instead of weekly) or to an increase in income (Y). An increase in $M_D{}^T$ shifts the ($M_D{}^T + M_D{}^P$) line to the right (from ($M_{D1}{}^T + M_D{}^P$) to ($M_{D2}{}^T + M_D{}^P$)), and therefore shifts the M_D line to the right (from M_{D1} to M_{D2}). The new intersection with M_S shows that the equilibrium level of interest rates will increase. An increase in money demand, for example by employers who have agreed to pay a month's wages rather than a week's wages, means that people want to hold more money than they are holding. They will therefore sell some assets, which will cause prices to fall and yields to rise.

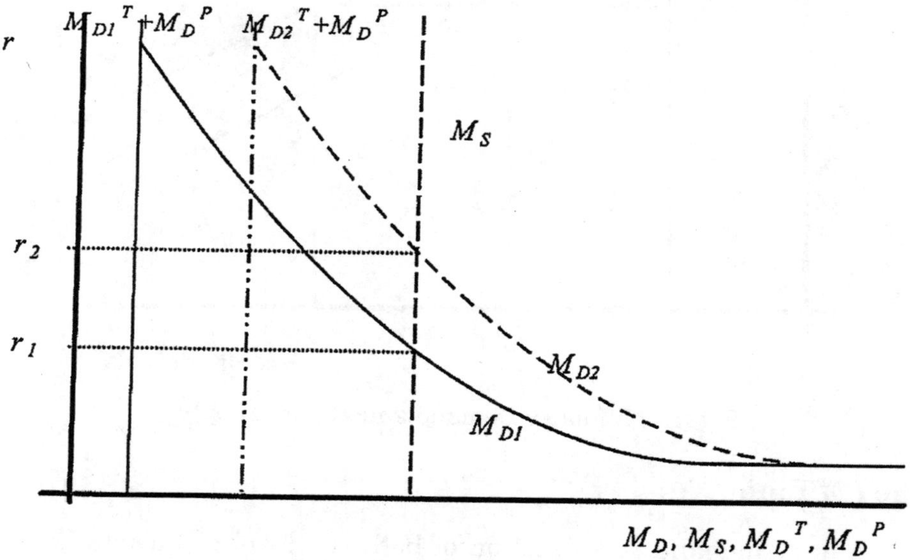

Figure 36. Money Demand and Money Supply.

A shift in the M_D function might be caused by a shift in the $M_D{}^S$ function. For example, by announcing that it would prefer interest rates to rise, the Reserve Bank of India (the central bank) is likely to create the expectation that they will rise. Since this would imply a fall in the value of financial assets, the announcement is likely to lead to a decrease in the demand for bonds. This will cause the price of bonds to fall and the rate of interest to rise. The reverse would happen if the Reserve Bank of India indicated that its preference was for a decreased level of interest rates. Such announcements, which are effectively an instrument of monetary policy, influence the outcome by causing a shift in the speculative demand for money (M_D^S) function.

Shifts of the M_D function can occur simultaneously with shifts of the M_S function. In this case, the conclusion depends on which line has shifted by the greater horizontal distance. In particular, if both M_D and M_S increase or decrease by the same amount there will be no change in the level of interest rates (r). A loose monetary policy may be used to neutralise the effect on interest rates of an autonomous increase in money demand, and *vice versa*.

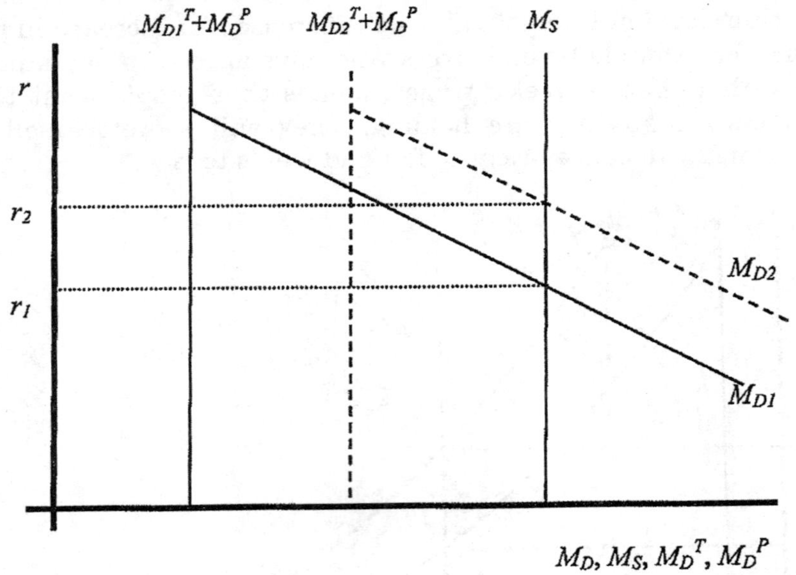

Figure 37. Money Demand and Money Supply.

The *LM* Line

Money demand is a function of both the level of income (Y) and the level of interest rates (r). It follows that the equilibrium level of interest rates can occur only at certain combinations of Y and r. A high level of r decreases the demand for speculative balances (M_D^S); in order for total money demand (M_D) to remain equal to money supply (M_S), there must be a corresponding increase in the demand for transactions and precautionary balances ($M_D^T + M_D^P$), which, if all other variables are assumed to be autonomous, must be caused by an increase in Y. A stable level of interest rates can therefore occur when

r is high and Y is high. It can equally occur when r is low (so $M_D{}^S$ is high) and Y is low (so $(M_D{}^T + M_D{}^P)$ is low). This is illustrated in Figures 38 and 39.

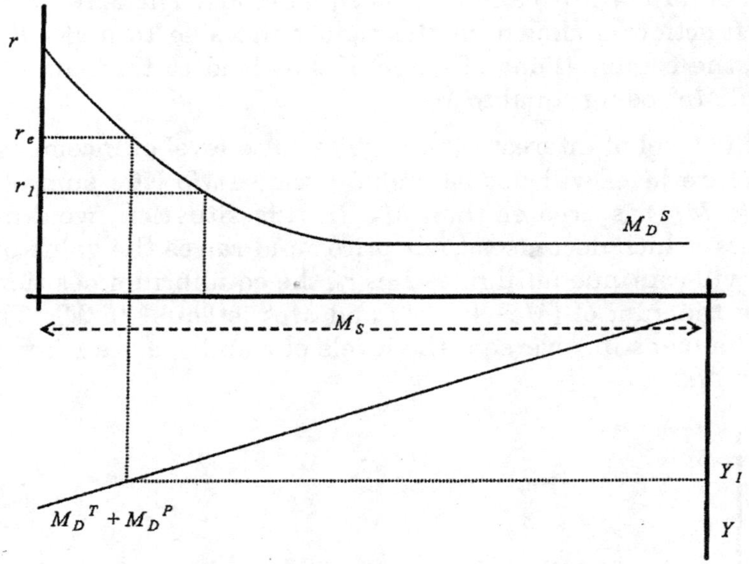

Figure 38. Equilibrium in the Money Sector.

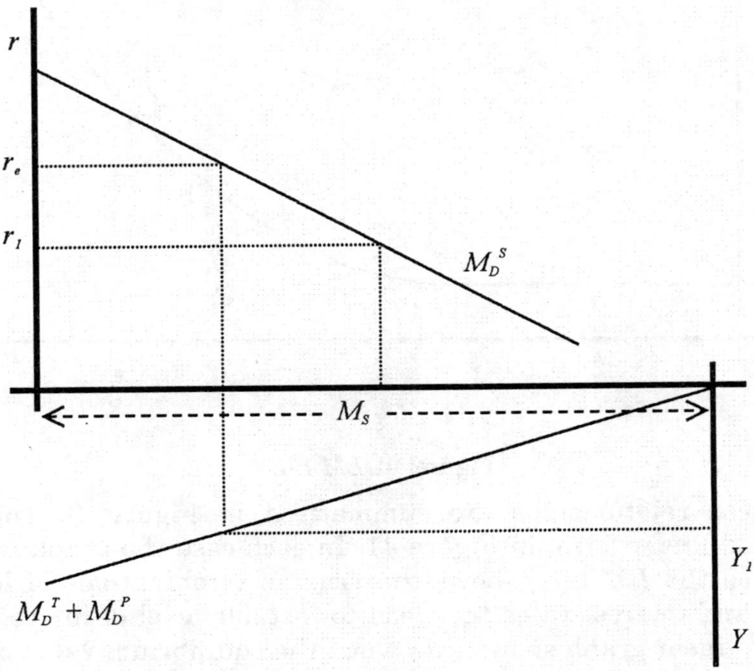

Figure 39. Equilibrium in the Money Sector.

Figures 38 and 39 show the inverse effect of r on $M_D{}^S$ and the positive effect of Y on $(M_D{}^T + M_D{}^P)$. The money supply (M_S) is assumed to be constant. The equilibrium value of r occurs when M_D, which is the sum of $(M_D{}^T + M_D{}^P)$ and $M_D{}^S$, is equal to M_S. The zero for the $(M_D{}^T + M_D{}^P)$ function is shown on the right-hand side to make it easy to identify the combinations of r and Y that lead to the sum of $(M_D{}^T + M_D{}^P)$ and $M_D{}^S$ being equal to M_S.

If the level of interest rates is r_1 and the level of income is Y_1, the interest-rate level will not be stable because M_D (the sum of $(M_D{}^T + M_D{}^P)$ and $M_D{}^S$) is greater than M_S. In this situation, wealth-holders sell assets, which decreases their prices and raises the value of r. This process will continue until r reaches r_e, the equilibrium position, which is where the sum of $(M_D{}^T + M_D{}^P)$ and $M_D{}^S$ is equal to M_S. The same process happens in reverse if the levels of r and Y are such that M_D is less than M_S.

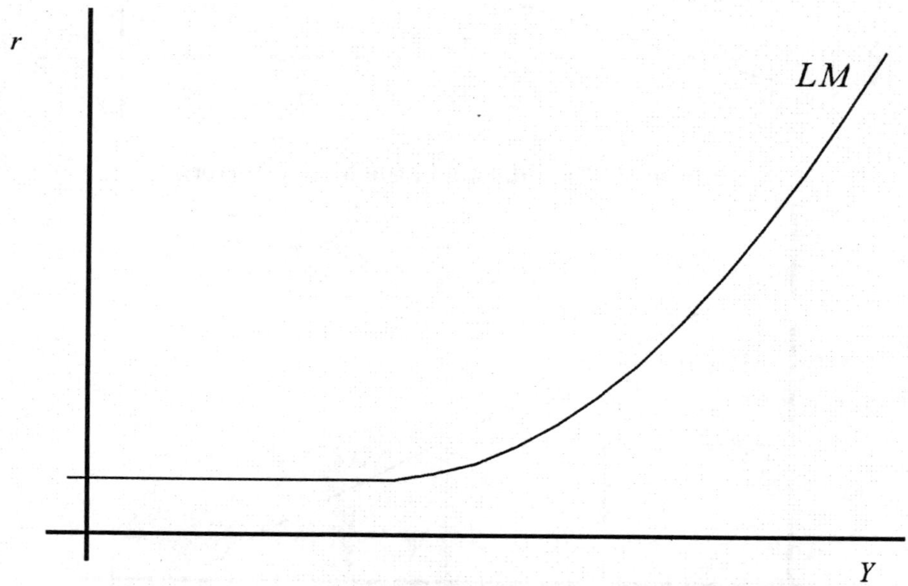

Figure 40. *LM* Line

These relationships are summarised in Figure 40 and, in a simplified linear form, in Figure 41. In each case the graph, which is known as the *LM* line, shows the locus of combinations of levels of income and interest rates that lead to a stable level of interest rates. The non-linear graph shows that when the equilibrium value of r is at its minimum level it might be combined with a range of values for Y; this information is lost on the linear graph. Like the *IS* line, the *LM* line is not a function; it does not describe the effect on Y of a changing value of r and nor does it describe the effect on r of a changing value of Y. If the level of interest rates is not at its equilibrium point, then the current situation is not described by any of the points on the *LM* line. If M_D does not equal M_S, then people will buy or sell assets, changing prices and therefore demand for, and supply of, assets, until M_D does equal M_S. At this point, asset prices will be stable and, therefore, so will interest rates. Equilibrium in the money market has been achieved, and the economy is at one of the combinations of Y and r that is on the *LM* line.

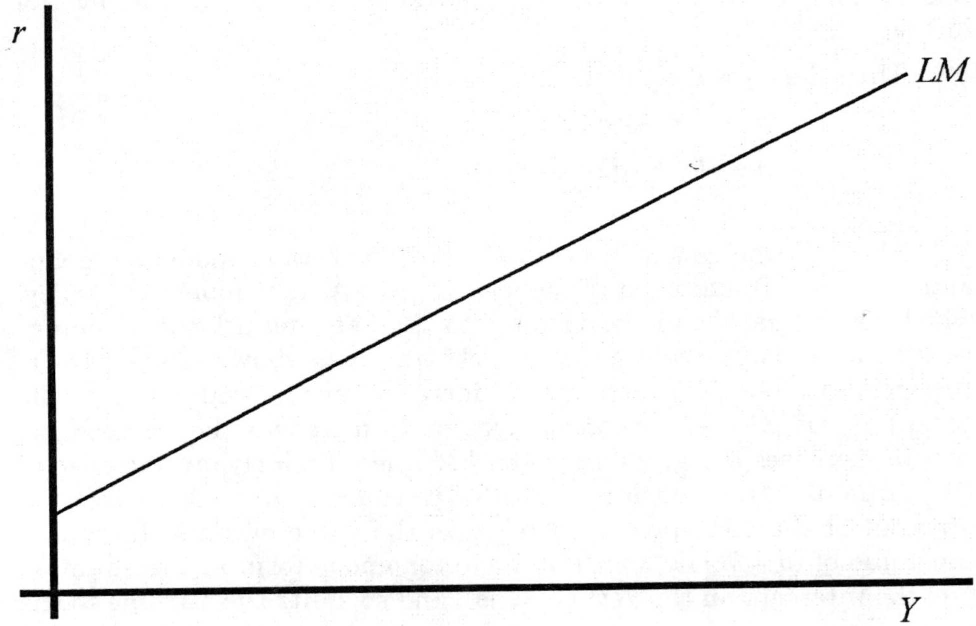

Figure 41. *LM* Line

The *LM* line is based on the M_S, $M_D{}^T$, $M_D{}^P$, and $M_D{}^S$ functions, and will move to a new position if any of these functions shifts. For example, an increase in $M_D{}^T$, which might be caused by a decreased frequency of payments, increases money demand at each level of income. It therefore shifts the *LM* line to the left. Similarly an increase in the money supply decreases interest rates at each level of income and shifts the *LM* line to the right. Shifts of the *LM* line may be parallel or changes of gradient. There will be a change of gradient following a change in the sensitivity of any of the elements of money demand to a change in the level of income or of interest rates. For example, a clockwise rotation of the *LM* line indicates an increased sensitivity of M_D to a change in r or a decreased sensitivity of M_D to a change in Y.

The *LM* line shows those points where M_D is equal to M_S. Its equation can be derived by setting the value of M_S equal to the behavioural equation for M_D. Money demand is a function of the level of income (for M_D^T and M_D^P) and of the level of interest rates (for M_D^S):

$$M_D = p + qY - sr$$

In this equation, qY shows the effect of Y on $(M_D^T + M_D^P)$ and sr shows the effect of r on M_D^S. The autonomous term (p) identifies the part of $(M_D^T + M_D^P)$ that is determined by variables other than Y plus the part of M_D^S that is determined by variables other than r. A linear relationship is probably reasonable for small changes in the level of interest rates.

Thus the equation for the *LM* line is:

$$M_S = p + qY - sr$$

$$r = \frac{p - M_s}{s} + \frac{qY}{s}$$

The *LM* line can be used to show the effects of monetary policy and of other influences on the money supply. A tight monetary policy, which decreases M_S, moves the line to the left, and a loose monetary policy moves it to the right. The *LM* line also shows the effects of changes in the M_D function. An increase in the value of q (the sensitivity of $(M_D^T + M_D^P)$ to changes in Y) increases the value of q/s and so increases the gradient of the *LM* line. Similarly, an increase in the value of s (the sensitivity of M_D^S to changes in r) decreases the gradient of the *LM* line. An increase in the value of s also decreases the value of $(p - M_S)/s$, which is the autonomous term in the equation (i.e. the intercept on the vertical axis), and so shifts the *LM* line to the right. An increase in the value of p (or a reduction in M_S) shifts the *LM* line to the left.

The possible determinants of upward (parallel) and clockwise shifts of the *LM* line are shown in Table 9. The directions of changes in the values of the parameters in the equation of the *LM* line are shown. Downward and anti-clockwise shifts are caused by changes of the same parameters in the opposite direction.

TABLE 9 Causes of *LM* shifts

Upward:	$p\uparrow$	$M_S\downarrow$	$s\downarrow$
Clockwise:	$q\downarrow$	$s\uparrow$	

The *LM* diagram is further developed in Chapters 6 and 12.

6

The Interaction of the Goods Market and the Money Market

The *IS* line and the *LM* line, each of which describes the combinations of levels of income (Y) and interest rates (r) that lead to equilibrium, refer to different, but not unrelated, aspects of the economic system. The *IS* line is the locus of equilibrium points in the real market (also known as the goods market); it shows combinations of r and Y where the level of output of goods and services is stable. The *LM* line is the corresponding locus in the money market; it shows combinations of r and Y where the equilibrium level of interest rates occurs.

Superimposing the *IS* and *LM* lines, as in Figure 42, enables the interaction of the two equilibrium processes to be analysed. The linear form of the *LM* line is sufficient for this discussion since the minimum level of interest rates is not of current importance.

If the current situation in the economy is not represented by a point on the *IS* line, then the level of income (output) (Y) will change until it is. This does not have an immediate effect on the level of interest rates (r), so the movement is towards the *IS* line by moving in a horizontal direction on the *IS–LM* graph (Figure 42). Similarly, if the current combination of Y and r is not on the *LM* line, then the level of interest rates will change until it is. There is no immediate effect on the level of income, so the movement is towards the *LM* line in a vertical direction.

It frequently happens that neither the real market nor the money market is in equilibrium. In this situation the combination of r and Y is neither on the *IS* line nor on the *LM* line. This applies at, for example, **A** in Figure 42, which is above the *LM* line and to the right of the *IS* line, which implies that output will be falling (a horizontal movement towards the *IS* line) and interest rates will also be falling (a vertical movement towards the *LM* line). The precise net effect of these two movements depends on the relative strengths of the two forces; it will necessarily be downwards and to the left, but it might be almost horizontal or almost vertical. The way the direction of such a move appears on the diagram depends also, of course, on the scales used on the axes.

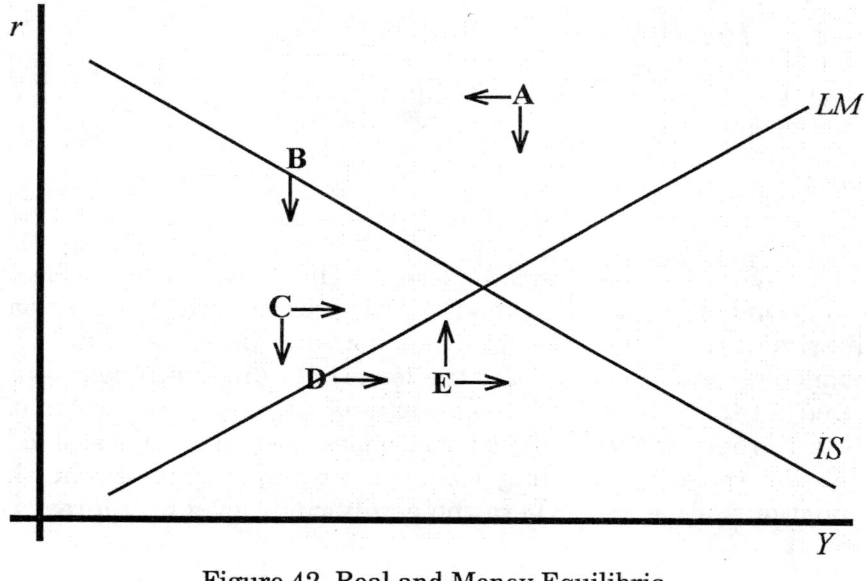

Figure 42. Real and Money Equilibria

If there are no autonomous shifts of the *IS* and *LM* lines, this downward and leftward movement will continue until the *IS* line is reached at **B**. At this point, because it is on the *IS* line, the level of income will be stable, but the level of interest rates will continue to fall, as the vertical movement towards the *LM* line continues. This involves a movement to **C** which is to the left of the *IS* line, and, when this has occurred, income will begin to rise (a rightward movement towards the *IS* line) as interest rates continue to fall (a downward movement towards the *LM* line).

If this process is not disturbed by autonomous shifts, it will continue until the *LM* line is reached at **D**. The level of interest rates is stable here, but output will continue to rise by a rightward movement towards the *IS* line, which means a movement to **E**, which is to the right of the *LM* line. There will then begin a simultaneous movement to the right (towards *IS*) and upward (towards *LM*).

The overall effect is shown on Figure 42 as a spiral movement. The eventual equilibrium is at the intersection of the *IS* and *LM* lines, which is the only point at which both Y and r are stable. It is likely that there will be shifts of either (or both) of the *IS* or the *LM* lines before the final equilibrium is reached; if this happens, the economy will start to move towards the new equilibrium before the previous one has been reached.

The real market and the money market have separate but related equilibrium processes. As each market moves towards its equilibrium point, it will disturb the other market's equilibrium. If aggregate demand (E_P) is greater than aggregate supply (Y), the current situation is to the left of the *IS* line, and Y will increase. This increases money demand (M_D) so that it is now greater than money supply (M_S), and this leads to an increase in interest rates (r). A higher value of r will decrease investment (I) and therefore E_P (of which it is a component). This decreases Y, which leads to lower M_D, and thus to lower r, which leads to higher I, higher E_P, and higher Y (and then to higher M_D, higher r, lower I ....). This is a probably an infinite process, and would be shown on Figure 42 as an oscillation around the intersection of *IS* and *LM*. The overall equilibrium point, at that intersection, is a mathematical limit rather than a point that is likely to be reached (even in the absence of autonomous shifts).

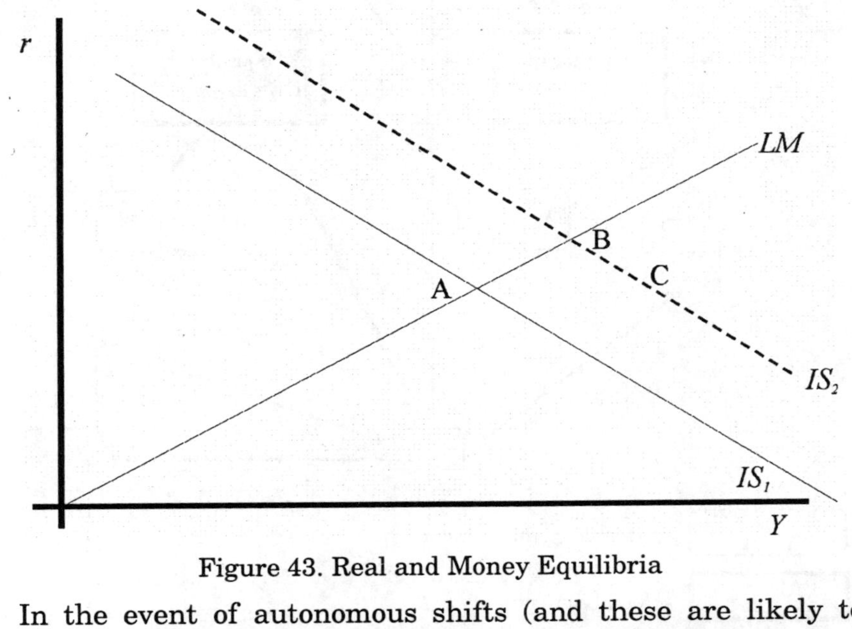

Figure 43. Real and Money Equilibria

In the event of autonomous shifts (and these are likely to be frequent), the position of the overall equilibrium will move to the new intersection of *IS* and *LM*, and the economy will move towards this point. Such a shift might be caused by an increase in government spending (G), which is an autonomous element of aggregate demand

(E_P). The effect of this is shown in Figure 43 as a parallel shift of the *IS* line from IS_1 to IS_2. The initial equilibrium is at **A**. The new equilibrium position is at **B**, around which, after a delay, the economy will oscillate. Shifts of the *LM* line, caused by autonomous changes in money demand (due, for example, to changes in the frequency of payments) or in money supply (due, for example, to a tightening of monetary policy or a change in the demand for loans) are also likely. Depending on the nature of the new situation, shifts of the *IS* and *LM* lines might involve changes of gradient. It is likely that the adjustment to the new equilibrium following a shift of the *IS* line or of the *LM* line will not be complete before another shift occurs.

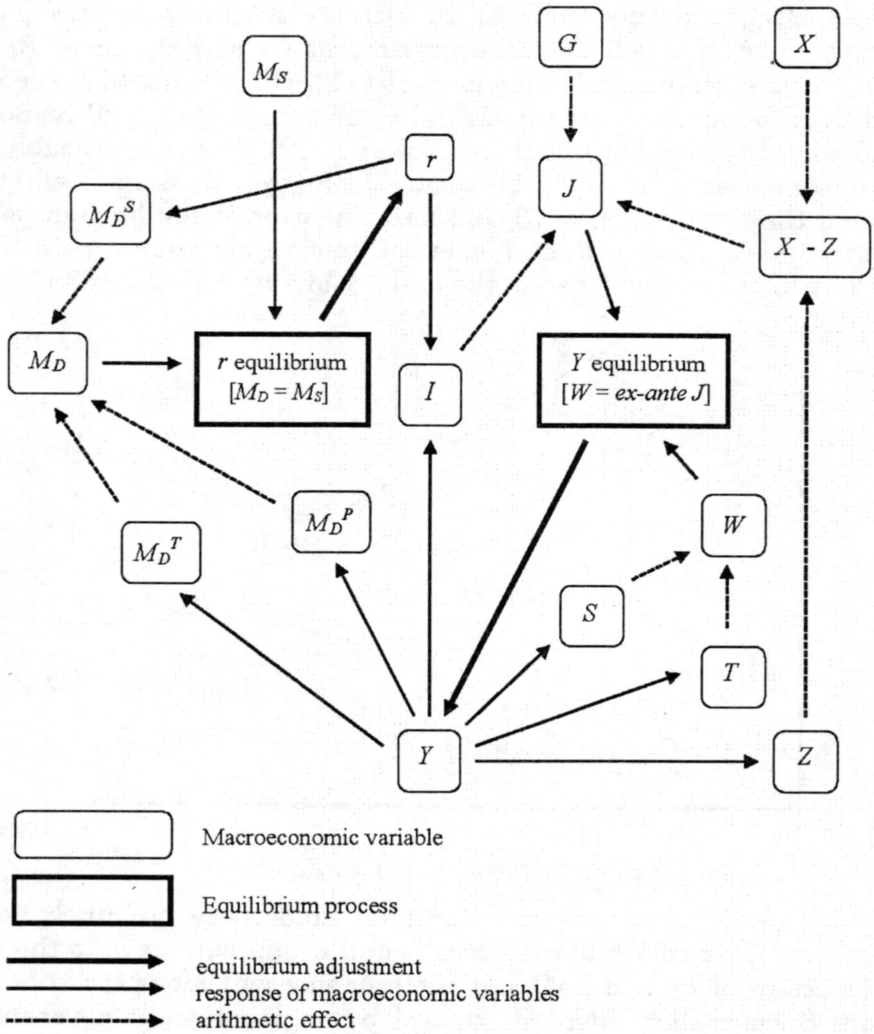

Figure 44. The Keynesian Macroeconomic Model

The relationships between the equilibrium processes in the real and money markets are summarised in Figure 44. In this diagram, an arrow indicates the direction of causation between two variables. Where two or more arrows converge on a single variable, it means that it is jointly determined.

The right-hand side of Figure 44 refers to the real-market equilibrium process, which determines the level of income (Y), and the left-hand side refers to the money-market equilibrium process, which determines the level of rates of interest (r). The top half of the diagram shows the influence of r on the demand for speculative balances ($M_D{}^S$) (in the money market) and on investment expenditure (I), a component of planned injections (J) (in the real market). The lower half of the diagram shows the influence of Y on demand for transactions and precautionary balances ($M_D{}^T + M_D{}^P$) (in the money market). It also shows its influence on savings (S) and net taxation (T), which are the components of withdrawals (W), and on imports (Z) and investment, which are components of planned injections (J) (in the real market). The level of investment is influenced both by Y and by r.

If W does not equal *ex-ante* J, then, as explained in Chapter 2, Y will change until they are equal, and if the sum of ($M_D{}^T + M_D{}^P$) and $M_D{}^S$ is not equal to M_S, then r will change until it is. However, as Y changes, it disturbs the equilibrium of r by changing M_D (because it changes $M_D{}^T$ and $M_D{}^P$), and if r changes it disturbs the equilibrium of Y by changing J (because it changes I). As each of the two markets moves towards its equilibrium, it disturbs the equilibrium in the other market.

There are, therefore, three conditions that must be satisfied for the macroeconomy to be in equilibrium. Aggregate demand (E_P) must be equal to aggregate supply (Y), money demand (M_D) must be equal to money supply (M_S), and the levels of Y and r must be consistent with each other, so that stability in both markets is possible.

With the exception of Y and r, which are determined purely by the equilibrium processes described in Chapters 2 and 5, all of the variables shown in Figure 44 are subject to autonomous disturbances. Three of the variables shown are entirely autonomous: G and X (which are discussed in Chapter 2) and M_S (which is discussed in Chapter 4). Prices and exchange rates are assumed constant; the determinants of these are explained in Chapters 8 and 11. Also ignored are the effects of r on international capital flows; this issue is discussed in Chapters 11 and 12. Arrows with broken lines identify relationships that are purely arithmetic. The components of M_D are, by definition, $M_D{}^T$, $M_D{}^P$

and $M_D{}^S$. Similarly, the components of J are I, G, and $(X-Z)$, the components of W are S and T, and the components of $(X-Z)$ are X and Z. For each of the two equilibria, a heavy arrow is used for the initial effect of the adjustment process.

According to the explanation of the multiplier process in Chapter 2, an autonomous change in aggregate demand (ΔA) leads to a much greater change in income (ΔY), and the ratio between these two is the multiplier (K). Implied in this model is a constant level of interest rates (r). This assumption is relaxed on the *IS–LM* diagram, on which r is allowed to vary. Figure 43 shows that an autonomous increase in aggregate demand, which shifts the *IS* line from IS_1 to IS_2, would increase Y, by a multiplied amount, from **A** to **C**. If r is allowed to vary, however, the increase in money demand ($M_D{}^T + M_D{}^P$) that results from the increase in Y leads to wealth-holders selling bonds. This decreases the price of bonds and increases r, which will discourage some investment spending (I) and decrease Y, again by a multiplied amount. When the new equilibrium is reached, therefore, the increase in Y (from **A** to **B**) shows that a change in r has decreased the multiplier effect of an autonomous increase in demand. Similarly, an autonomous decrease in aggregate demand decreases Y (by a multiplied amount) which decreases M_D and leads to a lower value of r, which leads to an increase in I and a multiplied increase in Y. In this case also, a change in the value of r has decreased the value of K.

An autonomous change in money demand ($M_D{}^T + M_D{}^P + M_D{}^S$) or in money supply ($M_S$) also affects the level of income (Y). An increase in M_S (or an autonomous decrease in M_D) shifts the *LM* line to the right. Excess money demand means that wealth-holders will sell bonds which decreases the price of bonds and increases r. This decreases I and causes a multiplied decrease in Y. The reverse occurs if there is a decrease in M_S or an autonomous increase in M_D (a shift of the *LM* line to the left).

The relationship between shifts of the E_P line and shifts of the *IS* line is illustrated in Figure 45. If aggregate demand increases causing a shift of the E_P line from E_{P1} to E_{P2}, then, in absence of any change in the level of interest rates (r), equilibrium income will increase from Y_1 to Y_2 . The *IS* line will shift from IS_1 to IS_2. This causes a disequilibrium in the money market as the combination of Y_2 and r_1 is not a point on the *LM* line. At this point, to the right of the *LM* line, money demand is greater than money supply, so people sell bonds, the price of bonds falls, and the rate of interest rises. This decreases investment expenditure (I) and shifts the E_P line from E_{P2} to E_{P3}. The new equilibrium is at Y_3, where E_{P3} intersects the 45° line and *LM* intersects IS_2.

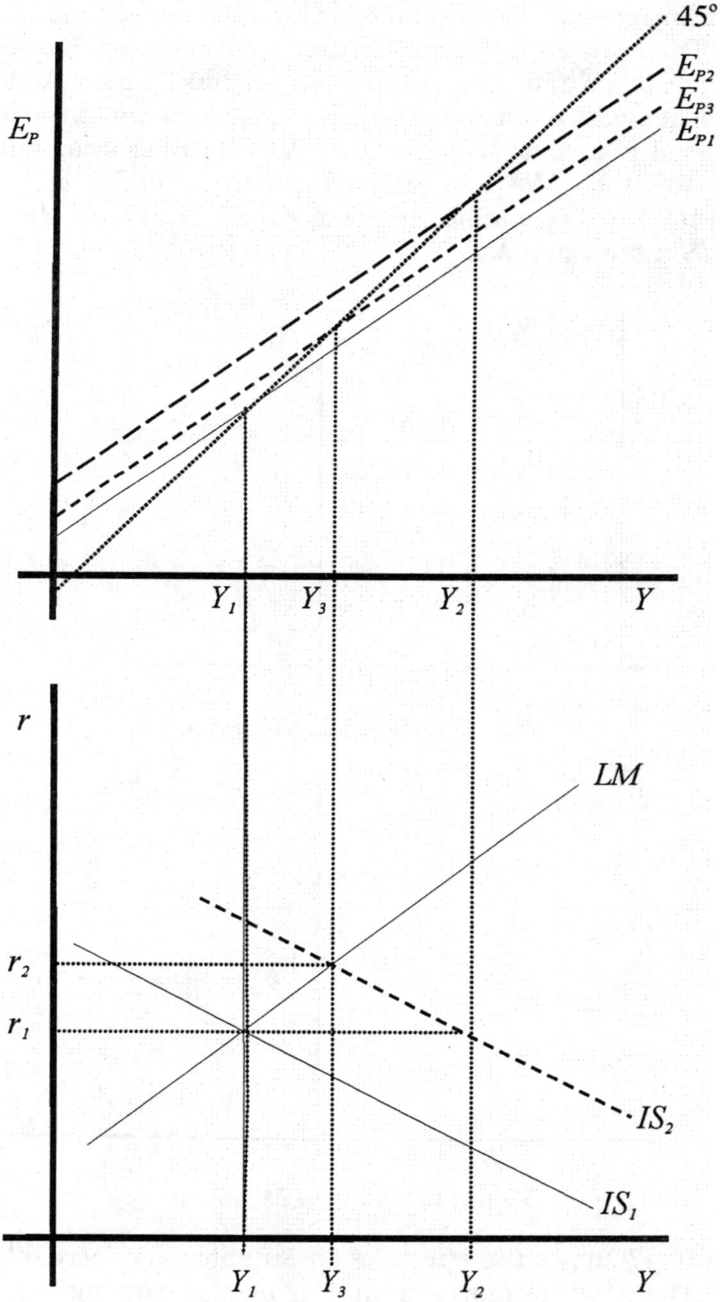

Figure 45. Shift of *IS* and E_P

Figure 46 illustrates the effects of an increase in the money supply. If the M_S line moves from M_{S1} to M_{S2}, there will be an excess money supply and the equilibrium interest rate will, in absence of a change in income, fall from r_1 to r_2. The *LM* line will move from LM_1 to LM_2. This causes a disequilibrium in the goods market as the combination of Y_1 and r_2 is not a point on the *IS* line. At this point, aggregate demand exceeds output, so firms will increase production and the level of income will increase. As *Y* increases, money demand increases (because $M_D{}^T$ and $M_D{}^P$ are functions of *Y*) and M_D shifts from M_{D1} to M_{D2}. The equilibrium is at r_3 and Y_3, where M_{S2} intersects M_{D2} and *IS* intersects LM_2.

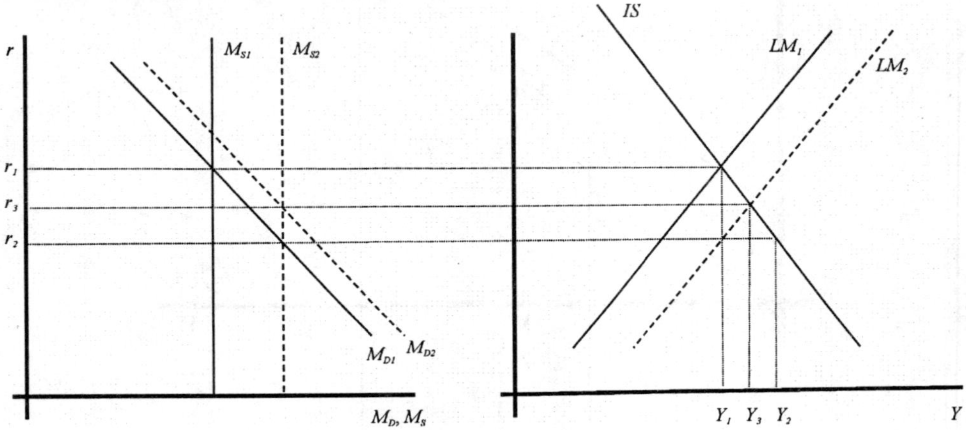

Figure 46. Shift of *LM* and M_s

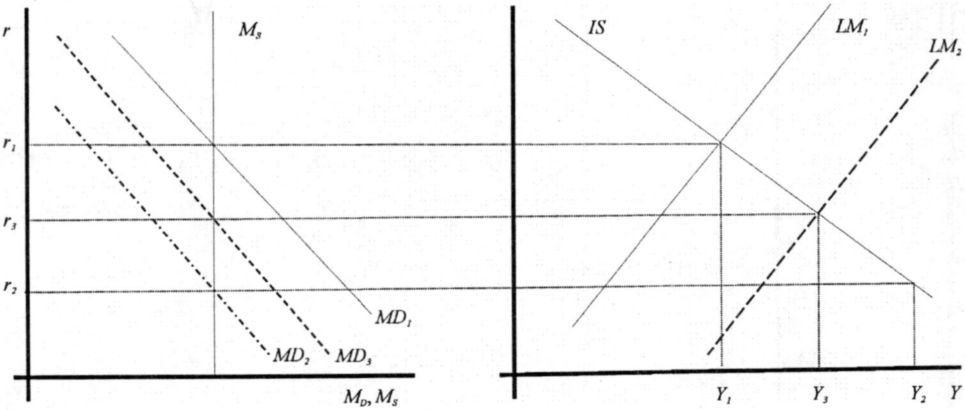

Figure 47. Shift of *LM* and M_D

Figure 47 shows the effects of an autonomous decrease in money demand. The M_D line moves from M_{D1} to M_{D2} causing excess money supply. The *LM* line moves from LM_1 to LM_2. People buy bonds, the price of bonds rises and the rate of interest falls, assuming a constant value of *Y*, from r_1 to r_2. The combination of r_2 and Y_1 is not on the *IS* line, so output increases. This causes an increase in money demand (from M_{D2} to M_{D3}). The equilibrium levels of income and of interest rates are Y_3 and r_3, at the IS–LM_2 and M_{D3}–M_S intersections.

Changes in the equilibrium level of Y also cause shifts in the AD line (see Chapter 8).

Overshooting

It is possible that some degree of overshooting might occur. This means that although the effects of an autonomous change in either the real market or the money market will be moderated by a change in the other, there might be a delay before the full effect of this occurs. This is illustrated in Figure 43. Following an increase in expenditure that shifts the IS line from IS_1 to IS_2, the economy might not move directly from the initial equilibrium (at **A**) towards the new equilibrium (at **B**), but might instead move from **A** towards **C** and then towards **B**. The autonomous increase in aggregate demand leads to a multiplied increase in output and moves the economy towards **C**. This point is below the LM line; the increase in income has increased money demand (M_D) above money supply (M_S). This causes people to sell assets, so their prices fall, and rates of interest (r) rise. This leads to a reduction in investment (I) and a multiplied reduction in income (Y); the economy is now moving towards the new equilibrium at **B**. The effect of this overshooting is that the level of income initially rises above its final equilibrium level. Overshooting might also occur following a shift in the LM line. In this case, a shift of the money supply function (M_S) or of the money demand function (M_D) leads to an initial adjustment of the level of interest rates (r) beyond its final value.

Fiscal and Monetary Policy

The IS–LM diagram can be used to illustrate the effects on the levels of income and of interest rates of changes in fiscal and monetary policy. Fiscal policy, through changes in net taxation and in government spending, changes the level of aggregate demand and shifts the IS line. Monetary policy affects the money supply and shifts the LM line. In each case, as shown in Chapters 3 and 5, a tight policy shifts the appropriate line to the left (leading to a decrease in income) and a loose policy shifts the appropriate line to the right (leading to an increase in income). However, a tight monetary policy tends to increase the level of interest rates (r) (by decreasing money supply (M_S)), while a tight fiscal policy tends to decrease the level of interest rates (by decreasing income (Y) and therefore decreasing demand for money ($M_D{}^T + M_D{}^P$)). The reverse happens when a loose monetary or fiscal policy is used.

Monetary and fiscal policy can be used alone or together and will be used in whatever combination supports the policy objectives of the government. For example, an increase in income is likely to result from the use of a loose fiscal policy and/or of a loose monetary policy. The target variable might, however, be the level of interest rates; a reduction in interest rates will follow the use of a tight fiscal policy and/or a loose monetary policy, and *vice versa*.

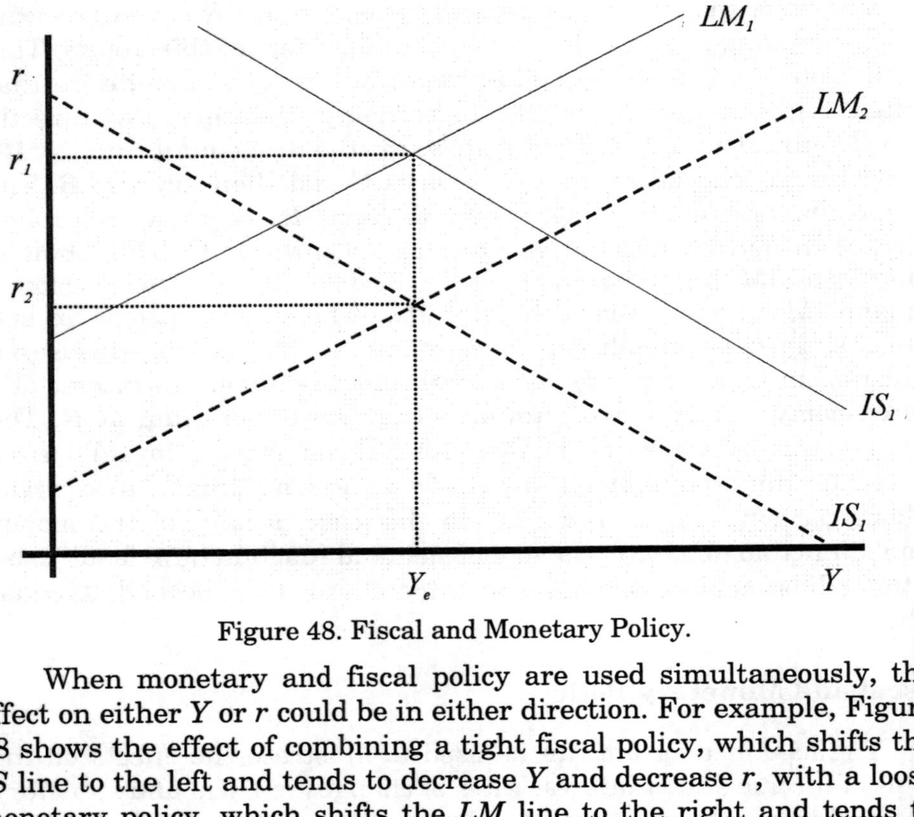

Figure 48. Fiscal and Monetary Policy.

When monetary and fiscal policy are used simultaneously, the effect on either *Y* or *r* could be in either direction. For example, Figure 48 shows the effect of combining a tight fiscal policy, which shifts the *IS* line to the left and tends to decrease *Y* and decrease *r*, with a loose monetary policy, which shifts the *LM* line to the right and tends to increase *Y* and decrease *r*. The effect on *r* is clearly downwards, but the effect on *Y*, which is shown in the diagram as zero, depends on which of the two policies has the greater force. If monetary policy is more powerful than fiscal policy, the *LM* line will move further than the *IS* line, and *vice versa*. Similarly, the combination of a tight fiscal policy (which shifts the *IS* line to the left) with a loose monetary policy (which shifts the *LM* line to the right) will lead to a decreased value of *r* and to an indeterminate effect on *Y*.

TABLE 10 Monetary and Fiscal Policy

		Fiscal Policy (*IS* shifts)		
		Loose ($E_P \uparrow$)	Tight ($E_P \downarrow$)	Neutral
Monetary Policy (*LM* shifts)	Loose ($M_S \uparrow$)	$Y\uparrow$ r?	Y? $r\downarrow$	$Y\uparrow$ $r\downarrow$
	Tight ($M_S \downarrow$)	Y? $r\uparrow$	$Y\downarrow$ r?	$Y\downarrow$ $r\uparrow$
	Neutral	$Y\uparrow$ $r\uparrow$	$Y\downarrow$ $r\downarrow$	Y no change r no change

In each case, the direction of the likely effects on Y and on r is shown.
A question mark indicates an indeterminate outcome.

The effects of combinations of monetary and fiscal policy are summarised in Table 10 and in Figure 49.

Figure 49 shows the relationships between fiscal policy, monetary policy, and changes in Y and in r. Arrows represent the direction of causation. The diagram shows that the immediate effect of monetary policy is on r (with subsequent effects on Y) and that the immediate effect of fiscal policy is on Y (with subsequent effects on r). Changes in r affect Y by influencing investment expenditure (I) which has a multiplied effect on Y, and changes in Y affect r by influencing transactions and precautionary demand for money ($M_D{}^T + M_D{}^P$). Other effects of monetary and fiscal policy are ignored; these include the effects on the price level (see Chapter 8) and on the exchange rate (see Chapters 11 and 12). It is assumed in Figure 49 that the level of income (Y) is the sole stimulus of changes in monetary and fiscal policy. Such policy changes could also be determined by changes in, for example, the level of interest rates (r), the price level, or the exchange rate.

It was discussed in Chapter 3 that the effect of fiscal policy depends on how it is financed. If a change in government spending is combined with an equal change in net taxation (T), then the *IS* line shifts by a smaller amount than if the amount of government borrowing changes. Another possibility is that an increase in government spending is financed by an increase in the money supply (or that a reduction leads to a reduction in the money supply); this shifts the *LM* line to the right (for increased M_S) or to the left (for decreased M_S) and therefore leads to a change in the level of interest rates (r).

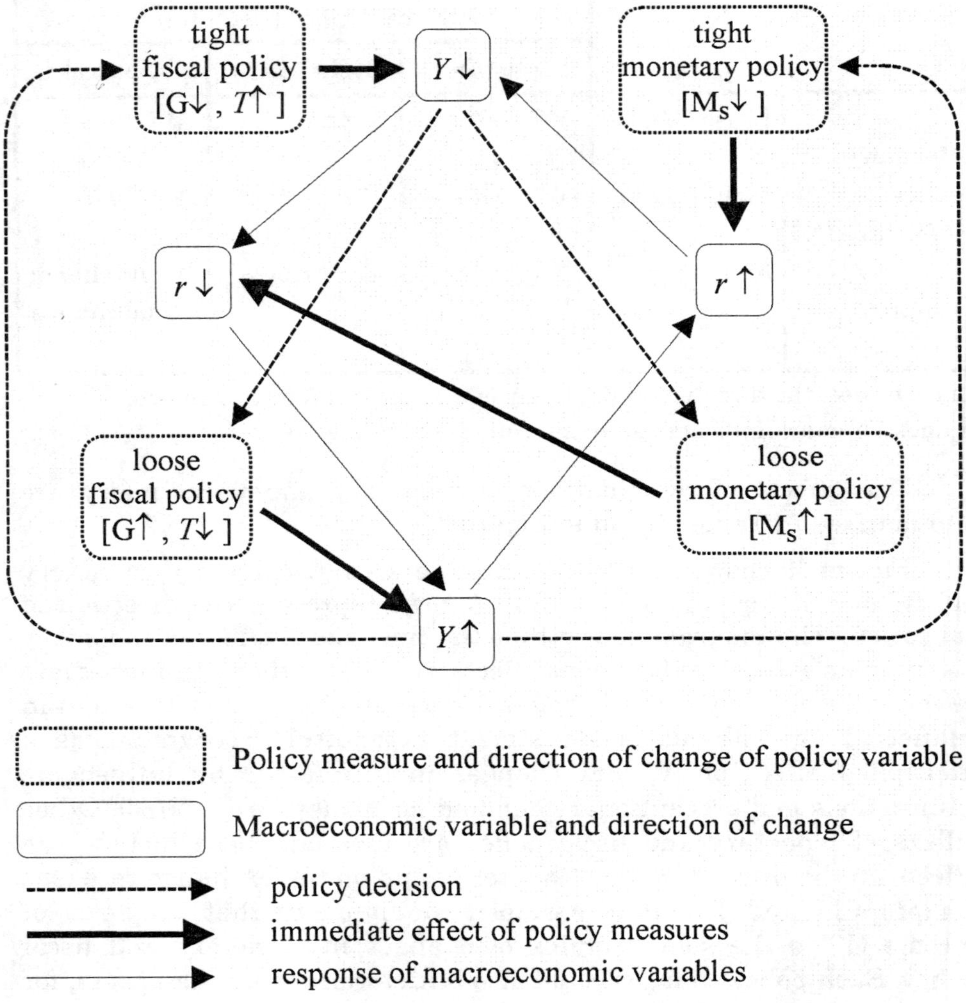

Figure 49. Monetary and Fiscal Policy.

The final possibility is that government expenditure is financed by borrowing or by the sale of government-owned assets. In this case, the *IS* line does not shift (because E_P has not changed) and the *LM* line does not shift (because neither M_S nor M_D has changed). The long-term consequences of deficit financing by borrowing or by asset sales are not shown on the *IS–LM* diagram. These include debt-servicing costs (in the case of borrowing) and the loss of profits (in the case of asset sales).

A change in the government budget balance might be due neither to a change in government spending (G) nor to a change in net tax rules. It might arise because a change in Y has led to an induced change in net taxation (T); an increase in aggregate output leads to an increase in net tax revenue and *vice versa*.

Depending on the nature of the government's response, a budget surplus or deficit will shift the *IS* line, or the *LM* line, or both, or neither. The macroeconomic consequences of a non-zero budget balance therefore depend on how governments respond to this situation.

7

Digression on Pre-Keynesian Economic Theory

The macroeconomic ideas that were current at the time that Keynes was writing have become known as the Classical theory. They date from Adam Smith (1723–90) whose book *An Inquiry into the Nature and Causes of the Wealth of Nations* was published in 1776. Other important Classical economists are David Ricardo (1772–1823) and John Stuart Mill (1806–73).

One of the themes of the Classical macroeconomics is the power of the market system, when it is allowed to operate without restriction, to lead to an efficient allocation and use of resources. This is called the doctrine of *laissez faire*: by not interfering the government can ensure that the outcome is desirable.

In the Classical macroeconomic theory, prices of individual commodities are assumed to be flexible and to act as powerful incentives for market participants to change their behaviour. For example, a commodity that is in excess demand will show an increase in price, and this will stimulate producers to increase their level of output and customers to decrease their level of demand. Similarly, if there is excess supply then prices will fall, output will fall, and demand will rise. This means that market forces operate in such a way as to ensure that there is full employment. Inadequate demand for output cannot, according to the Classical theorists, be a cause of unemployment; if demand for output is too low, then prices will fall, and so demand increases.

In the Classical theory, the incentives provided by prices are powerful and lead to behaviour that is in the interests of the whole community. Customers buy where goods are cheapest, so firms have an incentive to be efficient so that they can produce cheaply. Workers have an incentive to work hard, in order to increase their incomes. They will also choose the employer offering the highest wages, and therefore firms have an incentive to be generous to their workers. It sounds like an ideal world, but it differs considerably from observed experience.

The Classical economists applied their ideas to all parts of the economy. The labour market was thought to respond to price changes in the same way as do other parts of the economy. Should unemployment arise, and this might occur in the short term following, for example, a bankruptcy, then the demand for labour (the number of workers that employers wish to employ) would be less than the supply of labour (the number of workers that wish to work). This would lead to a cut in wage rates (the price of labour) and therefore to an increase in demand for labour, thus ending the unemployment. This approach ignores the fact that labour is not homogeneous (different people have different skills), and it also ignores the significance of the level of aggregate demand, which is such an important variable in Keynesian theory.

The Keynesian reply to the Classical view on unemployment is that many prices, including wage rates, are sticky rather than flexible. This means that they do not respond quickly to changed circumstances and they might not respond by a sufficient amount to bring demand and supply into equilibrium. In a situation of unemployment, the Keynesian view is that wages might not fall immediately, or at all, and that the wage cuts that do occur are unlikely to lead to a substantial increase in the demand for labour. Further, the Keynesian view is that wage cuts decrease the spending power of those people who are still in employment; this decreased demand leads to increases in stocks of unsold output and thus to decreased output and decreased employment. The Keynesian view is that demand for labour is derived from demand for output, and is likely to increase only if aggregate demand increases. Employers are not likely to recruit additional workers just because they are cheap, but they are very likely to want additional workers when their customers decide to increase the amount of output they wish to buy.

The Classical economists also used a proposition that has become known as Say's Law (after Jean-Baptiste Say (1767–1832)) which states that supply creates its own demand. This means that the productive process generates the spending power (in employees' wages and employers' profits, and in rent and interest) to buy the output that has been produced, and so somebody will buy whatever goods are produced. In this approach, changes in economic activity are driven by changes in supply, whereas the Keynesian view is that they are driven by changes in demand. One of the implications of Say's Law, as of other aspects of the Classical theory, is that full employment will occur spontaneously. It follows that measures to assist the unemployed are unnecessary and, because they provide a disincentive to work, likely to be harmful.

The Classical theory of the level of interest rates differs from Keynes' theory. In the Classical approach, interest is regarded as the price paid for the use of borrowed money. It is determined by the demand for loanable funds (D_{LF}), which is assumed to be discouraged by high interest rates, and the supply of loanable funds (S_{LF}), which is assumed to be encouraged by high interest rates. The demand for loanable funds (D_{LF}) is a similar concept to investment (I) since most investment projects are financed with borrowed money, and the supply of loanable funds (S_{LF}) is the same concept as savings (S) since, in the Classical theory, all income not spent is made available for borrowing. This means that an increase in S_{LF} implies that people are saving more, which means that people are spending less on consumption.

The Keynesian view of the demand for money to borrow (D_{LF}) is not totally different to the Classical theory. Both theories assume that the level of interest rates has an inverse effect on the amount of borrowing. In the Classical theory, however, the level of interest rates is the only determinant, while in the Keynesian approach it one of several determinants (which include income and business confidence), and probably not the most important.

There are, however, marked differences between the Keynesian and the Classical approaches to the level of savings (S), which has the same meaning as the Classical concept of the supply of loanable funds (S_{LF}). In the Classical theory, S_{LF} shows a positive relationship with the level of interest rates (r), and therefore consumption (C) shows an inverse relationship with the level of interest rates. In the Keynesian theory, the level of savings is determined principally by the level of income, and also by the level of confidence, but not by the level of interest rates. People will save more if they can afford to save more, or if they believe that some personal disaster (such as illness or unemployment) is imminent, but are very unlikely to do so in response to a higher level of interest rates.

Figure 50 describes the Classical theory of the level of interest rates. The vertical axis shows the independent variable; both the demand for loanable funds and the supply of loanable funds are functions of the level of interest rates (r). If the level of interest rates is at r_1, S_{LF} exceeds D_{LF}; this means that banks and similar bodies find that more money is being deposited than borrowers wish to borrow. Their response will be to decrease the level of interest rates; this will encourage borrowers and discourage depositors. At r_1, therefore, the system is not in equilibrium, and the level of interest rates will fall. If interest rates are at r_2, S_{LF} is less than D_{LF}, and banks will increase interest rates to attract depositors and discourage borrowers. The equilibrium is reached when the level of interest rates is at r_e.

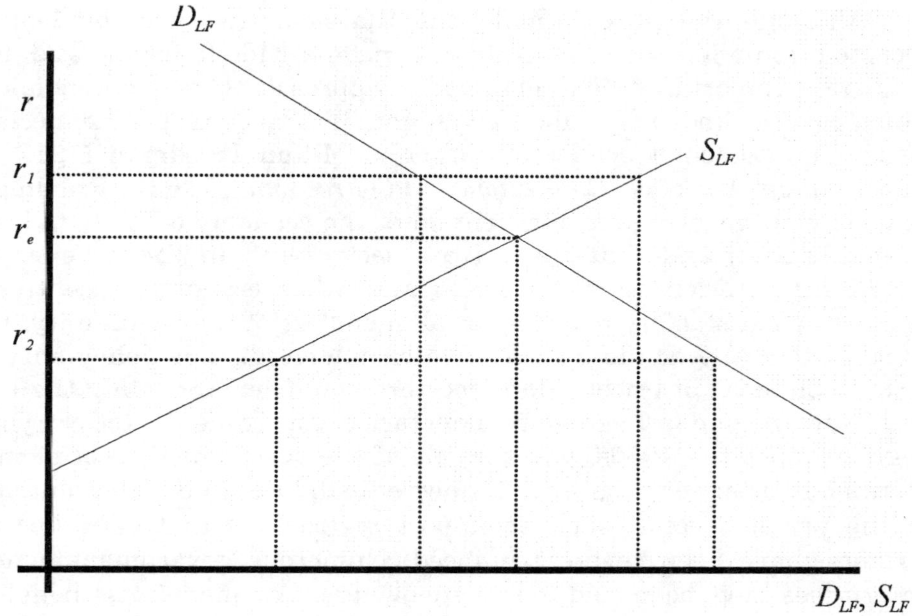

Figure 50. Demand for and Supply of Loanable Funds.

The experience of individual banks is often consistent with the Classical theory. A bank that increases its interest rates is likely to receive additional deposits. This is not, however, an increase in S_{LF}. It is not an increase in the aggregate level of savings (S) leading to an increase in the pool of funds available for lending; it is a movement of funds from one bank to another. The level of interest rates influences those who already own assets, but is unlikely to influence the decision to consume or to save.

Probably the most important difference between the Classical and Keynesian approaches is that, unlike his predecessors, Keynes believed that the economy cannot be relied upon to move automatically to a full employment outcome, and that therefore government intervention is necessary. In addition, in the Classical view, any short term adjustment that is necessary takes place via changes in prices, which are flexible and a powerful incentive. In the

Keynesian view, however, adjustment towards the equilibrium point is principally through changes in the level of output.

The Classical approach to the causes of inflation is discussed in Chapter 9.

Monetarism

Although the pure form of the Classical theory is no longer accepted, some ideas developed from it have a wide following and are of current importance. The monetarist approach to macroeconomics, which is also known as the New Right, is based on pre Keynesian ideas. The principal academic author is Milton Friedman (1912–) whose main book is *Capitalism and Freedom* (1962). Friedman believes that government intervention in the economy is likely to lead to inefficiency, and that the private sector will, in the absence of significant interference with prices and other economic incentives, evolve to a satisfactory outcome for all members of the community. He believes that the dominant objective of macroeconomic policy should be a stable level of prices. Many western countries, including the UK and New Zealand, have had monetarist governments (of varying degrees) since the 1980s, and the role of the government in economic affairs has been very significantly decreased since then. Interventions in the private sector, such as import restrictions and subsidies to farmers, have been severely reduced. Numerous government owned enterprises have been sold to private owners. The monetarist belief is that exposing the economy to market forces, with minimum restraint, will encourage efficiency, innovation, and effort.

The nature and effects of monetarism are discussed further in Chapters 8, 9, 10, and 14.

8

The Role of the Price Level in Aggregate Demand and Supply

In the theoretical models explained in Chapters 2 to 7, it was assumed that there were no changes in the general level of prices; it was assumed that the rate of inflation was zero. The absence of a supply constraint was also assumed: this means that output (Y) would be able to increase by the full amount of an increase in demand (E_P). In this chapter, the price level is incorporated as an additional variable into the Keynesian and Classical models, with particular emphasis on its relationship with the level of income. In addition, allowance is made for the fact that productive capacity is not infinite; due to insufficient availability of appropriately-skilled labour, or of other resources, it might not be possible to produce the quantity of goods and services that are demanded. Chapter 9 contains material on the nature, causes, and other effects of inflation.

The Price Level and Aggregate Demand

There is an inverse relationship between the price level (P) and aggregate demand (E_P). As prices rise, if other things remain unchanged, people can afford to buy smaller quantities of output. An increase in the price level does not imply that all prices are rising, and it does not imply that all prices are rising at the same rate. Further, the inverse relationship between the price level and the level of aggregate demand does not necessarily imply that demand falls for those products whose prices have risen. For example, the increase in the price of oil and related products in 1973 did not lead to a dramatic cut in demand for these commodities, but it did cause a reduction in aggregate demand. Demand for petrol, for example, is inelastic in the short term; when the price rises, people decrease the quantity they purchase by only a very small amount. In this situation, however, because of the higher prices, they spend a much greater amount of money on petrol that previously, and so have less money left for other goods and services, and this causes a significant reduction in aggregate demand.

The price level also influences the level of aggregate demand through its effect on the real value of assets, including bank deposits and cash, whose value is fixed in money terms and not, like other forms of wealth such as houses, land, gold, and company shares, determined by supply and demand. An increase in the price level therefore decreases the real value of certain forms of wealth which, perhaps especially in the case of retired people, is likely to lead to a reduction in autonomous consumption (a) and, after a delay, to a multiplied reduction in aggregate demand. The effect on real wealth (and hence on consumption expenditure) of changes in the price level will be decreased if interest is paid on money-defined assets, and will be zero if the interest rate is at least equal to the rate of increase of prices.

The inverse relationship between the price level and the level of aggregate demand can also be derived from the *IS–LM* diagram.

One of the assumptions on which the *LM* line is based is a constant real money supply (M_S). If the nominal money supply (the number of rupees) is constant, an increase in the general level of prices is equivalent to a reduction in the real money supply, as the same amount of money will, at higher prices, pay for a smaller quantity of goods and services. The inverse relationship between a change in the price level (P) and the change in real money supply (assuming a constant nominal money supply) is proportional. If prices double then the real value of a certain number of rupees has halved. If the value of P is multiplied by x then the real value of the money stock is divided by x. During a period of inflation, therefore, the decreased value of a constant nominal money stock implies that the *LM* line moves to the left.

The *IS* line responds to an increase in the price level in the Indian economy through its effects on international trade. An increase in domestic prices makes foreign goods more competitive; it is therefore likely to increase the volume of imports and decrease Indian output as people substitute foreign for local goods. This shifts the *IS* line to the left. Similarly, an increase in the price of manufactured goods produced in India will decrease the amount of exports as foreign customers switch to suppliers in other countries. This also moves the *IS* line to the left. The volume of exports of commodities such as minerals, cotton, and fruit is not affected by changes in the level of prices in India, as the prices of these commodities are determined in wholesale markets in other countries. However, rising prices in India decrease the quantity of goods and services that producers in India can buy with a constant amount of earnings, and this shifts the *IS* curve to the left.

This discussion of the effects on the *IS* line of an increase in the general level of prices in India is, of course, based on the assumptions that international trade is unrestricted and that exchange rates are fixed. These issues are pursued further in Chapters 11 and 12.

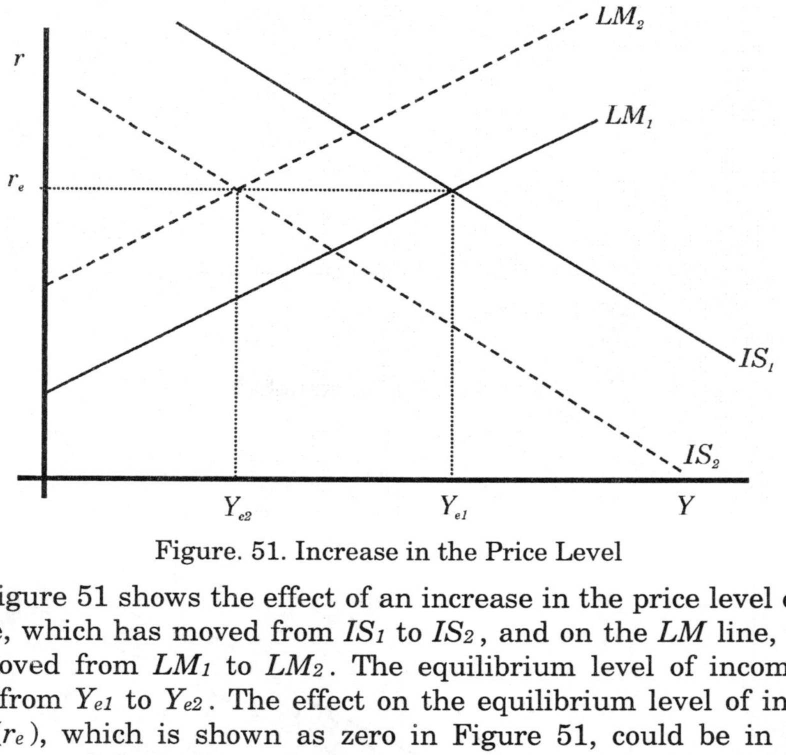

Figure. 51. Increase in the Price Level

Figure 51 shows the effect of an increase in the price level on the *IS* line, which has moved from IS_1 to IS_2, and on the *LM* line, which has moved from LM_1 to LM_2. The equilibrium level of income has fallen from Y_{e1} to Y_{e2}. The effect on the equilibrium level of interest rates (r_e), which is shown as zero in Figure 51, could be in either direction, and depends on which of the *IS* shift and the *LM* shift is the stronger force.

The graph of aggregate demand as a function of the price level, shown in Figure 52, is referred to as the aggregate demand schedule (*AD*). The horizontal axis is labelled *Y* because the equilibrium level of output (Y_e) is determined by the level of aggregate demand (E_P), and Y_e falls when E_P falls. The independent variable (*P*), which is shown on the vertical axis, is a weighted average of prices. The *AD* line can also be regarded as the locus of *P* and *Y* combinations where both the money market is in equilibrium (M_D is equal to M_S) and the market for new goods and services is in equilibrium (*Y* is equal to E_P).

It is therefore the locus of points where the *IS* line and the *LM* line intersect.

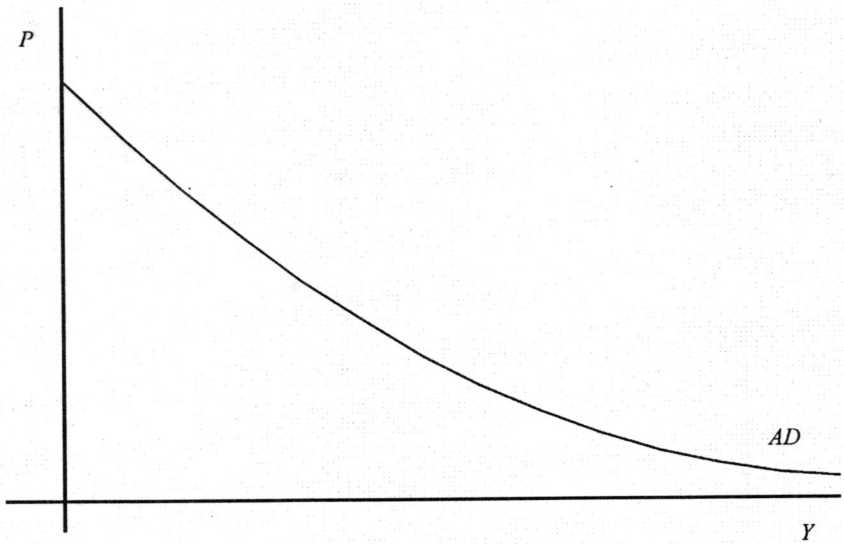

Fig. 52. Aggregate Demand Schedule.

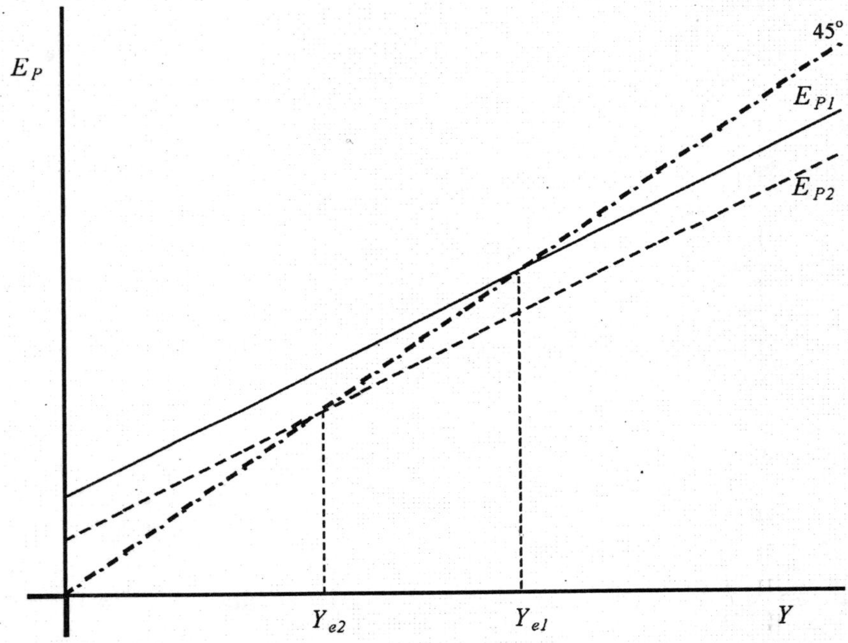

Fig. 53. Effect of an Increase in the Price Level

The effect of an increase in the price level (P) on the level of aggregate demand can also be shown on a graph of aggregate demand (E_P) against income (Y). A shift of the *IS* line to the right is equivalent to a downward shift of the E_P function, as shown in Figure 53. There is a multiplied reduction in the equilibrium level of income from Y_{e1} to Y_{e2}.

The Price Level and Aggregate Supply

The Classical analysis of the relationship between the price level (P) and the level of aggregate supply differs from the Keynesian approach.

According to the Classical theory, the economy necessarily tends towards the full-employment level of output, and is not affected by changes in the price level. The relationship is therefore shown as the vertical line in Figure 54. Because it represents part of the Classical theory, the existence of flexible prices is implied in this diagram.

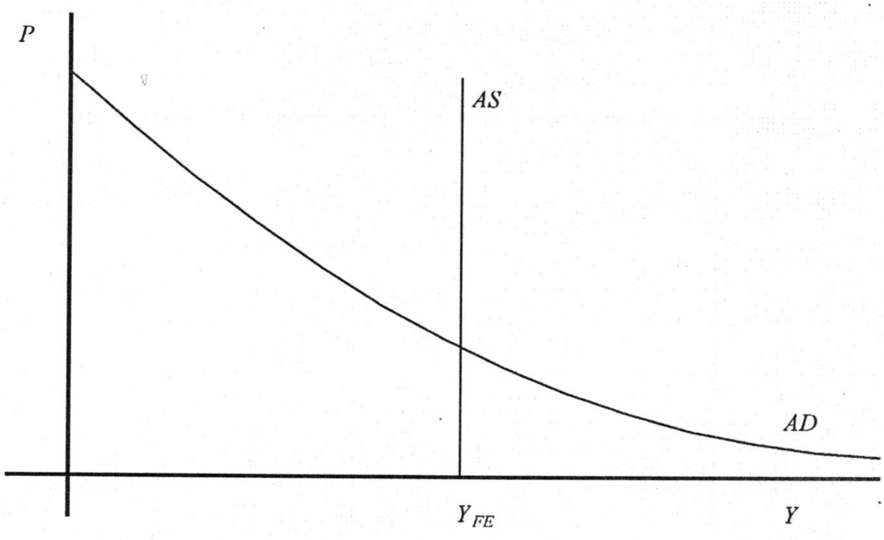

Fig. 54. Aggregate Demand and Aggregate Supply with Flexible Prices.

Keynes' view was that, if the full-employment level of income (Y_{FE}) has not been reached, the economy will be able to increase output in response to an increase in aggregate demand (E_P) without affecting the price level (P). Once the full-employment level of income is reached, however, further increases in demand cannot lead to increased output, and result instead in a higher price level. This approach is described by the aggregate supply schedule (*AS*) in

Figure 55. The *AS* line shows the level of output (*Y*) as a function of the price level. The horizontal part of the line indicates that output is infinitely elastic, and responds fully to changes in demand, until it reaches its maximum (at the full-employment level of income (Y_{FE})) when the line becomes vertical.

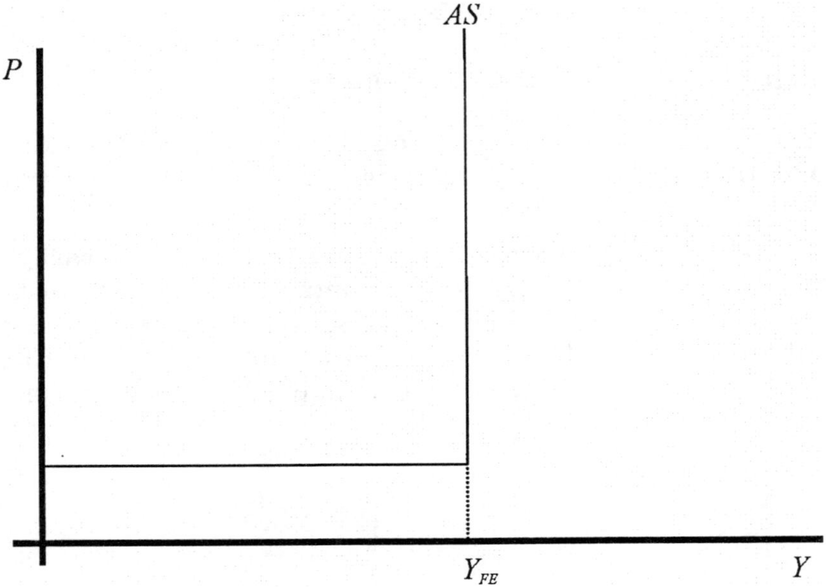

Fig. 55. Keynes' Approach to Aggregate Supply.

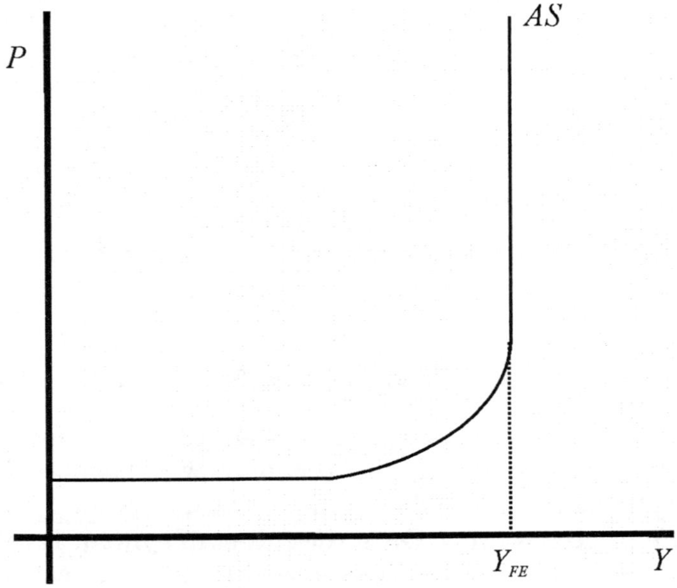

Fig. 56. Keynesian Approach to Aggregate Supply.

Figure 56 shows an adaptation of the Keynesian view that reflects recent macroeconomic experience. In this diagram the *AS* line begins to rise before the full-employment level of income is reached. This allows for the fact that it is likely that some industries reach their maximum output before others, and so the stimulus to increase prices begins to take effect before the whole economy has reached full employment.

Equilibrium Output and Price Levels

The interaction of aggregate supply (shown on the *AS* line) and aggregate demand (shown on the *AD* line) determines the equilibrium level of income (Y_e) and of prices (P_e). If, at a particular level of prices, aggregate demand is not equal to aggregate supply, then stocks of unsold goods will rise or fall, prices are likely to fall or rise, and the level of output (Y) might change. In firms that produce to order, the indicator is not the size of unplanned changes in stocks but the length of the order book; in firms that provide services, the indicator is the length of the queue. The economy moves towards the equilibrium point, at which the quantity of newly-produced output that people wish to buy at current prices is equal to the quantity that the producers wish to sell at current prices. This is at the intersection of the *AD* line and the *AS* line.

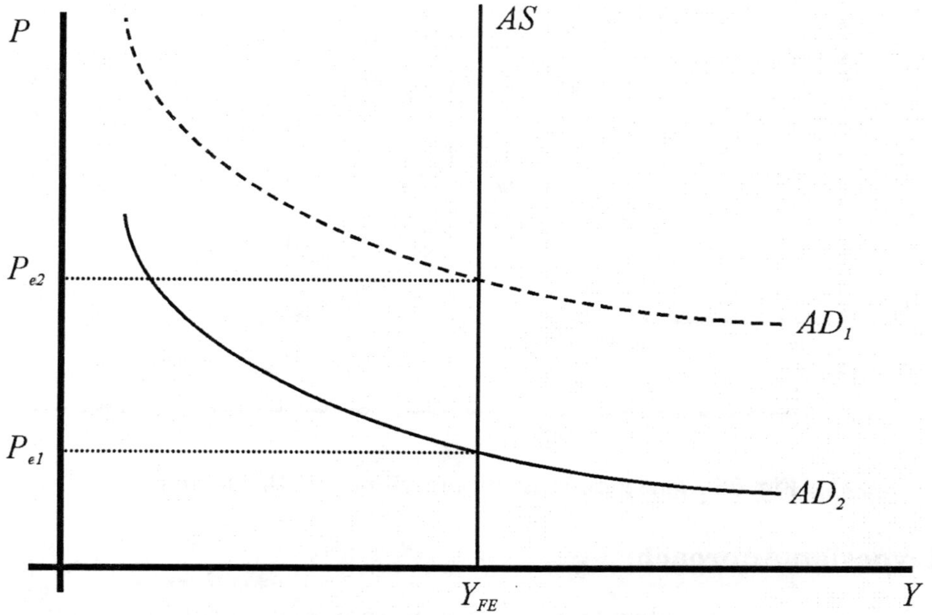

Fig. 57. Aggregate Demand and Supply with Flexible Prices.

Classical Approach

Figure 57 shows the Classical interpretation of the *AS–AD* diagram. The equilibrium point is at the intersection of the two lines. If aggregate demand were to increase, perhaps as a result of a loose monetary or fiscal policy or due to an increase in expenditure on investment or net exports, the *AD* line would move to the right, from AD_1 to AD_2. At the new equilibrium point, there is no change in income, which remains at the full-employment level (Y_{FE}), but the price level has risen from P_{e1} to P_{e2}.

According to the Classical view, increased output can occur only if the *AS* line shifts. A move to the right of the *AS* line implies that the productive capacity of the economy has improved. This could be caused by investment in more or better equipment or in education, or it might be caused by an increase in the population or in the labour force participation rate. Figure 58 shows that such a shift increases output (from Y_{e1} to Y_{e2}) and decreases the price level (from P_{e1} to P_{e2}). If both the *AS* line and the *AD* line move to the right the effect on the price level could be in either direction.

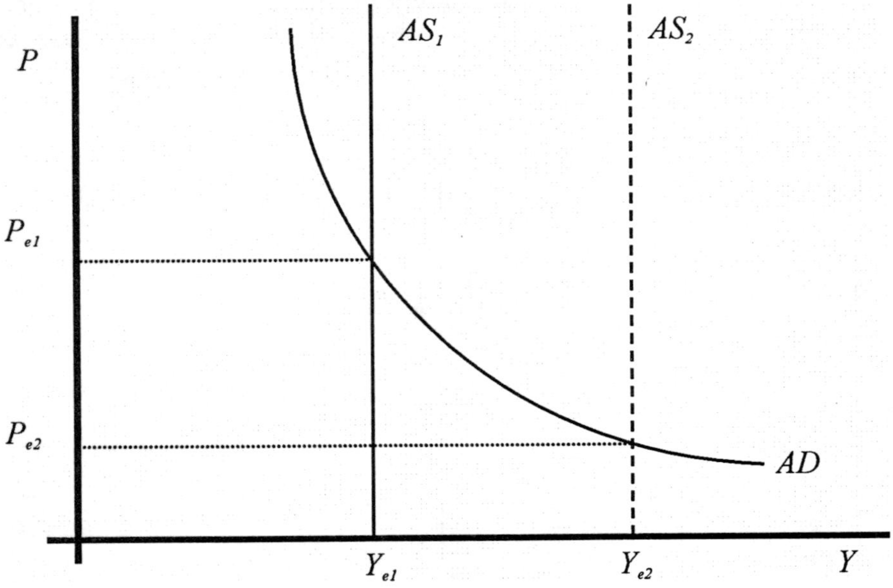

Fig. 58 Aggregate Demand and Supply with Flexible.

Keynesian Approach

Figure 59 describes the Keynesian approach to the likely effects on the level of prices and output of shifts in aggregate demand.

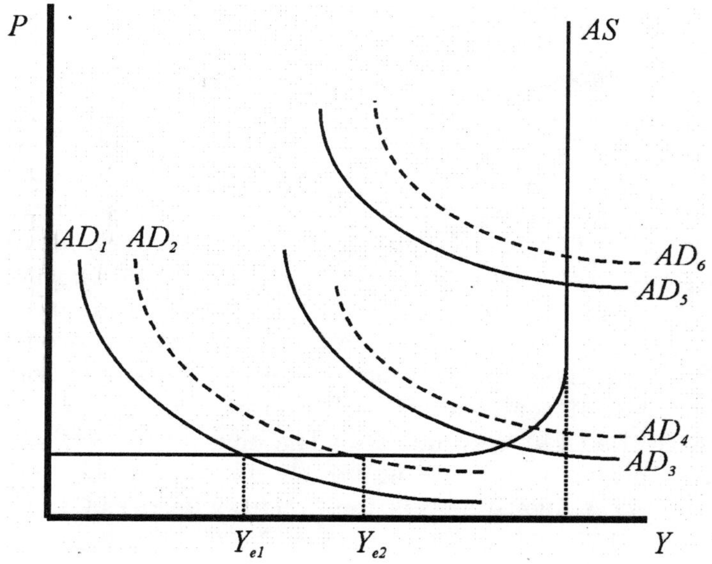

Fig. 59. The Keynesian view on Shifts of Aggregate Demand.

If the *AD* line in Figure 59 moves from AD_1 to AD_2, output increases (from Y_{e1} to Y_{e2}) without an increase in the price level. This describes the situation of the 1930s, in numerous countries, in which there was substantial spare capacity and output could be increased without incurring greater costs per unit of production.

The effect of an increase in aggregate demand during a period of full employment is shown by the movement of the *AD* line from AD_5 to AD_6; in this situation, output has reached its maximum, and the whole effect of the increase in demand is reflected in changes in the price level.

The third type of situation is when the economy is near, but not at, full employment. This has occurred in many countries since the 1980s. An increase in aggregate demand in this situation is shown by the shift of the *AD* line in Figure 59 from AD_3 to AD_4; this leads to adjustment of both income and price levels.

The gradient of the *AS* line influences the value of the multiplier (*K*). If there is an increase in aggregate demand during a severe depression, when the *AS* line is horizontal (from AD_1 to AD_2 in Figure 59), prices will not rise and *Y* will increase to match the new level of demand. In this situation, *K* has its maximum value. If aggregate demand increases when unemployment is low (from AD_3 to AD_4) there will be a decreased multiplier effect because there will be some constraint on the expansion of output and therefore an increase in the price level. The value of *K* is therefore decreased. If the increase in demand occurs when the economy is at the full-employment level of output, when the *AS* line is vertical (from AD_5 to AD_6), there will be no increase in *Y* and the value of *K* will be zero.

The Keynesian *AS* line can shift in two ways. If productive capacity increases, the line moves to the right. This might occur, for example, as a result of an increase in population (by changes in net immigration or by changes in birth and death rates), of an increase in the participation ratio (the proportion of the population seeking paid employment), of an improvement in the health or skills of employees, or of investment expenditure (*I*) (leading to greater productivity of labour). If any of these changes occur there will be an increase in the level of output that corresponds to full employment (Y_{FE}). A shift of the *AS* line to the right does not alter the horizontal part of the curve; it does not change the price at which goods and services can be produced during a severe depression (such as occurred in the 1930s). This type of shift is shown in Figure 60 by the movement of the *AS* line from AS_1 to AS_2; the equilibrium price level would fall (from P_{e1} to P_{e2}) as industry became more efficient, and the equilibrium level of income would rise (from Y_{e1} to Y_{e2}) as customers responded to the lower prices by increasing their level of demand. If this type of shift were combined with a rightward shift of the *AD* line, there would be a further increase in the level of income but the net effect on the price level could be in either direction. If the rightward movement of the *AS* line occurs with a decrease of aggregate demand (a shift to the left of the *AD* line), the equilibrium price level will fall again but the equilibrium level of income could increase or decrease from its initial value.

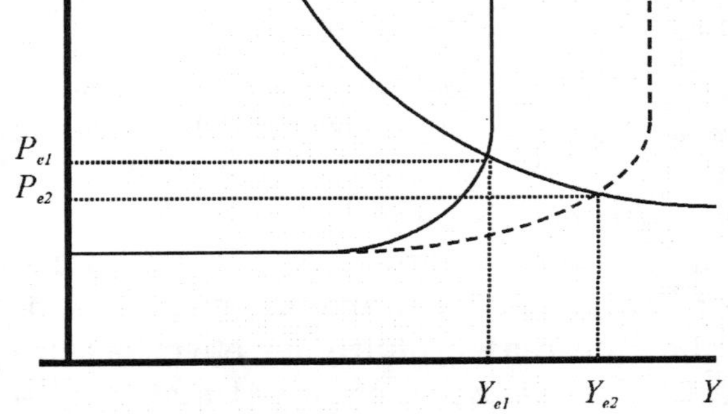

Figure 60. Aggregate Supply Shift

The second type of shift of the Keynesian *AS* line is a vertical shift, as shown in Figure 61. This type of shift of the *AS* line results from a change in production costs per unit. Examples of autonomous increases in costs that would move the *AS* line upwards are the introduction of increased sales taxes and an increase in world oil prices. This type of shift does not affect the vertical part of the *AS* line; it does not change the level of income (Y_{FE}) at which full employment occurs. An upward movement of the *AS* line (from AS_1 to AS_2) tends to increase prices (from P_{e1} to P_{e2}) as higher business costs are passed on to customers, and to decrease output (from Y_{e1} to Y_{e2}) as customers respond to the higher prices by reducing their demand for output (and *vice versa*). If the upward movement of the *AS* line occurs with an increase in aggregate demand (a rightward shift of the *AD* line), the equilibrium price level will rise further but the equilibrium output level might move in either direction from its original position. If this type of shift of the *AS* line is combined with a movement of the *AD* line to the left, then the equilibrium level of income will decrease further but the equilibrium price level might show a net movement upward or downward.

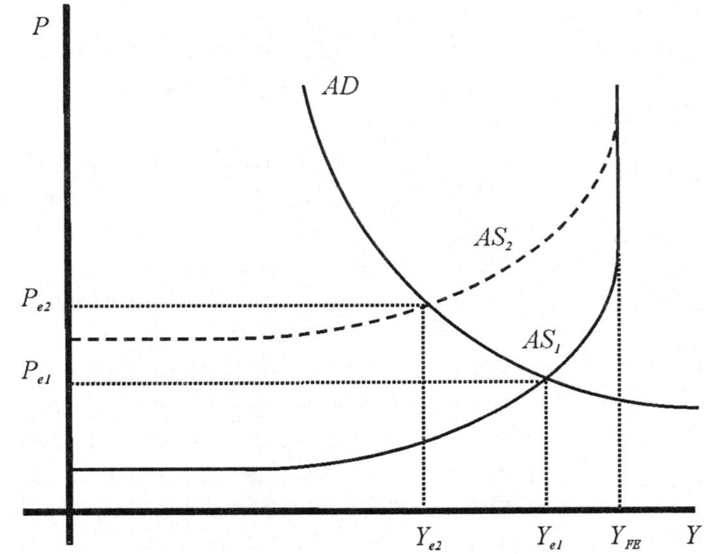

Figure 61. Aggregate Supply Shift

Sometimes a single event produces shifts both in the *AD* line and in the *AS* line. For example, a large increase in wage rates will move the *AS* line upwards (by increasing the cost of production) and will move the *AD* line to the right (because, at each level of prices, consumption expenditure (C) will increase following an increase in employees' disposable income (Y_d)). In this case, the effect on the price level (P) will be upward and the effect on income (Y) could be in either direction.

Analysis of changes in supply conditions might be complicated by simultaneous vertical and horizontal shifts of the *AS* line. It is possible that a single disturbance will produce both a vertical and a horizontal shift of the *AS* line and that these might be combined with a shift of the *AD* line. For example, an increase in investment expenditure (I) implies that the *AS* line shifts to the right because it increases the economy's capacity to produce and thus leads to an increase in the level of output that occurs when there is full employment (Y_{FE}). The *AS* line also shifts downwards because the increase in I leads, in addition, to greater efficiency at each level of output and thus to a decreased cost per unit of production. An autonomous increase in I also leads to a multiplied increase in aggregate demand and so shifts the *AD* line to the right. The equilibrium effect of an increase in I will therefore be an increase in Y and a change in P that could be in either direction.

Outcomes

The Classical and Keynesian approaches to the relationship between the level of income (Y) and the general level of prices (P) lead to very different conclusions.

In the Classical view, which assumes that prices are flexible and have a major influence on human behaviour, the economy will tend automatically towards the full-employment level of output. Income can be increased only by increasing the productive capacity of the economy; increases in the level of aggregate demand merely cause the price level to rise. Monetarists, including many of the economic advisers to British governments, United States governments, and others, since the 1980s, have used this theory to justify their emphasis on the supply side, rather than on the demand side, of the economy. It is also used to justify their belief in the importance of removing constraints on the adjustment of prices (including wage rates) in both directions. The social effects, including decreased wage rates, that might arise from the exertion of market power are assumed to be a reasonable price to pay for longer-term benefits.

The conclusions of the Keynesian view on the relationship between the levels of aggregate output (Y) and prices (P) are more complex. According to this approach, full employment is unlikely to occur spontaneously, and changes in aggregate demand will have a major influence on the levels of both income (and employment) and of prices. For this reason, Keynesian economists are usually keen for governments to manage the level of aggregate demand; this implies the frequent use of fiscal and monetary policy. The theory also shows that changes in supply conditions in India, including the cost of imported materials (which is determined outside India), might have significant effects on both Y and P.

9

Inflation: Causes, Effects, Policy

Inflation is defined as a process of persistent increases in the general level of prices. This has been a world-wide phenomenon for much of the last century, and the achievement of price stability has been a major aim of many governments. In December 2007, for example, the annual rate of consumer-price inflation in India was 5.7% [Source: Ministry of Statistics and Programme Implementation, India].

There are two types of inflation. It might be creeping inflation, which is slow enough not to severely disrupt economic activity in the short term, although it might have serious effects in the longer term, or it might be galloping inflation (also called hyper-inflation) which is so rapid that it causes the collapse of the economic system.

Galloping Inflation

Only a small number of cases of galloping inflation have occurred since the beginning of the twentieth century. It happened, for example, in Germany in 1922–23, in Greece in 1943–44, and in Hungary in 1945–46. In each of these cases (and there are others), prices rose, and so money lost its value, so fast that economic incentives were grossly distorted. It became a matter of very great urgency to spend money as soon as it was received, and before its purchasing power diminished sharply. Ultimately, galloping inflation destroys the incentive to work, since this is paid for in money that rapidly becomes useless, and, when this happens, production and distribution activities cannot operate. In every case of hyper-inflation, people have suffered from extreme deprivation, including malnutrition and even starvation. These acute social effects also have political consequences, as people become receptive to extreme policies in situations of acute hardship which have been neither prevented nor cured by existing politicians and their policies.

Galloping inflation does not just mean fast inflation. It means extremely fast inflation. Average prices in Germany multiplied by more than 10^9 between August 1922 and November 1923. In Hungary between August 1945 and July 1946, they multiplied by more than 10^{27}.

Galloping inflation has never occurred in India, and nor is it likely that it will. For this reason, although it remains a problem that cannot be totally ignored, it is not considered to be of current importance. Throughout the rest of this book, therefore, inflation should be taken to mean creeping inflation.

Creeping Inflation

There are two types of creeping inflation. This is a classification by cause rather than by speed. The two types are demand-pull inflation and cost-push inflation.

Demand-pull inflation occurs when aggregate demand (E_P) is greater than the full-employment level of output (Y_{FE}). In this situation, people wish to buy, and can pay for, a greater quantity of output than the system can produce. This type of inflation is consistent with Keynesian views on the role of the level of aggregate demand. Demand-pull inflation might appear when major sectors of the economy face an excess level of demand for output even if this is combined with a significant amount of spare capacity in the economy as a whole.

Demand-pull inflation occurred in many countries after the end of the Second World War. Demand was high because people (including firms and governments) wished to replace things that had been destroyed during the fighting. They had the ability to pay because savings had accumulated during the war, when spending opportunities had been restricted. There was also a sudden increase in the birth rate which led to an increase in the demand for housing and for other goods and services. Simultaneously, the productive capacity of most economies had been reduced. A significant proportion of buildings and other capital goods, especially in Europe, had been destroyed or taken into military use, and conscription and casualties had reduced the availability of labour. For all of these reasons, demand for many commodities exceeded the maximum supply, and prices rose.

Cost-push inflation means increases in the price level caused by the pressure of increases in business costs. Firms who face increased costs cannot reasonably be blamed for passing these costs on to customers in the form of higher prices; costs must be met before profits can be made.

There are numerous possible causes of cost-push inflation. It might, for example, be due to increases in the prices of imported inputs (components, raw materials, and fuel). When the world price of oil rose sharply in 1973, for example, all firms in India faced increased costs, and had a very strong incentive to raise their prices. Increases in the prices of imported intermediate goods can be caused by a fall in the value of the Indian rupee, so that an increased quantity of Indian money has to be paid for a certain amount of foreign money.

Cost-push inflation might also follow an increase in net tax rates. This applies to all types of taxes and subsidies. Sales taxes are levied on firms but are usually added, in whole or in major part, to prices. Subsidies are paid to firms but usually have a major impact on prices. Increased taxes on personal incomes might lead to demands for higher wages; if these are successful, prices will almost certainly rise. Taxes on profits are also likely to lead to higher prices, as firms try to achieve their target rate of after-tax profit.

Increased rates of interest also cause cost-push inflation. Most firms are in debt much of the time, and the interest they pay is a business cost; increases might be added to prices. Some governments have controlled the level of interest rates in an attempt to prevent this problem.

Monopoly power might lead to cost-push inflation. Firms might exploit the absence of competition, when customers have no choice of supplier, by raising prices to their profit-maximising levels. For this reason, many governments attempt to restrict the power of monopolies.

Cost-push inflation might also be caused by powerful trade unions, since all or most of increased wage costs are likely to be added to prices.

Finally, cost-push inflation might occur as a result of inefficient management. Higher prices can result from, for example, obsolete methods, obsolete equipment, or inadequately trained labour.

These six causes of cost-push inflation (import prices, taxes, interest rates, monopoly power, strong labour unions, inefficient management) are not mutually exclusive. A single event might fit more than a single category. A successful wage demand by a powerful trade union, for example, might be an example of monopoly power, as are the increases in the price of oil announced by the Organisation of Petroleum-Exporting Countries (OPEC) in 1973 and later years.

The six types of cost-push inflation listed include several very different phenomena. It could be argued that the only thing that they have in common is that they might result in inflation other than through the effects of increased demand. Cost-push inflation is therefore a generic term that refers to any occurrence of inflation that cannot be explained by the Keynesian approach to the relationship between aggregate demand (E_P) and the full-employment level of output (Y_{FE}).

Demand-pull inflation and cost-push inflation, despite their distinct causes, frequently occur together and cause or encourage each other. For example, rising prices (which might be due to excess demand) are likely to encourage monopolists to feel that they can raise their prices without being noticed, and hence without customer resistance. This is an example of demand-pull inflation encouraging cost-push inflation. The reverse process also occurs. Monopolists who have made substantial profits (by raising prices, thus causing cost-push inflation) will increase demand when they spend their additional income; if output is at or near the full-employment level, this might cause demand-pull inflation. In practice, therefore, demand-pull inflation and cost-push inflation occur together and each tends to stimulate the other.

Each of the two types of inflation also tends to build on itself. A firm whose actions to lead to cost-push inflation is likely to encourage other firms to do the same. Equally, a period of demand-pull inflation means that people have rising disposable incomes which lead to further increases in demand and, hence, to further rounds of inflation.

One of the problems of inflation is that, if not checked, it tends to accelerate. Once this process begins, it might become self-justifying. For example, firms who believe that the prices of their inputs are certain to rise will have an incentive to raise the prices of their output in advance of the anticipated increases in their costs, especially if they believe that other firms are doing the same. Inflation causes inflation expectations which cause more inflation.

Although there is a clear theoretical distinction between cost-push and demand-pull inflation, the two phenomena cannot in practice be disentangled. The distinction is, however, of importance because the effects on the economy of each of these two types of inflation might be different, and the policies designed to cure each of these problems are also different.

Effects of Demand-Pull Inflation

The obvious feature of a period of inflation, of any cause, is an increasing level of prices (including increasing wage rates) which is, of course, the definition of inflation. This does not necessarily mean that the prices of all commodities are rising at the same rate. It does not even mean that prices of all commodities are rising; some might be falling.

A characteristic of economies which are experiencing demand-pull inflation is that the level of output is at or near the full-employment level. This is part of the definition of demand-pull inflation. It follows that there will be a very low level of unemployment. All of this arises as firms try to respond to a level of aggregate demand that it is beyond the capacity of the economy to satisfy.

Attempts to increase output during a period of demand-pull inflation might lead to over-full employment. This means that the economy is producing at a level which is not consistent with efficiency in the longer term. It might mean that firms have responded to a shortage of skilled labour by using inadequately trained workers for skilled work. This will probably lead to an increased cost per unit of output, as such workers might work slower than their skilled colleagues, they might require additional supervision, they might produce a higher proportion of defective output that has to be discarded, and they might have a higher accident rate. Over-full employment might mean that employees are working very long hours per week; as a result of the overtime premium on wage rates, this causes costs per unit of output to rise significantly. It can also happen that equipment is over-used; if adequate time is not allowed for servicing, machines become less efficient and might fail more frequently.

The high level of aggregate demand that is a feature of situations of demand-pull inflation causes stock levels (both of raw materials and of finished goods) to diminish as firms find that they can sell more than can be produced. This leads to delays and shortages, especially as many firms sell their output not to final customers but to other firms. This is another example of the inefficiencies that arise when the level of aggregate demand exceeds the maximum amount of output that can be produced.

A high level of output, caused by excess demand, leads to cost-push pressures. Low unemployment strengthens trades unions, as there is no alternative source of labour in the form of a pool of unemployed people. Increased wage rates increase business costs, as do the inefficiencies that result from over-full employment. These are among the ways in which demand-pull inflation causes cost-push inflation.

Demand-pull inflation has two types of effect on the government budget. Unless tax rules change, demand-pull inflation results in increased net tax revenue, as T is a positive function of Y (since, for example, people who are employed pay tax and do not receive social security payments), and thus leads to a reduced budget deficit (or increased surplus). Additionally, if the tax system is progressive (see Chapter 3), tax revenue will rise faster than prices; this is called fiscal drag.

Demand-pull inflation is usually combined with a decline in the quality of output. This is partly a consequence of over-full employment, since over-worked or under-skilled employees are unlikely to be able to produce the best quality of output, but it is also frequently a deliberate management decision. If firms find that demand exceeds their capacity to produce, so that they can sell all of their output without difficulty, then there is little incentive to maintain a high standard of quality. In this situation, producing more cheaply is unlikely to lead to lower sales.

Reduced quality of output leads to an increased level of aggregate demand, as goods do not last as long as previously. For example, if people respond to reduced quality by buying new cars every three years instead of every four years, demand for cars increases by 33%, from 2.5 to 3.3 per person in each period of ten years. Thus demand-pull inflation, which is caused by excess demand, causes demand to rise further, which leads to faster demand-pull inflation.

Demand-pull inflation might have an impact on international trade. It is, in particular, likely to lead to an increased demand for imports. There are four reasons for this. If exchange rates for the Indian rupee do not change, then increases in the prices of goods made in India mean that foreign goods become relatively cheaper than they were, and therefore more attractive to buyers. The second reason is that, if the flow of imports is not restricted, it is likely that additional goods will be imported to meet unsatisfied demand. At a time when aggregate demand exceeds maximum output, customers who prefer locally produced goods might be willing to buy imports (Z) if the alternative is to join a long queue. The third reason is that a high level of output (Y) leads to a high demand for imported materials, fuel, and components; Z is a positive function of Y. The fourth reason for increased demand for imports is that reduced quality of local goods improves the relative attractiveness of foreign goods.

The demand for manufactured exports is likely to fall for the same reasons. If there are no changes in exchange rates, then inflation in India means that foreign buyers have an incentive to choose a supplier in another country. In addition, goods that might have been exported might be diverted to the buoyant domestic market; firms who can sell their output locally have little incentive to sell in other countries.

The volume of exports of primary commodities (cotton, fruit, minerals, etc.) is unlikely to be affected by demand-pull inflation in India, as the prices of such goods are determined in wholesale markets in other countries, though a high level of demand in the local market might reduce the amount available for export.

Since demand-pull inflation tends to encourage imports and discourage manufactured exports, it has a negative effect on the balance of trade. This is discussed in Chapters 11 and 12.

Demand-pull inflation leads to a reduced incentive to save (S). If the level of unemployment is low, jobs are secure, and employers are offering a large amount of overtime work, then the prevailing mood will be optimistic. A high level of savings is encouraged by a fear of hardship, and this is not frequent during periods of demand-pull inflation (and low unemployment). In addition, people might feel that the interest they receive on their accumulated money does not adequately compensate for increases in prices; it might be better to buy things before their prices rise further.

There might be significant consequences of a reduced rate of saving. People who save less are spending more, so demand-pull inflation, which is caused by a high level of demand, leads, by discouraging saving, to an even higher level of demand and thus to even faster demand-pull inflation.

Saving releases resources for investment (I). If people reduce the amount they save, then firms might be prevented from borrowing to finance investment projects. This might inhibit the expansion of such firms' productive capacity, and ensure the continuation of excess demand and therefore of demand-pull inflation. It might also restrain the modernisation of firms' equipment, which means that the cost per unit of output will be higher than it would otherwise have been. This inefficiency leads to cost-push inflation.

Demand-pull inflation is sometimes regarded as a stimulus to the economy. People might be encouraged to borrow and spend, especially when confidence is high (which it will be when unemployment is low), if debts can be repaid in depreciated money. This means that the level of demand is further increased at a time when it is already higher than the economy can satisfy. This effect depends partly, of course, on the level of interest rates.

Any kind of inflation has distributional effects. Rising prices do not affect everyone equally. People (and firms) whose wages (and profits) are rising faster than the general level of prices are benefiting from inflation, while those whose wages or profits are rising slower than the general level of prices are suffering from inflation. In general, inflation strengthens those who are already in a relatively strong position, and makes the relatively weak relatively even weaker. People whose skills are in excess demand are likely to receive wages that rise faster than the wages paid to people whose skills are in excess supply. Members of strong trades unions are likely to benefit relative to non-union labour. These types of changes in the distribution of income are also likely to occur in the absence of inflation; one of the effects of demand-pull inflation is to make them happen very much faster and therefore to make them become much more apparent.

Inflation also leads to a redistribution of wealth. Some assets rise in rupee value as prices rise; these include houses and land. Money, however, does not. People who hold their wealth in the form of money will find that the real value of this wealth diminishes during a period of inflation, though this effect is often reduced by the payment of interest. The form in which wealth is held is not random; in general, wealthier people are likely to hold a high proportion of their (substantial) wealth in the form of assets such as land and houses, and poorer people are likely to hold a high proportion of their (small) wealth in the form of money. For this reason, inflation tends to make the rich relatively even richer and the poor relatively even poorer.

The distributional effects might have significant political effects. A situation that penalises those least able to protect their own interests is generally regarded as unjust.

The effects of demand-pull inflation are summarised in Table 11.

TABLE 11 Effects of Demand-Pull Inflation

Effects
Increasing prices
High output; low unemployment
Reduced government budget deficit
Reduced quality of output
Increased imports; decreased manufactured exports
Reduced incentive to save
Redistribution of income and of wealth

Effects of a Depression

The inverse of demand-pull inflation is a depression, when a high level of unemployment is caused by a level of aggregate demand that is too low to keep the economy at the full-employment level of output. A severe depression occurred in many countries in the 1930s. Like demand-pull inflation, the explanation of this problem is consistent with the Keynesian approach to the significance of the level of aggregate demand. High unemployment caused by a low level of aggregate demand is also called a slump, a recession, or a downturn. Although each of these terms has specific connotations, they describe the same phenomenon. Other causes of unemployment are discussed in Chapter 10.

During a depression the effects of demand-pull inflation, shown in Table 11, are reversed. The price level falls, as firms try to attract customers by reducing prices, and employees accept wage cuts in order to retain their jobs. The low level of aggregate demand leads to low output and to high unemployment. Quality of output tends to rise during a depression, as firms compete against each other for customers. The volume of imports tends to be low, because the low level of output means that there is a reduced need for imported intermediate goods, and because local goods of low price and high quality are in excess supply. Manufactured exports might be encouraged by their price and quality.

The incentive to save during a depression is very substantial. Confidence is low; people are frightened of losing their jobs. In the 1930s, a large proportion of people were, because of unemployment and low wage rates, unable to save, but the savings rate among those who could afford to save was high. Tragically, a low level of confidence is often self-justifying. If people believe that unemployment is going to rise, they will increase the proportion of their disposable income that is saved; this reduction in spending persuades firms to reduce output and therefore increases unemployment (by a multiplied amount). Fear of unemployment might therefore cause unemployment. This supports the Keynesian views that behaviour that is an appropriate response by an individual to a particular set of circumstances might not be in the interests of the whole community, and that there is, therefore, a role for the government to counteract changes in the level of demand in the private sector.

Effects of Cost-Push Inflation

Unlike both depression and demand-pull inflation, cost-push inflation is not a single phenomenon with a clear theoretical explanation, and its effects depend on its cause. If cost-push inflation leads to a low level of demand, it causes all the problems of a depression but, if it is associated with a high level of demand, then, if income is at or near the full-employment level, it causes all the problems of demand-pull inflation. The increase in the price of oil in 1973 had little immediate effect on the quantity demanded of oil, but caused a decreased level of demand for a large number of other products; this led to cost-push inflation combined with an increased level of unemployment and other features of a depression. In contrast, when cost-push inflation is caused by large increases in wage rates, this will probably lead to an increase in demand, as employees spend much of their increased wages, and might, therefore, cause demand-pull inflation. The conclusion is that cost-push inflation might be combined with demand-pull inflation, or with depression, or with both.

Policy Responses

There are four types of policy measure that can be used by governments to reduce the severity of inflation.

Fiscal policy means changes in net tax rates and/or in the level of government spending that are designed to change the level of aggregate demand. This type of policy can be used both during periods of demand-pull inflation and during periods of depression. Increases in net taxation (T) and cuts in government spending (G) tend to decrease demand (E_P) and can be used against demand-pull inflation; decreases in net taxation and increases in government spending lead to a multiplied expansion of aggregate demand and can be used in times of depression. Cost-push inflation is not caused by the level of aggregate demand, and therefore cannot be solved by fiscal policy.

Monetary policy means government decisions that directly affect the level of the money supply (Ms). Such decisions influence the availability, and therefore the price (interest rate), of borrowed money. This type of policy is also intended to influence the level of aggregate demand; preventing or discouraging borrowing is intended to influence the amount of spending. A tight monetary policy, which reduces the availability of loans, can be used during periods of demand-pull inflation, and a loose monetary policy can be used in an attempt to stimulate demand when the level of unemployment is high. Neither is relevant during cost-push inflation, which is not caused by the level of aggregate demand.

Rationing means direct restrictions on the level of demand. It means that the government specifies the maximum amount of particular commodities that people are permitted to purchase. Severe rationing of food and other essential commodities was introduced in the UK, and in other European countries, during and after the Second World War. The exigencies of war meant that many important products, including food, were in very short supply, and rationing was imposed to ensure that everyone received a fair share of the limited quantity available. It was also a function of rationing to inhibit increases in the price level (P); had rationing not been introduced, demand would have greatly exceeded supply and food prices would have risen very substantially. In this type of extreme situation, in which the poorest people might have faced starvation, rationing can be regarded as a policy against demand-pull inflation. It is, however, relevant neither to cost-push inflation nor to depression.

The fourth type of policy is a prices and incomes policy (also known by other names including price controls and wage-price freeze). This means direct restrictions on wage rates and on prices of output. Under this type of policy, the government specifies the price increases that are permitted. This is an attempt to cure cost-push inflation by forbidding it.

Variants of prices and incomes policies, designed to influence the level of business costs, include direct controls on interest rates and on the exchange rate. The administrative fixing of the level of interest rates is likely to lead to a disequilibrium in the money market and thus to a scarcity of borrowed funds. The effects of a fixed exchange rate are explained in Chapters 11 and 12. Another variant is indexation, of which the precise rules vary but usually compel employers to pay percentage increases in wage rates that are equal to recorded percentage increases in the price level. This is designed to protect employees from the effects of rising prices and to protect employers from rapidly increasing wage costs, but is not likely to solve the problem of inflation.

Unfortunately, economic problems can rarely be solved by statutory prohibition of their effects, and a prices and incomes policy is likely to be successful in delaying, but not in preventing, price increases. A major practical problem is that there are some prices which cannot be controlled by the government; these include the prices of imported intermediate goods. It is difficult, therefore, for this type of policy to be seen to be fair. Firms might feel justified in objecting to the fixing of their output prices if some of their costs are continuing to rise. Similarly, wage-earners might feel aggrieved if consumer prices rise when wage increases are not permitted.

Prices and incomes policies usually have a limited life because they are ultimately unenforceable. Such policies are workable when people co-operate willingly with them, but are very difficult to police if the restrictions are widely perceived to be inequitable. In general, prices and incomes policies survive for less than two years, and are useful only to the extent that they provide a respite from persistent increases in the price level.

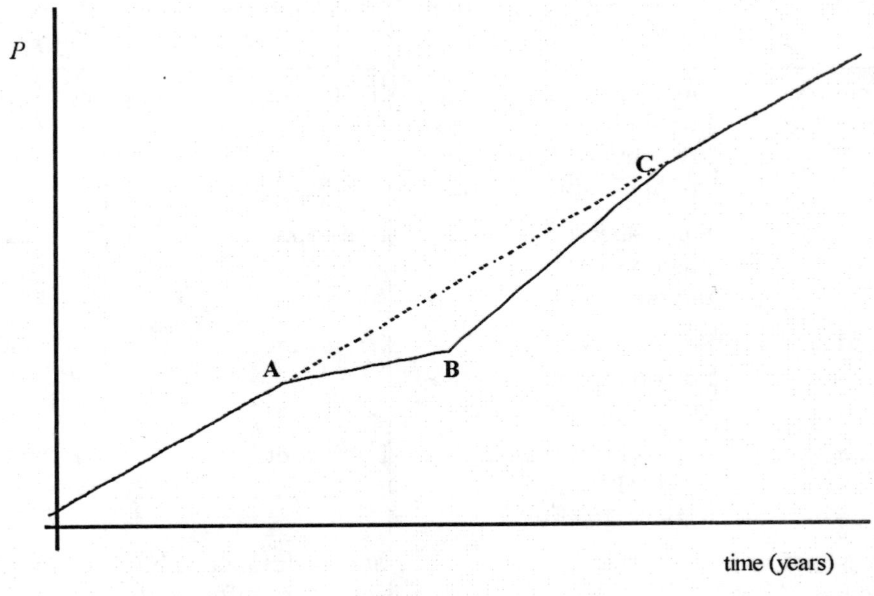

Fig. 62. Prices and Incomes Policy

Figure 62 shows the usual effects on the price level (P) of a prices and incomes policy. It shows that the rate of increase of prices is reduced by the introduction, at **A**, of controls on prices and wage rates.

However, when the policy comes to an end, at **B**, there is a surge of price increases, as firms try to recover from customers the sales revenue that was lost when price increases were not permitted, and employees obtain the wage increases that they felt they should have received earlier. When this recovery period is complete, at **C**, the price level usually returns to its rate of increase that was observed before the introduction of restrictions on price increases.

Application of Policy Measures

Table 12 summarises the main effects of using each of the types of policy against demand-pull inflation, cost-push inflation, and depression. It is assumed that each of these three problems occurs on its own, and that each of the types of policy is used on its own. Effects relating to international trade are ignored, as are other microeconomic and macroeconomic problems. The interaction between exchange-rate policy and domestic macroeconomic policy, which is summarised in Table 17 (Chapter 12), is also ignored.

TABLE 12 Effects of Policy against Inflation and Depression

	Demand-pull inflation (1950s)	Cost-push inflation (1970s)	Depression (1930s)
Monetary policy (ΔM_S)	Some success, but: other finance sources reduced investment (I) cost-push (higher r) unemployment	Irrelevant	Irrelevant
Fiscal policy (ΔT)	Some success, but: cost-push hardship unemployment	Irrelevant	Irrelevant
Fiscal policy (ΔG)	Some success, but: reduced amenities cost-push unemployment	Irrelevant	Successful policy
Rationing	Successful policy, but: restriction of liberty difficult to enforce	Irrelevant	Irrelevant
Prices and Incomes Policy	Irrelevant	Successful policy, but: short-term effect only delayed inflation difficult to enforce	Irrelevant

A tight monetary policy is likely to have some degree of success in reducing the pressure of demand-pull inflation; restriction of the availability of bank loans will have some effect in reducing spending. However, some people who are refused bank loans will find other sources of finance. They might spend their accumulated savings, or borrow from friends, or borrow from a non-bank financial intermediary that is not subject to the rigours of monetary controls. Further, although monetary policy can be used to control the amount of bank lending, it cannot control the uses to which the remaining loans are put, and it is possible that a tight monetary policy might prevent spending, including investment spending, which would be of benefit to the whole of the economy.

A tight monetary policy which significantly reduces demand will cause a multiplied increase in unemployment especially if the previous level of aggregate demand was less than the full-employment level of output.

Contractionary monetary policy causes increases in the level of interest rates since a reduction in the money supply will mean that it is likely to be less than money demand. Interest rates paid on loans obtained from non-banks in an attempt to avoid the effects of the policy are also likely to be high. Increased interest payments are an increased business cost which might be added to the price of output. A tight monetary policy might, therefore, stimulate cost-push inflation.

Monetary policy is not relevant during periods of cost-push inflation, which is not caused by a high level of aggregate demand.

Monetary policy will not be successful in stimulating demand during a severe depression. In the 1930s, very many businesses had substantial spare capacity, and there was therefore, despite the low level of interest rates, little incentive to invest in additional equipment. Demand for loans was also low in the household sector; people who are frightened of losing their jobs are keen to save rather than to borrow. Increasing the availability of loans does not increase the level of aggregate demand when the economy is suffering from a depression.

On the *AS–AD* diagram (Figure 59), which shows aggregate demand and aggregate supply as functions of the price level (P), a tight monetary policy during a period of demand-pull inflation is shown as a leftward shift of the *AD* line when the economy is at or near the full-employment level of income (Y_{FE}); this leads to a reduction in P. A loose monetary policy during a period of depression is very unlikely to increase the level of aggregate demand (because demand for loans is low) and so does not shift the *AD* line.

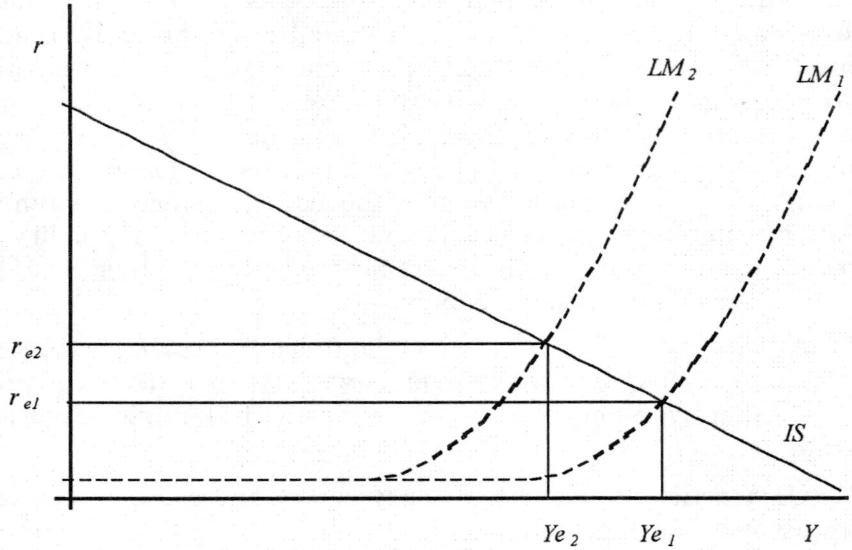

Fig. 63. Monetary Policy during Demand-Pull Inflation.

The application of *IS–LM* analysis to the use of a tight monetary policy during a period of demand-pull inflation is shown in Figure 63. Equilibrium combinations of income (Y) and interest rate (r) levels are shown for the real (or goods) market (*IS*) and for the money market (*LM*), and a tight monetary policy is shown as a shift of the *LM* line from LM_1 to LM_2. This increases the level of interest rates and reduces the level of income. The effect of a loose monetary policy during a severe depression is shown in Figure 64 as a shift of the *LM* line to the right; since interest rates are at their minimum level (because Y is significantly less than Y_{FE}), this affects neither the value of r nor the value of Y. The increase in the money supply is not used to buy bonds (because bond prices are at their maximum and there is no chance of a capital gain) so bond prices do not rise and r does not fall. Therefore there is no stimulus to increase investment (I) and so there is no increase in Y. Monetary policy is ineffective when the *IS–LM* intersection is on the horizontal part of the *LM* line. This situation is known as the liquidity trap (see Chapter 5).

In Table 12, fiscal policy using changes in net taxation (ΔT) is treated separately from fiscal policy using changes in government spending (ΔG). Like a tight monetary policy, a tight fiscal policy will have some effect in reducing the pressure of demand-pull inflation. Increases in net taxation (ΔT) reduce disposable income and so reduce induced consumption spending (which has a multiplied effect on the level of aggregate demand). This, of course, probably causes unemployment. Higher taxes are also likely to lead to price increases (cost-push inflation) by increasing business costs and shifting the *AS* line upwards, and might also cause hardship.

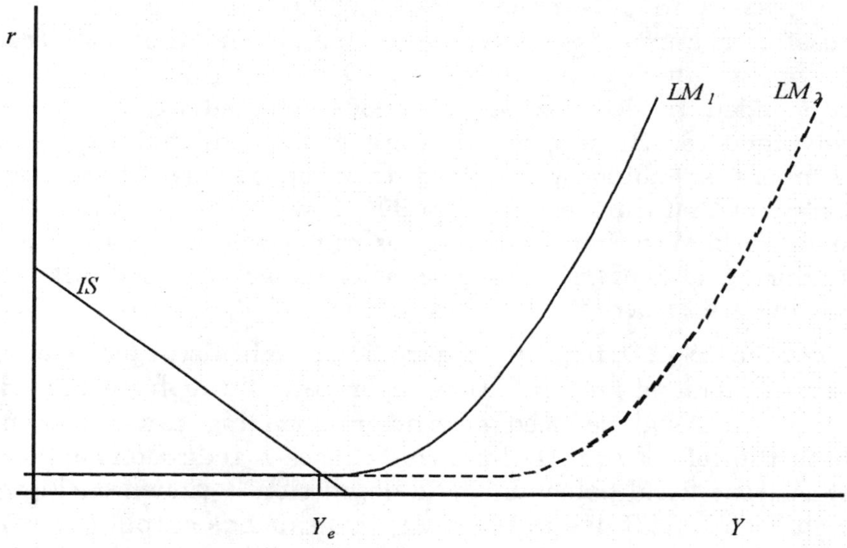

Fig. 64. Monetary Policy during a Depression.

A tight fiscal policy during a period of demand-pull inflation might involve cuts in government spending (ΔG). These reduce the level of aggregate demand (by a multiplied amount) and therefore result in some reduction in the pressure of demand-pull inflation. This type of policy will also, however, necessarily lead to the reduction or withdrawal of some of the services provided by the government to firms and to households, and this might have significant social and economic consequences. A decrease in the range of services provided to firms without charge by the government might reduce the efficiency of firms. It might also result in firms providing some additional services themselves. In either case, business costs will increase, and, if these increases are added (even in part) to the price of output, cost-push inflation will be stimulated. Reduced government spending also probably causes unemployment.

Cost-push inflation is not caused by excess demand in the economy, so the use of fiscal policy is not relevant to this problem.

A loose fiscal policy can be used to stimulate increased demand during a depression. However, this will not be achieved through reductions in tax rates. If unemployment is high, and the level of confidence is low, people will respond to a reduced tax burden by increasing their savings rather than by increasing their spending. Cuts in tax rates will not, therefore, lead to increased aggregate demand during a depression.

Increases in government spending are, however, likely to be successful in stimulating increased demand, and therefore creating employment, during a depression. This is the type of policy recommended by Keynes in the 1930s. His advice was, however largely ignored. His opponents were concerned that expansion of government spending would lead to a budget deficit, which was regarded, at that time, as unacceptable. It was not until the end of the Second World War that there was general acceptance of Keynes' view that, during a depression, government budget deficits financed by borrowing are an acceptable policy outcome.

On the *AS–AD* diagram (Figure 59), a tight fiscal policy during a period of demand-pull inflation, operating through increased net taxation or through reduced government spending, can be shown as a shift to the left of the *AD* line; this causes a reduction in the price level. A loose fiscal policy during a depression is shown on Figure 65 as a shift of the *AD* line to the right; this expands output (from Ye_1 to Ye_2) and employment but has no effect on P because the *AS* line is horizontal. If, however, the instrument of the loose fiscal policy is a reduction in tax rates, then the savings rate is likely to increase. This shifts the *AD* line to the left again, moving it to, or very near to, its original position; in this case, the level of unemployment will not decrease.

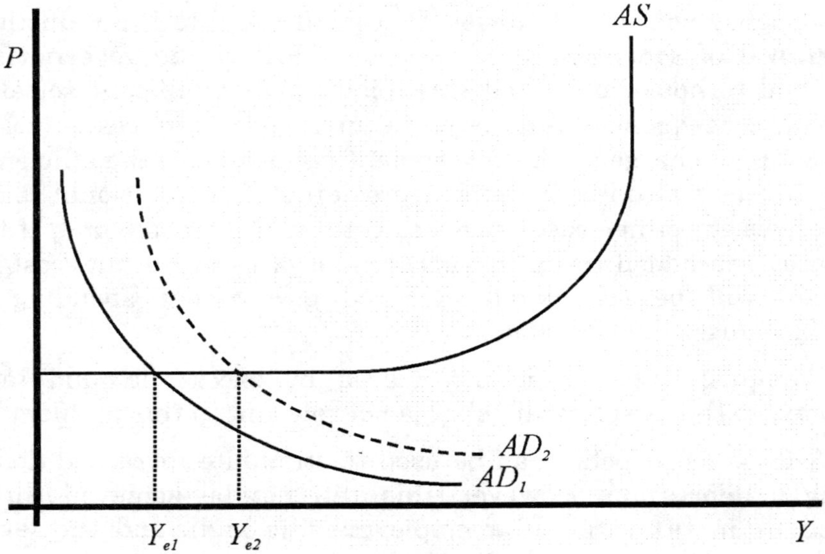

Fig. 65. Fiscal Policy during a Depression.

A tight fiscal policy during a period of demand-pull inflation is shown on an *IS–LM* diagram as a shift of the *IS* line to the left. A loose fiscal policy during a depression is shown on Figure 66 as a shift of the *IS* line to the right; in this case the *LM* line is horizontal, so income (and employment) expand but there is no effect on the level of interest rates.

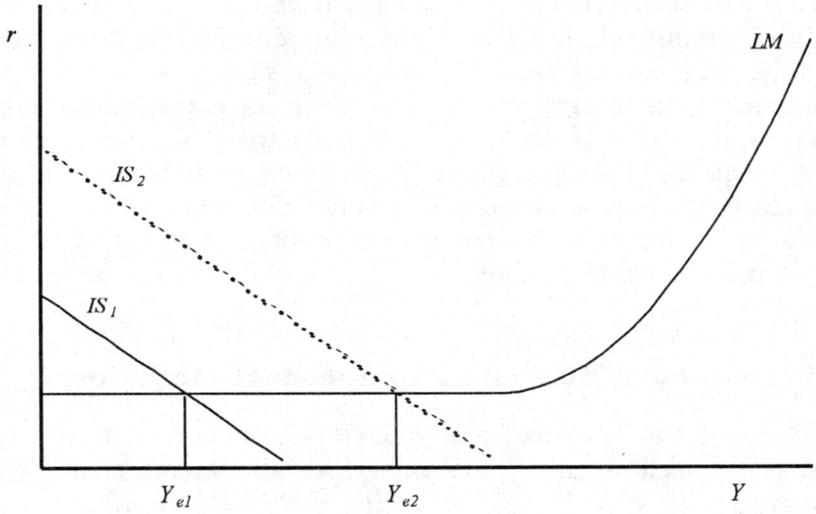

Fig. 66. Fiscal Policy during a Depression.

Rationing was used extensively, especially in Europe, to prevent demand-pull inflation during and after the Second World War. The social and political effects are such, however, that it can be used only during a time of great national crisis. Rationing is seen as a restriction of individual liberty; people resent intensely not being allowed to spend their money as they see fit. The effect of this is that a black market is likely to develop; illegal deals are impossible to regulate, as both the buyers and the sellers are guilty, so there is no-one who will inform the police. A black market further reduces the supply on the legal market, causing further resentment. Rationing is not, therefore, of current importance in India.

Rationing is of no relevance during periods of cost-push inflation and of depression, neither of which is caused by excess demand for important commodities.

Prices and incomes policies do not directly influence the level of aggregate demand, and so cannot be used against the problems of demand-pull inflation and of depression. Such policies can, however, be used against cost-push inflation, but are very likely to be workable in the short term only. Prices and incomes policies are intended to reduce the cost of running businesses and are shown on the *AD–AS* diagram as a downward shift of the *AS* line.

Table 12 refers to only three types of macroeconomic problem (which are assumed not to occur simultaneously), and to only five types of policy (which it is assumed are not used together), and international trade effects are ignored. It should therefore be treated as a gross simplification. Of the fifteen combinations that are shown in the table, only one (increased government spending during a severe depression) is an unreserved success. Tragically, the advice given by Keynes and others to use this policy in the 1930s was generally ignored. The real world is, of course, more complex than is implied in Table 12, because macroeconomic problems occur together and might require conflicting policy responses. An additional complication is that solving one economic problem is very likely to cause (or accelerate) others.

The Classical and Monetarist Approaches to Inflation

Much of the Classical and monetarist theory on the nature of inflation is based on interpretations of an adaptation of an equation which was originally devised by Irving Fisher (1867–1947). A recent version of the equation is:

$$M_S V \equiv PY$$

M_S is the money supply, V is the velocity of circulation, which means the average number of times that each rupee is used to make a payment for final output (not intermediate goods) in a year, P is the price level, and Y is the annual amount of aggregate output. This is an identity; it must be true at all levels of income because of the way in which the symbols are defined. $M_S V$, the amount of money in the economic system multiplied by the number of times it is used to buy final output, measures the value of purchases of final output; and PY, the quantity of output multiplied by its average price, measures the value of output sold. The value of output sold must necessarily be equal to the value of output purchased.

The Classical view is that V has a constant value because people's spending behaviour does not change. They also regarded Y as constant since, except perhaps in the very short term during the adjustment of prices following a disturbance, income will be at the full-employment level. If V and Y are constant, it follows that there is a directly proportional relationship between M_S and P; if the money supply increases by $x\%$, then the price level will increase by $x\%$. This is called the quantity theory of money, and constitutes the Classical theory of inflation, which is that inflation is caused by increases in the money supply.

The Keynesian view of the Fisher equation is that it is valid as an identity, but that the Classical assumptions about V and Y are not valid. Income is not always at the full-employment level and nor can the velocity of circulation be regarded as necessarily constant. The Keynesian view is that if the money supply (M_S) changes, some combination of the other three variables (V, P, Y) will adjust. The main effect of an increase in M_S is likely to be shown on the level of income (Y), unless it has already reached the full-employment level (Y_{FE}) and cannot increase further. In this situation, the main effect will be on the price level (P); this is called demand-pull inflation.

The monetarist approach is a development of the Classical theory. The monetarists accept that the velocity of circulation (V) might not be constant, but believe that it is not a function of the money supply (M_S). Changes in M_S therefore affect the price level (P) and the amount of output (Y) but not the velocity of circulation. The monetarist view is that the main effect is on P, though there might be significant effects on Y in the short term. In the longer term, monetarists believe that the effects on Y will diminish towards zero. Monetarist governments believe that reducing the money supply is an appropriate policy at a time of inflation, and the unemployment that this causes will decrease significantly in the longer term.

Monetarists support their view that the most efficient method of controlling inflation is to control the money supply by referring to the strong statistical correlation shown between money supply data and price level data. The Keynesian reply, however, is that correlation does not necessarily prove causation, and it might be that it is increases in the price level that cause the money supply to rise. For example, if prices rise, then people will seek larger loans that they otherwise would, and these will lead to the creation of larger new bank deposits than would otherwise occur, which constitute an increase in the money supply over the level that would have occurred if prices had not risen. It is also possible that increases in the money supply and in the price level are simultaneously caused by changes in some third variable.

The Phillips Curve

Using data relating to the British economy, A W Phillips (1914–75) was able to demonstrate a stable relationship between the annual rate of change of money wages (and, by inference, the price level) and the unemployment rate. This work was published in 1958, and produced a diagram, of the form shown in Figure 67, which has since become known as the Phillips curve. This graph is not a statement of a theoretical proposition; it is a description of observed macroeconomic behaviour. Since his data showed a good fit to the curve, Phillips' work was widely regarded as evidence that the Keynesian approach to the importance of the level of aggregate demand was correct; an inverse relationship between the rates of unemployment and inflation is consistent with the Keynesian theory that too much demand causes one and insufficient demand causes the other.

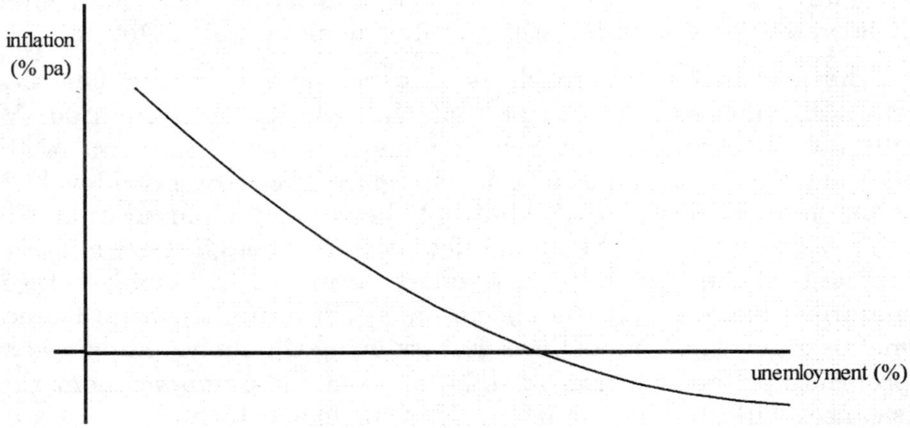

Figure 67. Phillips Curve

Figure 67 shows that high rates of inflation were combined with low rates of unemployment in, for example, the 1950s, while the reverse occurred during periods of depression (including the 1930s), when economic conditions were often so severe that wage levels (and prices) showed a negative rate of change.

From the late 1960s, and especially from the increase in the world price of oil in 1973, the stable relationship described by the Phillips curve came to an end. Many countries, including the United States and the UK, experienced increases both in the rate of inflation and in the rate of unemployment. This encouraged monetarists to criticise the Keynesian approach, since it indicated that the level of aggregate demand did not have the precise role described by Keynes.

Monetarists believe that in the long run there is no relationship between the rates of inflation and of unemployment. In this approach, the Phillips curve is vertical, which means that the economy will tend towards a rate of unemployment (called the natural rate of unemployment) which can co-exist with any rate of increase in the price level. It follows that controlling the level of aggregate demand is not likely to be a reliable method of controlling the rate of inflation. Monetarists believe that the position of the Phillips curve in the short term is largely determined by the level of inflation expectations; if people believe that prices are likely to rise they will behave in a way that causes them to rise. For example, businesses might increase their output prices when they anticipate an increase in the prices of their inputs. This is an example of cost-push inflation.

Keynesians believe that the shifting of the Phillips curve to the right since the late 1960s does not alter the importance of the relationship that it describes. There is frequently an inverse relationship between the rate of unemployment and the rate of increase of the price level in the short run.

Measurement of the Price Level

The prices of different commodities change at different rates and sometimes in opposite directions. A simple average of the prices of all goods and services would not be a useful statistic since some prices are of greater importance than others. An increase in the price of a new piano, for example, would be of no significance for the overwhelming majority of Indian households, while a change in the price of rice affects almost all of them. It is necessary therefore to calculate a price index based on an appropriate weighted average of prices.

The Ministry of Statistics and Programme Implementation, India, publishes data for numerous price indices in order to record changes in the price level as it affects different parts of the economy. These include index numbers of wholesale prices (by type of product), index numbers of consumer prices (for industrial workers and for agricultural labourers and also by region), and all-India average rural retail prices of selected commodities.

10

Unemployment: Causes, Effects, Policy

The unemployment rate is an important indicator of economic and social conditions and a low unemployment rate is usually regarded as a policy objective. In India during 2004–05, for example, the average unemployment rate was 2.1% for rural males, 3.1% for rural females, 4.4% for urban males, and 9.1% for urban females [Source: Ministry of Statistics and Programme Implementation, India].

Unemployment is of economic significance because it implies that an important resource is not being fully utilised. It represents a lost opportunity to produce output; it represents income that has been foregone. Unemployed workers might also lose their skills and, in extreme cases, become unemployable; unemployed labour is therefore not just an under-utilised resource, it might also be a deteriorating resource. Unemployment also, by reducing tax revenue and increasing the amount of government transfer payments, has a negative effect on the government budget. In addition, there are frequently severe psychological effects for people who are unemployed, and, to the extent that unemployment is correlated with increased crime, there might be social effects that impose a financial and non-financial cost on the whole of the population.

Measurement of Unemployment

The concept of unemployment refers to a resource that is not in productive use but could easily be brought into use. Unemployment does not, therefore, include all the people who are not in paid employment but only those who would find work quickly if the demand for labour increased. The definition of an unemployed person is someone who is not in employment, who is both able and willing to work, who is sincerely looking for employment, and who is willing to accept any offer of employment that is appropriate to his/her skills and experience. It is not easy, however, to apply this definition to the collection of data.

In official Indian data, the labour force at a particular time consists of those who are working (engaged in any economic activity) and those who are seeking work (including those who are available for work). The principal-status approach counts a person among the employed during year if he or she has spend more time within the labour force than out of it and more time working than in seeking work. This approach counts a person among the unemployed during year if he or she has spent more time within the labour force than out of it and more time in seeking work than working. The unemployment rate is defined as the ratio of the number of persons unemployed to the number of persons in the labour force (which is the total of the employed and of the unemployed).

Causes of Unemployment

Like inflation, unemployment is not a single phenomenon with a single cause. It is a collection of phenomena which have different causes but which might encourage each other. Classification of the causes of unemployment varies between economists, but it is useful to identify four principal types.

Unemployment might arise because of insufficient demand in the economy. This is Keynes' theory of unemployment; it means that the quantity of output that people (including the government) wish to buy, and can afford to pay for, is less than the economy is capable of producing. This condition was described, in Chapter 9, as a depression.

There might be a problem of structural unemployment. This means that people have not been able to adjust to a change in the structure of the economy, perhaps following a change in technology. For example, there might be unemployed coal-mining workers if the primary source of energy has evolved from coal to oil. Miners might be out of work because they are too old, or unwilling, to learn new skills, or they might be unwilling to move to a new location to find work. Structural unemployment means that people have the wrong skills, or are in the wrong place, to find employment. This type of unemployment is likely to be a long-term problem.

Frictional unemployment, however, is a short-term problem. It means that employees might have a short gap between leaving one job and starting the next. This might arise because of lack of information;

it might take time for an employer with a vacancy to find a suitable employee, and it might take time for an unemployed worker to find an employer with a vacancy that matches his or her skills.

Seasonal unemployment is the fourth type. This might be demand-determined or it might be supply-determined. Supply-determined seasonal unemployment occurs when there is a seasonal pattern to the production process. This includes fruit-picking, and it also includes the construction industry in countries that experience severe weather conditions in winter. Demand-determined seasonal unemployment arises when the level of demand shows a strong seasonal pattern, and it is not possible to store output for later sale (as in the case of service industries). This applies particularly to the tourist industry

These four types of unemployment are not mutually exclusive. This means that a particular individual might fall into more than one category. It is not possible, therefore, to use this classification in the preparation of unemployment statistics.

According to the Classical theory, unemployment is not possible, except in the very short term, because wage rates (the price of labour) will adjust until demand for labour is equal to the supply of labour. The Classical economists were, however, aware that an inadequate flow of information (between employers with vacancies and unemployed people looking for work) could also lead to unemployment.

The monetarist approach is that unemployment occurs partly because there exist aspects of the economic system that prevent flexibility of prices (and wage rates). These include statutory minimum wage rates and powerful trades unions.

Policy against Unemployment

If unemployment is caused by insufficient demand, then the appropriate policy is one that leads to an increased level of aggregate demand. The appropriate mix of loose fiscal policy and loose monetary policy will depend on the desired effect on the level of interest rates. This was discussed in Chapter 6. As with other aspects of economic policy, political considerations might also be important.

To decrease the problem of structural unemployment, the government might introduce training schemes for unemployed people, and financial assistance might be offered to unemployed people who are willing to move from areas of declining employment to areas where jobs are more plentiful. Subsidies might also be offered to companies who move into areas of high unemployment, or who provide additional training opportunities for unemployed people.

Frictional unemployment may be targeted by facilitating the flow of detailed information between unemployed people and employers with vacancies. In India, this is the role of the employment exchanges, run by the government, to which employers notify their vacancies and at which unemployed people can register and seek information about available work.

Seasonal unemployment is very difficult to solve. No-one knows how to make fruit ripen in the winter. It is, however, possible to encourage tourists (especially from other countries) to take their holidays at times when facilities are under-used.

The monetarist view is that unemployment will fall if the price mechanism is allowed to operate freely according to market conditions in each location. This means that wage rates should be allowed, or encouraged, to fall when the supply of labour exceeds the demand for labour. Monetarist governments sometimes also provide a subsidy to firms who recruit additional employees; this is also intended to increase demand for labour by reducing its price. The Keynesian view is that demand for labour does not respond to the price of labour, but is derived from the demand for output, and that decreasing wages will induce a reduction in the demand for output (because employed people have less money to spend), which will increase unemployment further.

The Target Level of Unemployment

The level of measured unemployment that the government regards as acceptable depends partly on the interpretation of the published data. Some economists believe that a zero level of registered unemployment cannot be achieved, because there is a minimum level, perhaps between 1% and 2% of the labour force, which consists of people who are almost unemployable. These people might be, for example, ill, disabled, or unable to develop new skills.

Government policy on unemployment will also be influenced by the prevailing view on the relationship between the level of unemployment and other macroeconomic variables. In particular, it might be believed that a high level of unemployment is a necessary condition for a reduction in the rate of inflation. This is the Phillips relationship, which was discussed in Chapter 9. Policy targets relating to interest rates, exchange rates, or the government budget deficit might also constrain policy related to unemployment.

Keynesians believe that the reduction of the level of unemployment should be regarded as a high priority. Monetarists generally believe that the level of unemployment need not be specifically targeted; in the longer term, as the rate of inflation is decreased, and impediments to the free operation of the price mechanism are removed, the economy will become more efficient and output (and employment) will expand. Monetarists believe, however, that a residual amount of unemployment (the "natural rate of unemployment") will, in the long term, persist regardless of other circumstances.

11

Exchange Rates and International Payments

Payments across international boundaries differ from payments within an economy because different countries use different currencies. The completion of such payments therefore necessarily involves the exchanging of one currency for another.

International trade is one of the many reasons for money to be paid across an international boundary. Expenditure on imports and exports, which together comprise international trade, refers to payment by a person or company in one country for work done in another. There is no economic distinction between visible trade (in goods) and invisible trade (in services). Thus tourism and banking are export industries if the customers are from other countries, and Indian residents who take their holidays in other countries are importing services. The difference between the value of imports and the value of exports is called the balance of trade, which is positive (in surplus) if export receipts exceed payments for imports and *vice versa*.

The balance of trade should not be confused with the balance of payments, which refers not merely to payments related to trade but to all payments between India and the rest of the world. A major contribution to the balance of payments is frequently made by movements of short-term capital (also called hot money). This means large sums of money that move between countries to maximise short-term gain. If interest rates in India rise relative to those available in other countries, large companies and wealthy individuals might move some of their money into Indian financial institutions. Similarly, if Indian interest rates fall, or foreign rates rise, then short-term capital will leave India.

Movement of long-term capital is a different phenomenon, and refers to the purchase or sale of an existing asset in one country by a firm or individual in another. Such purchases include buildings and land.

Included in the balance of payments is international aid, the contributions made by governments of richer countries to the welfare of poorer countries. Such aid, which might be in the form of loans or gifts, does not always have purely humanitarian motives. There might be political considerations, and it might also be important for exporting countries to maintain the prosperity of their customers, so that they can afford to import.

There are also flows of personal payments between countries. These include gifts, inheritances, the savings that migrants take with them, and the remittances that migrants from low-income countries send to family members in the countries from which they came.

Also forming part of the balance of payments are the subscriptions paid by the Indian government to international bodies such as the United Nations (in the United states), the World Health Organisation (in Switzerland), and the Food and Agriculture Organisation (in Italy).

The balance of payments may also be divided into the current account (the balance of trade plus net foreign property income plus net foreign transfers) and the capital account (short-term and long-term capital flows).

TABLE 13 Principal Components of the Balance of Payments

Imports
Exports
Short-term capital
Long-term capital
International aid
Personal payments
Subscriptions to international bodies

The principal types of payments that can occur across international boundaries are listed in Table 13. They refer to very different activities, but have in common that they all involve the buying and selling of currency.

Manufactured goods (and also services such as tourism) that are produced in India and sold to residents of other countries are usually priced in Indian rupees because the producing firm has to pay its costs (including taxes) in Indian rupees. Foreign importing firms or individual buyers will therefore need to obtain Indian rupees in exchange for their own currency before they can pay for Indian goods and services.

The prices of primary commodities (cotton, minerals, fruit, etc.) are, however, determined by the forces of supply and demand in world markets, and Indian exporters of such goods have no influence on the prices they will receive from foreign buyers. These prices will be specified in a foreign currency such as the British pound or the United States dollar, and Indian exporters will sell this foreign money in return for Indian rupees.

In the case of exports of both manufactured goods (and services) and of primary commodities, therefore, Indian money is likely to be purchased in exchange for foreign money in order to complete the transaction. Demand for Indian exports generates demand for Indian rupees. Similarly, expenditure on imports leads to a demand for foreign money (with which to buy the foreign goods) in exchange for Indian money, so demand for imports generates a supply of Indian rupees.

The same applies to all the other parts of the balance of payments, including personal payments and movements of long-term capital. When money leaves India, Indian rupees will be offered for sale, and when money enters India, foreign money will be sold for Indian money. For example, if a property company in India buys a building in Singapore, the price must be paid in Singapore dollars, so the Indian company will buy Singapore dollars in exchange for Indian rupees. An Indian living in the United Arab Emirates who sends money to his relatives in India will either send a sum in UAE dirhams, which the recipients will sell for Indian rupees, or will send a sum in Indian rupees that was bought in exchange for UAE dirhams.

It was explained in Chapter 4 that the overwhelming majority of money is in the form of (intangible) bank deposits, which are the liabilities of banks. This applies equally to the currency markets. It is possible to buy and sell foreign banknotes (and even, in some cases, foreign coins), but this is a very small part of the market for foreign currency. Most transactions, and almost all major transactions, involve the buying and selling of bank deposits. An Indian firm that wishes to import goods from Japan will buy a deposit denominated in yen at a bank in Tokyo, and will pay for this using Indian rupees drawn from its bank deposit in India; payments can then be made in Japanese currency.

Rates of Exchange

The price of a currency in terms of another is called the rate of exchange. The value of a foreign currency unit might be expressed in terms of local money or *vice versa*. It was equally correct, in 2008, to say that one Indian rupee was worth US$0.023 or to say that one United States dollar was worth Rs. 42.69.

Unless there is government intervention, exchange rates are determined by the market mechanism. This means that the exchange rate will adjust until the supply is equal to the demand. If the quantity of Indian rupees that is offered for sale is greater than the quantity that people wish to buy then the value of the Indian rupee will fall, and *vice versa*. A decrease in the value of a currency is called a depreciation, and the reverse is called an appreciation.

Rationale for Government Intervention

Governments frequently intervene in currency markets in order to influence exchange rates. There are several possible reasons for this.

The government of a country whose exports are dominated by primary commodities might wish to minimise the fluctuations in its producers' incomes. Although sellers of such goods cannot influence the price that is paid (in foreign currency), additional fluctuations in the exporters' income as a result of the conversion from foreign currency to the exporters' currency can be eliminated by fixing its exchange rate. This decreases the amount of hardship (and perhaps even bankruptcy) experienced by farmers in the years that their incomes are lower that usual. By improving their level of confidence, it might also encourage farmers to invest, which generates not only an immediate multiplied increase in aggregate demand (and therefore income) but also increased levels of efficiency and of output capacity.

The second possible reason for governments to stabilise exchange rates is to encourage foreign firms to buy manufactured exports. The prices of such goods are generally specified in their producer's currency, though foreign buyers generally assess their liabilities in terms of their own currencies. If the exchange rate fluctuates, this does not alter the amount of the producer's currency that must be paid; it might, however, make a substantial difference to the sum when expressed in foreign currency. For example, a firm in the United States that agrees, at a time when the Indian rupee is worth US$0.03, to pay Rs. 10 lakh for a consignment of Indian goods might feel that it has accepted a liability of US$30000 but if, on the day that the debt is paid (which might be many months later), the Indian rupee is worth US$0.04, it will cost the importer the sum of US$40000. Thus, if the United States firm believes that the Indian rupee is likely to appreciate, it is likely to be discouraged from buying Indian goods. It helps foreign buyers if they can feel confident of the amount of their own currency they will be liable to pay for an agreed amount of the exporter's currency. Increased export sales increase aggregate demand (E_P) and lead to a multiplied increase in income (Y) (and employment).

Sometimes a government's intervention in the determination of exchange rates takes the form of a deliberate decrease in the value of its currency unit. This is intended to decrease the foreign price of the country's manufactured goods (and also services). If the Indian government decreases the value of its currency (in terms of other currencies such as the Unites States dollar), then goods and services that are priced in Indian rupees will cost a smaller amount of foreign currency than they did before the change; foreign buyers will need to pay a smaller sum of their own money for each Indian rupee. If the demand for exports of manufactured goods is elastic (which means that the demand increases by a larger percentage than the decrease in price), then the total value of exports will increase. This will, of course, have a multiplied effect on the level of aggregate demand (E_P) and, hence, on the levels of output and employment. This is shown by a shift of the *IS* line and of the *AD* line to the right. Similarly, a decrease in the value of the Indian rupee increases the prices (in Indian rupees) of foreign goods bought in India, as a greater number of Indian rupees is needed to pay for each unit of foreign currency. If the value of the elasticity of demand for imports is greater than one, the value of imports (Z) will fall and the level of aggregate demand for Indian output ($C + I + G + (X - Z)$) will rise. This is also shown by a shift of the *IS* line and of the *AD* line to the right.

Depending on the elasticities of demand for imports and for exports of manufactured goods (and for services), a decrease in the value of the Indian rupee might move the *IS* line and the *AD* line to the left. For example, if the demand for imports is inelastic, then an increase in the price of imports will have little effect on the demand for imports, but will greatly increase the sum of money paid for them. This will decrease the amount of expenditure on Indian output, which shifts the *IS* line and the *AD* line to the left. This occurred following the increase in the price of oil in 1973. No local substitute for imported oil was available, and the burden of its increased price was felt in an increased level of unemployment, as individuals and firms decreased their expenditure on other items to finance their increased spending on (an almost unchanged amount of) imported oil.

A decrease in the value of the Indian rupee increases the income of producers whose output is sold in other countries and priced in foreign currency, since each unit of foreign money is now worth a larger number of Indian rupees than previously. Increases in such producers' incomes generate multiplied increases in aggregate demand. This is shown by a shift of the *IS* line and of the *AD* line to the right.

A government might decide to increase the value of its currency in order to decrease the rate of increase of the price level. Imports become cheaper to Indian customers if fewer Indian rupees are needed to buy a particular amount of foreign money. It might also be thought that the increased pressure of competition faced by Indian firms that follows from encouraging customers to buy imported goods can act as a useful stimulus to greater efficiency in India. If imported goods become cheaper than they were, then Indian firms that produce similar goods might have to become markedly more efficient in order to achieve the price decreases that are needed to attract customers.

An increase in the value of the Indian rupee has the opposite effect on the *IS* line and on the *AD* line to a decrease in its value.

Methods of Government Intervention

There are two principal ways in which a government can influence the exchange rate for its currency. It might specify the exchange rate at which it will permit its currency to be traded, or it might participate, as a buyer or as a seller, in the currency market. Governments that control the exchange rates at which their currencies may be traded might specify the value of their currency unit either in terms of a single foreign currency or in terms of a basket of foreign currencies For example, the Indian government has defined the value of its currency in British pounds (until 1971, 1972–75), in United States dollars (1971–72), and against a trade-weighted basket of currencies (1975–78). From 1993 to 2000, the Indian market for currencies was allowed to operate without direct government intervention. From 1978 to 1993 and since 2000, the Indian government has intervened occasionally in an attempt to avoid severe fluctuations.

When a government controls the price at which its currency might be traded, there is no guarantee that the demand (the quantity that people wish to buy) will be equal to the supply (the quantity that other people wish to sell). Dealers are likely to find, at the end of each business day, that their stock of local currency has either risen (if supply exceeds demand) or fallen (if supply exceeds demand). In this situation, the government acts as the residual buyer or seller of its own currency. This was the procedure in India until its fixed exchange rate ended in 1978.

The costs incurred by a central bank when it sells its own currency are negligible, and in return for newly-issued money it receives foreign currency which is added to the reserves (the stock of foreign money held by the central bank on behalf of the government). The reserves are also known as the international reserves. When exchange rates are fixed, therefore, a balance of payments surplus (when demand for a country's currency is greater than the supply) leads to a sale of its own currency by a government which causes the country's money supply to rise by a multiplied amount and causes an increase in its reserves.

When the balance of payments is in deficit in a fixed exchange-rate system, the process happens in reverse. In this situation, the excess stock of its own currency is bought by a government in exchange for foreign currency. This, of course, causes the value of its reserves, and the money supply, to decrease.

An alternative to the system of an absolutely fixed exchange rate is a system where the exchange rate is allowed to fluctuate within narrow limits. This was the policy adopted by most major countries until the 1970s. A value (also called a peg or a parity) for each currency was announced, and also specified were the limits within which the exchange rate would be allowed to fluctuate. In 1967, for example, the British government announced that the peg for the British pound would be US$2.40 plus or minus US$0.02. This meant that the value of the pound would be allowed to vary between US$2.38 and US$2.42. This was not a restriction on the price that people were permitted to pay; it merely specified the point at which the British government would become one of the buyers, or one of the sellers, of British pounds.

Governments who buy or sell one currency for another are able to do this in amounts that are sufficiently large to influence its price (the exchange rate). In the exchange-rate system that operated in the UK until 1972, for example, balance of payments deficits led to an excess supply of British pounds which meant that the value of the pound fell. To prevent it falling below the specified limit, the Bank of England, which is the central bank of the UK[1], would influence the exchange rate by buying pounds for foreign currency, and the value of the UK reserves would fall. During balance of payments surpluses, the Bank of England sold pounds, and acquired foreign currency, in order to prevent the exchange rate for the pound breaching its upper limit.

Whether the exchange rate for a currency is fixed absolutely or within limits does not alter the overall effect of government intervention to fix the value of a currency. In both cases, a balance of payments surplus leads to an increase in the value of the reserves and of the domestic money supply (because the central bank is selling its own currency) and a balance of payments deficit causes a decrease in the value of the reserves and of the domestic money supply (because the central bank is buying its own currency). In both cases, a commitment to a fixed exchange rate removes the government's control over the money supply because maintaining a fixed exchange rate (even if only within limits) commits the central bank to issue (selling) or withdraw (buying) its own currency by the amount is needed to stabilise the market at the specified price. Such issues and withdrawals of currency change the volume of banks' balances at the central bank and therefore affect the availability of loans and, hence, have a multiplied effect on the money supply (see Chapter 4).

It is possible for a government that is maintaining a fixed exchange rate to sterilise the monetary effects of adjustment to a balance of payments deficit or surplus. This means buying or selling bonds by the amount that is necessary to return the money supply to its level before the purchase or sale of foreign currency that was needed to stabilise the exchange rate. A balance of payments deficit requires, if the exchange rate is to remain fixed, a government purchase of its own currency; to sterilise the monetary effect of this, the government will buy bonds. This will cause the price of bonds to rise and the level of interest rates to fall. The reverse happens if there is monetary sterilisation during a balance of payments surplus. Monetary sterilisation might be used if it is believed that a balance of payments surplus or deficit is temporary only and that conditions are very shortly going to improve. In this situation, sterilisation avoids fluctuations in the money supply (M_S) and therefore in the level of interest rates (r), investment (I), and income (Y).

---

[1] The misleading name of the central bank of the UK is a reminder that the Bank of England was founded in 1694, which is before the union of England with Scotland (1707) and with Ireland (1801).

Floating Exchange-Rate Systems

Since 1978, the Indian rupee has had a floating exchange rate; the Indian government has not specified a value for its currency unit. From 1993 to 2000, the precise policy was a clean floating exchange rate, which means that the Indian government did not undertake any market intervention with the intention of influencing the exchange rate. A managed (dirty) floating exchange rate system, in which the government intervenes in the market occasionally to decrease severe fluctuations, was operated between 1978 and 1993 and was reintroduced in 2000. Even under a floating exchange rate policy, however, the Indian government can influence the value of its currency through its monetary policy. A tight monetary policy raises the level of interest rates which is likely to stimulate a flow of short-term capital into India. This leads to an increased level of demand for the Indian rupee, which raises its exchange rate. Similarly, a loose monetary policy decreases interest rates and encourages an outflow of short-term capital, which causes the exchange rate to fall.

In an attempt to decrease the rate of inflation by controlling the money supply, a government using a floating exchange rate system might decide to operate a tight monetary policy. This would cause the level of interest rates to rise, which would probably attract funds from other countries. This would lead to an appreciation of the local currency unit, which would make imports cheaper (in local currency) and thus, by decreasing business costs and shifting the *AS* line downwards, decrease the rate of inflation. It would also, to an extent determined by the elasticities of demand for imports and for exports, increase the demand for imports and decrease the demand for exports, thus shifting the *IS* line to the left (see Chapter 3) and the *AD* line to the left (see Chapter 8). All of this is consistent with the monetarist approach to macroeconomic policy.

It is an advantage of the system of clean floating exchange rates that there is no need for use to be made of the reserves, which are frequently a scarce resource. In addition, if capital movements are not substantial, it is likely that exchange rates will reflect the real value (purchasing power) of each currency in its own country. The third advantage is that governments that adopt a clean floating exchange-rate system can operate an independent monetary policy, which can be (if they wish) unconstrained by exchange-rate considerations.

The disadvantage of operating a system of clean floating exchange rates is that substantial short-term fluctuations in the value of the currency unit are possible.

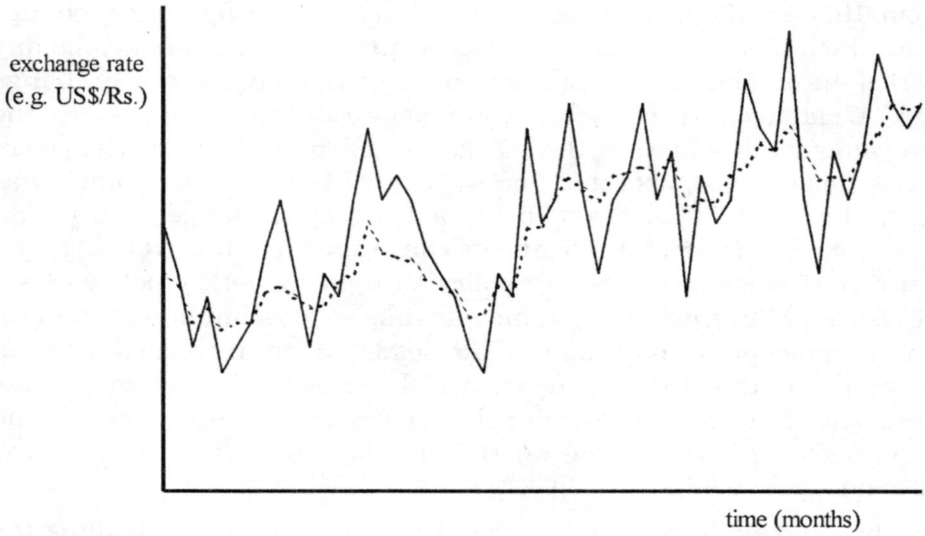

Figure 68. Exchange-Rate Smoothing

The second type of floating exchange-rate system is a dirty (or managed) floating exchange rate. In this system, which has been used by, for example, India from 1978 to 1993 and since 2000, the UK since 1972, Australia since 1983, and New Zealand since 2004, a value for the currency unit is not specified, but the central bank intervenes in the market from time to time in order to smooth any extreme fluctuations. The effect of this type of policy is shown in Figure 68; the continuous line shows the movement of the exchange rate in the absence of government intervention, and the broken line shows how intervention can be used to decrease the severity of fluctuations. The effectiveness of this policy depends, however, on the availability of accurate forecasts; government action to prevent a change in the exchange rate will increase rather than decrease volatility if the exchange rate spontaneously moves in the opposite direction to the one in which it was expected to move. This point is illustrated in Figure 69. The continuous line shows the path of the rate of exchange. At time *t*, it is forecasted that the value of the currency unit is likely to fall towards **A**, so the government buys its own currency with the intention of making the exchange rate move towards **B**. If, however, the forecast was inaccurate, and the exchange rate would spontaneously have moved towards **C**, the government purchases of its own currency would increase the fluctuation of the exchange-rate by making it move towards **D**. Inadequate forecasting of exchange-rate movements during a period of managed floating exchange rates has the effect that intervention might increase, rather than decrease, the amplitude of fluctuations.

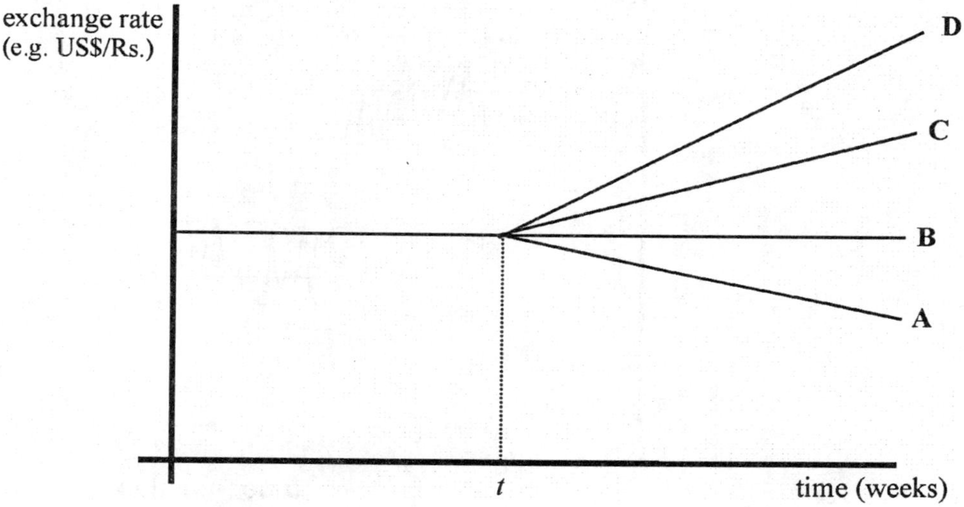

Figure 69. Importance of Exchange-Rate Forecasts

The advantage of the system of managed floating is that, depending on the accuracy of the available economic forecasts, extreme fluctuations in exchange rates can probably be avoided. There is less need for reserves than under a fixed exchange-rate system and, if capital movements are not substantial, the exchange rate is likely to be close to the purchasing power of the currency.

Adjustable Peg

Until the early 1970s, most major economies used the adjustable-peg system of exchange-rate regulation, under which each government specifies a value for its currency, though, if there are persistent balance of payments deficits, this might be altered. This type of policy framework was required by membership of the International Monetary Fund (IMF) from the start of its operations in 1947 until the collapse of the system in the 1970s. The IMF rules required each member-government to specify the value of its currency in terms of the United States dollar (or in terms of another currency, such as the British pound, whose value was specified in terms of the United States dollar), and to maintain this exchange rate within 1% of the specified parity. The peg could be changed only in cases of persistent balance of payments deficits.

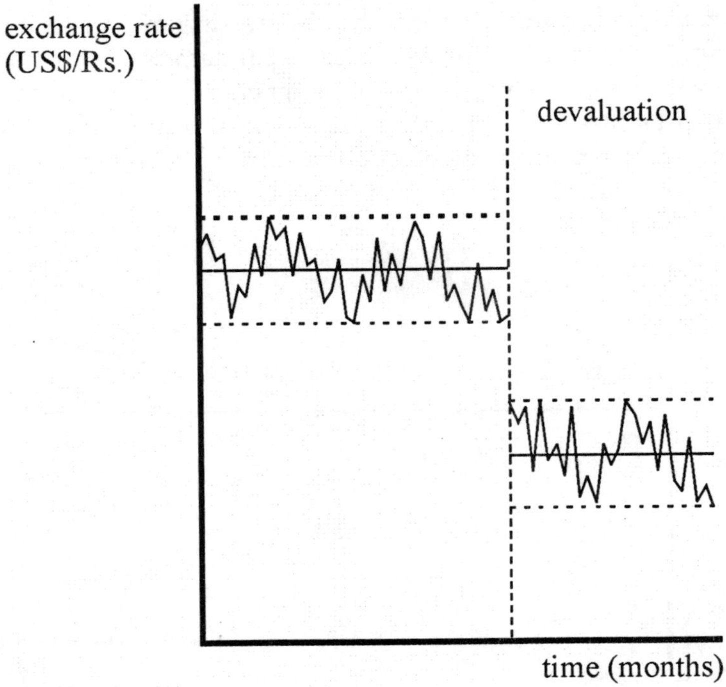

Figure 70. The Adjustable Peg

Figure 70 shows the behaviour of exchange rates under an adjustable-peg system. The important features are stability for long periods between occasional substantial changes. The parity of the British pound, for example, did not change during the eighteen years from its 30% devaluation in 1949 to its 14% devaluation in 1967. The diagram shows an exchange rate fluctuating within narrow limits. In many countries, the exchange rate was absolutely fixed.

The advantage of the adjustable-peg system is that it leads to long periods of stable exchange rates which are likely to encourage the expansion of international trade. The drawback is that reserves are needed, possibly in large amounts, to stabilise exchange rates.

Although countries that use the adjustable-peg system of exchange rates usually experience substantial periods of exchange-rate stability, changes in parities are occasionally necessary. These happen partly because inflation rates vary between countries and, when exchange rates are fixed, high-inflation countries find that their goods and services become uncompetitive both in foreign markets and at home because other countries can produce more cheaply. Consider, for example, the effects of a 10% increase in the Indian price level if the United States has stable prices and if the exchange rate for the

Indian rupee is fixed at US$0.10 (which represents its initial purchasing power). A consignment of goods made in India that is worth Rs. 10 lakh increases in price to Rs. 11 lakh, and so (ignoring transport costs, etc) goes on sale in the United States for US$110000. It previous price in the United States was US$100000. Equivalent goods made in the United States cost US$100000, and can be exported to India and sold for Rs. 10 lakh. In India, this consignment of Indian goods cannot compete with imports. In the United States, this consignment of Indian goods cannot compete with locally produced goods.

Under a system of fixed exchange rates, a country whose price level is persistently rising faster than the price level in other countries producing comparable goods will find that its economy contracts following a decline in export sales and an increase in the volume of its imports. In addition, its reserves will fall due to government purchases of its own currency. This is not a sustainable situation. Governments might respond by taxing imports (to raise their prices) or by restricting the volume of imports, or they might subsidise exports, or they might restrict outflows of capital. They might introduce a tight fiscal or a tight monetary policy to depress the demand for imports. A government in this situation might prefer a tight monetary policy since this has the additional effect of raising the level of interest rates which will stimulate demand for its currency by attracting a flow of short-term capital from other countries. If none of these policies succeeds in bringing the balance of payments back into balance, then the parity will be decreased; this is called a devaluation. For example, India devalued its rupee by 36.5% in 1966.

A devaluation is intended to decrease demand for imports by increasing their prices and to increase demand for exports by reducing their prices. If the value of the Indian rupee was decreased from US$0.10 to US$0.08 then, if transport costs are ignored, the price of an item costing Rs. 1000 would fall (in the United States) from US$100 to US$80, and the price of an imported commodity worth US$100 would rise (in India) from Rs. 1000 to Rs. 1250. A devaluation is also intended to restore commodity producers' real incomes that have been decreased during a period of domestic inflation. If the value of the Indian rupee is decreased, then each payment by foreign buyers to exporters of commodities that are priced in foreign currency will be worth an increased number of rupees.

Experience in many countries shows that devaluations are unlikely to solve the problems associated with persistent balance of payments deficits.

A significant problem with the use of devaluations is that demand for imports is frequently inelastic. Many countries, including India, import commodities that cannot be produced locally and for which there are no substitutes. In India, many of these are essential intermediate goods such as oil. When the prices (in Indian rupees) of these increase, as they will following a devaluation, the effect on the quantity demanded is likely to be very small (or even zero), and so the value of imports is likely to rise. This makes the balance of payments deficit even more serious. Like the change in the value of imports, the change in the value of manufactured exports depends on the elasticity of demand; a change of price might have little effect on the quantity demanded in this part of international trade too. In the case of commodity exports (cotton, fruit, minerals, etc), the price is determined (in foreign currency) in foreign markets, and so a devaluation has no effect on the price paid by foreign buyers, and thus cannot affect the level of demand. A devaluation will, however, increase the income of farmers and other producers of commodity exports (as they will receive more Indian rupees for each unit of foreign currency) which will lead to a multiplied increase in income (Y) and thus to increased demand for imports (Z) (which the devaluation was an attempt to discourage).

Devaluations are intended to shift the *IS* line and the *AD* line to the right by increasing the value of exports (X) and reducing the value of imports (Z), thus reducing the balance of payments deficit and increasing aggregate output (Y). Depending on the elasticities of demand for exports and for imports, however, the *IS* line and the *AD* line might shift to the left or to the right. If they shift to the left, the balance of payments deficit will worsen.

Goods such as imported oil have very inelastic demand. There are no substitutes for these commodities, and when their prices increase following a devaluation, or for any other reason, the quantity demanded decreases by a very small amount and the sum of money spent on them increases. This increase in expenditure on imports (Z) decreases expenditure in the domestic economy (by a multiplied amount) and the *IS* line and the *AD* line move to the left. In contrast, goods such as imported shoes have elastic demand because there are locally-produced substitutes. When there is an increase in the price of foreign shoes a significant number of purchasers buy locally-made shoes instead, which decreases the value of imports (Z), stimulates local production (by a multiplied amount) and shifts the *IS* line and the *AD* line to the right.

A second major disadvantage of a devaluation is that it will cause cost-push inflation (which is likely to be a serious and accelerating problem). Increases in the prices of essential imports necessarily lead to increases in the prices of output, and these will lead to pressure for increased wage rates, which will cause further price rises. The increased price level caused by a devaluation means that the prices of manufactured exports in foreign markets will fall by a smaller percentage than the amount of the devaluation, and might not fall at all.

A further problem of devaluation is that it necessarily leads to a sudden increase in business costs. Firms find that they have to pay substantially more of their own currency than had been expected to finance an agreed amount of foreign currency for imported goods. This might cause serious financial problems for some firms.

Any positive effects of a devaluation are likely to be destroyed by devaluations in other countries. Whenever a major country devalues its currency, smaller countries that depend on its market for their exports usually devalue theirs too, and this restores exchange rates to (or near to) their previous levels. When the British pound was devalued by 30.5% in 1949, for example, the Indian rupee was devalued by the same percentage, which meant that there was no change in the exchange rate between these two currencies.

Forecasts of a devaluation are also likely to encourage speculation, which, though probably of considerable benefit to the speculators, imposes a cost on the whole community. If, under a fixed exchange rate system, a devaluation of the Indian rupee is thought to be likely, people will exchange that currency for other countries' money. This increases the supply of Indian rupees, which, in order to maintain the fixed exchange rate, the Reserve Bank of India is required to use its reserves to buy. After the devaluation, speculators can sell their foreign money for a larger amount of Indian money than they started with. The Reserve Bank of India will respond by selling Indian rupees in exchange for foreign currency but at the devalued rate of exchange, so there is a net decrease in the value of the reserves.

Devaluations mean that the stability that is a feature of the adjustable-peg system alternates with the extreme instability caused by devaluations. In addition, devaluations are very unlikely to solve the problem of persistent balance of payments deficits, and almost certainly generate new problems (including cost-push inflation).

The inverse of a devaluation is a revaluation. This is an increase in the parity specified by a government for its currency. This device is occasionally used, while a fixed exchange rate is in operation, to decrease the cost (in local currency) of imports and thus to decrease the problem of cost-push inflation. For example, New Zealand revalued its dollar by 2% in 1976. Predictions of a revaluation are, like predictions of a devaluation, likely to lead to currency speculation.

Creeping Peg

Governments that introduce a creeping-peg (or crawling-peg) system of exchange-rate management are attempting to obtain the benefits of a fixed exchange rate without its disadvantages. In this system, a peg is specified with a time limit. In contrast to the adjustable-peg system, there is no commitment to maintain the existing exchange rate indefinitely (which means until the next devaluation changes the rules). The creeping-peg system implies that the peg will be re-considered at regular intervals.

This structure was used in, for example, New Zealand from 1979 to 1982. There were frequent small devaluations during this period which averaged about 0.5% per month (measured against a trade-weighted basket of currencies).

The advantage of the creeping-peg system is short-term stability combined with long-term flexibility. Firms that settle their debts quickly can be confident that exchange rates will not have changed substantially before they do so. The exchange rate changes sufficiently often to ensure that, if capital movements are not substantial, it does not diverge markedly from the purchasing power of the currency. Devaluations might be frequent, so each is too small to cause serious financial problems for firms and too small to encourage speculation.

European Developments

Recent events in Europe illustrate the nature of some of the political and economic constraints on exchange-rate policy.

From the end of the Second World War, most major countries (with several exceptions including Canada) used the adjustable-peg system of exchange-rate management. However, from the late 1960s, increasing capital mobility and the low level of reserves in many countries imposed strains on the system and it ultimately collapsed in the early 1970s.

In May 1972, the members of the European Economic Community (which, with an expanded membership, has now become the European Union) set up a system (that became known as the Snake) that was designed to control fluctuations in their currencies' exchange rates, but only when expressed in terms of other currencies in the group, and not when measured against external currencies. Sweden and Norway, neither of which was then an EEC member, also participated in the Snake. The agreement meant that the French government, for example, would ensure that the value of the French franc would show very limited fluctuation in terms of the Italian lira or the Netherlands guilder, but that there would be no attempt to stabilise its fluctuations against the United States dollar, the Japanese yen, or other currencies that were outside the agreement.

This was a narrower objective than the aim of the adjustable-peg system, which was intended to stabilise the value of each currency in terms of all other important currencies, but for which the amount of reserves held by governments had proved to be insufficient. It was felt that this limited objective could be realised with the amount of reserves available to member governments.

The agreement also had a political dimension. Stable exchange rates are likely to encourage international trade, and it was hoped that the agreement would stimulate trade within western Europe at the expense of the rest of the world. This was one of the objectives of the European Economic Community from its inception.

Exchange rates within the group of currencies were managed by market intervention; member governments bought and sold currencies in sufficiently large quantities to influence their exchange rates. There was an agreed maximum divergence between the strongest and weakest currencies. Figure 71 shows the behaviour of the exchange rates of two of the currencies that participated in the Snake arrangements. Exchange rates of the whole group of currencies fluctuated against external denominators such as the United States dollar.

Membership of the Snake was not stable. The UK and the Irish Republic withdrew in June 1972, and did not rejoin. Most of the other members withdrew and rejoined (some several times). Only the German Federal Republic remained a member of the Snake for the whole of its existence.

The Snake came to an end in 1979 and was replaced with the European Monetary System (EMS). The exchange-rate mechanism of the EMS had the same objectives as the Snake, but the procedure for allocating intervention responsibilities among member governments was more precisely specified.

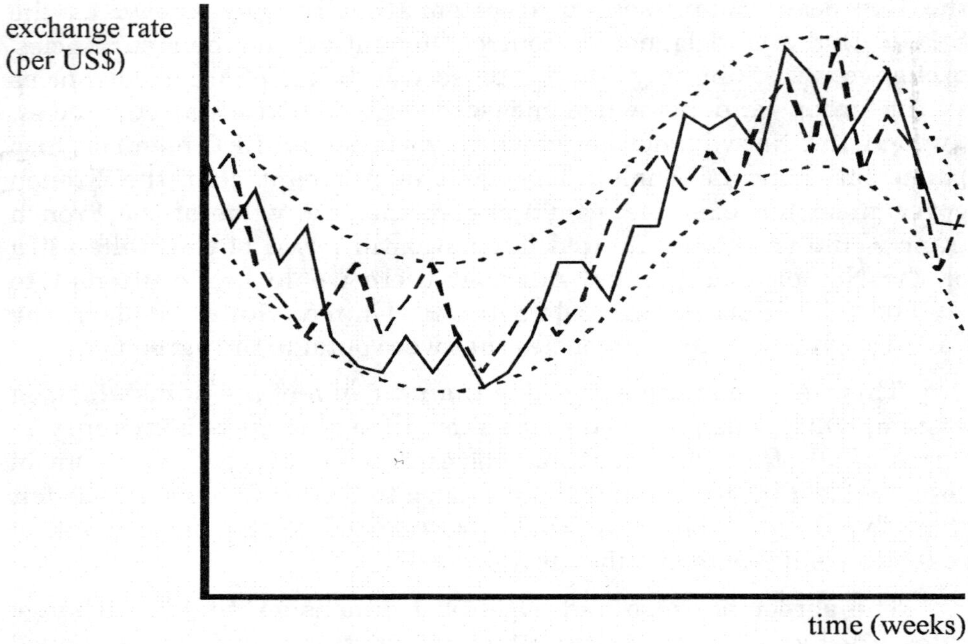

Figure 71. The Snake (only two currencies are shown).

Membership of the EMS involved an obligation on each EMS-member government to undertake to stabilise its currency value with respect to the value of a basket of EMS-member currencies called the European Currency Unit (ECU). Each country's currency had a weight in the ECU which was related to the importance of that country's trade within the EMS group of countries. An autonomous shift in the external value of any EMS-member currency changed the value of the ECU and therefore imposed exchange-rate adjustment obligations on all members of the system.

Incentives to join the EMS were comparable to those that applied to the Snake and included the desire for stable exchange rates with a country's principal trading partners and the desire to encourage trade within the group of EMS members rather than with countries in the rest of the world.

The UK decided not to participate in the exchange-rate mechanism of the EMS at its inception. It was influenced by the fact that the weight allocated to the British pound (0.13) in the definition of the ECU was insufficient to allow the UK government to delegate to other EMS members a large proportion of the exchange-rate stabilisation responsibilities that it would acquire under EMS rules. The outcome of EMS membership for the UK in 1979 would have been, therefore, in marked contrast to the outcome for France (with an ECU-weight of 0.20) and, especially, for the German Federal Republic (with an ECU-weight of 0.33). The proportion of the UK's exports that, at that time, was sold in EMS countries was low relative to the proportion of any other EMS-member's exports, and this was reflected in its ECU-weight. The relationship between the weight assigned to an individual EMS-member's currency in the definition of the ECU and the ability of that country to delegate adjustment responsibilities was that a particular percentage shift in the external value of the currency of a major member of the EMS had a greater effect on the value of the ECU than the same percentage disturbance to the external value of the currency of a less important member, and it therefore imposed greater exchange-rate adjustment responsibilities on the remaining EMS members than did the same percentage shift applied to the external value of the less important EMS-member currency.

A second reason for the refusal of the UK to join the EMS in 1979 was that membership would not have led to greater stability of its exchange rates with respect to the currencies of its major trading partners, which were, at that time, outside the EMS group of countries.

An important reason for the British government's continued refusal, for more than eleven years, to participate in the EMS was its concern about the loss of sovereignty that membership would imply. A floating exchange rate (even a "dirty" floating exchange rate such as was operated by the UK government from 1972 to 1990) permits an independent monetary policy, but EMS obligations make this impossible. Monetarist views on the efficacy of restraining the rate of inflation by controlling the rate of growth of the money supply were dominant during the early years of the EMS, and an independent monetary policy was seen as being particularly significant.

By 1990, when the UK government decided to join the EMS, a number of economic conditions had changed. It is significant that the proportion of UK exports sold in EMS countries had risen markedly. Following substantial speculative selling of British currency in September 1992, however, the UK withdrew from the EMS. One of the causes of this was the substantial flow of short-term capital from the UK, where interest rates were relatively low, to Germany, which was implementing a very tight monetary policy and hence had very high interest rates. This illustrates that a common monetary policy is one of the necessary conditions for the operation of agreements, such as the EMS, that are intended to limit exchange-rate fluctuations.

Despite the partial collapse of the EMS in 1992, a common currency, the euro, was introduced in 1999 by eleven members of the European Union, and a twelfth country joined the euro zone in 2001. From 1999, each national currency in this group had a rigidly fixed exchange rate with the euro (and, hence, with each other). In 2002, euro notes and coins replaced national currencies in the euro zone. The intention of the new currency arrangement is to decrease transactions costs and encourage economic integration. The Snake and the EMS can perhaps be regarded as transitional structures leading to the introduction of the euro, which is the single currency of a single integrated economy.

The countries that adopted the euro in 1999 are Austria, Belgium, France, Finland, Germany, Irish Republic, Italy, Luxembourg, Netherlands, Portugal, and Spain. Greece followed in 2001. Countries outside the European Union that previously had fixed exchange rates defined in terms of one of the currencies that has been replaced by the euro now have exchange rates that are fixed to the euro. These include Bosnia-Herzegovina, Bulgaria, and Estonia (whose currencies were previously pegged to the German mark), Cape Verde (whose currency was previously pegged to the Portuguese escudo), San Marino (whose currency was previously pegged to the Italian lira), and the members of the *Communauté Financière Africaine* and of the *Comptoirs Français du Pacifique* (whose currencies were previously pegged to the French franc). Denmark, Cyprus, Lithuania, Macedonia, and Malta have also pegged their currencies to the euro since 1999. Slovenia (2007), Cyprus (South) (2008), and Malta (2008) have adopted the euro. Bulgaria and Slovakia are likely to adopt the euro in 2009.

Nominal and Real Exchange Rates

An important distinction is between a nominal exchange rate and a real exchange rate. The nominal exchange rate for a currency is its value in terms of another currency. A nominal exchange rate is a price. Some central banks publish trade-weighted indexes of their exchange rates. These data, which are price indexes, indicate the general trend in the value of a particular currency in terms of the currencies are relevant to recent trade flows.

A country's real exchange rate is entirely different. It is not a measure of the value of a currency and it is not a price index. The real exchange rate is a measure of the competitiveness of an economy. It is an inverse index, which means that a high value of the real exchange rate indicates a low level of competitiveness and *vice versa*. The formula used in the calculation of the real exchange rate (RER) of a country (for example, India) includes the nominal exchange rate (NER) for its currency, the price level in the country (*P*), and the price level in other countries (*Po*). A simplified formula for the real exchange rate is:

$$\text{RER} \equiv \text{NER} \times \frac{P}{P_o}$$

An increase in India's nominal exchange rate (NER) makes Indian output less competitive relative to goods and services from other countries, as does an increase in the level of prices in India (*P*). The formula shows that either of these causes an increase in the real exchange rate (RER) (which implies a decrease in competitiveness). An increase in the price level in countries with which India trades (*Po*) decreases the value of the real exchange rate; it makes Indian goods more competitive, even if there has been no change in the level of prices in India and no change in the value of the Indian rupee.

A devaluation, which is intended to increase competitiveness when a fixed exchange rate is in operation, decreases NER and therefore decreases RER. The benefit is, however, likely to be lost through the higher cost of imported inputs (which increases *P*), and also because other countries might devalue too (which increases NER).

Under a floating exchange rate, NER (and thus RER) might be influenced by the level of interest rates. For example, a tight monetary policy, which leads to increased interest rates, might cause an inflow of short-term capital and thus a currency appreciation (increase in NER) and, as a result, a decrease in competitiveness (increase in RER). An increase in the level of interest rates leads to an increase in business costs and therefore an increase in *P*; this causes a further increase in RER and so reinforces the effect on international competitiveness of tight monetary policy when the exchange rate is floating.

Exchange-Rate Policies Compared

Ultimately, the differences between the effects of different types of exchange rate policy amount to differences of timing in exchange rate changes. An adjustable-peg policy causes stability in the short term, but in the longer term a depreciation that would have occurred gradually under a floating exchange-rate policy, or a series of very small devaluations that would have occurred under a creeping-peg policy, will appear as a single substantial devaluation. Differences of timing do, however, frequently have substantial economic effects. For example, if stable exchange rates encourage exports of manufactured goods (and also services) there will be a substantial multiplied effect on income (and employment). Equally, stable exchange rates decrease the amount by which the incomes of farmers (and of other producers of primary goods) fluctuate and therefore decrease the severity of hardship in their less successful years.

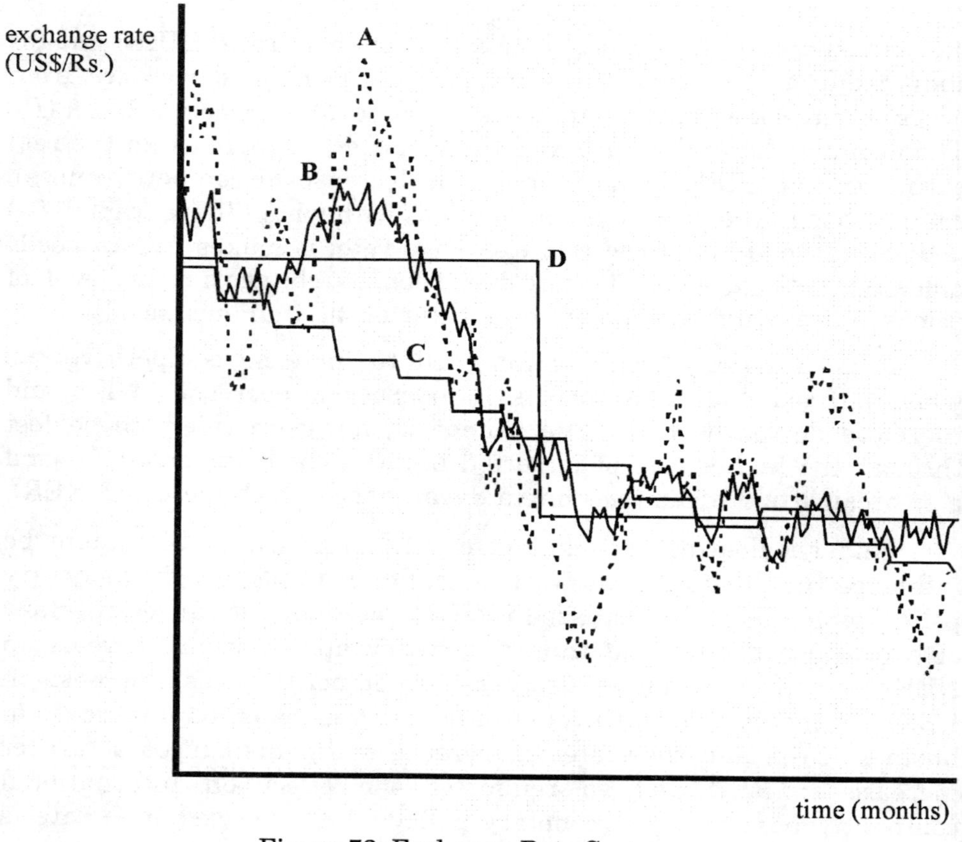

Figure 72. Exchange-Rate Systems.

Figure 72 compares the likely paths of the exchange rate for the Indian rupee at a time of rising prices under clean floating exchange rate (**A**), dirty floating exchange rate (**B**), creeping peg (**C**), and adjustable peg (**D**) policies. **A** shows the least short-term stability and the greatest independence of monetary policy; the other extreme is **D** which shows the greatest short-term stability (except at a devaluation) but the least monetary independence.

TABLE 14 Exchange-Rate Systems

	Advantages	Disadvantages
Clean Floating	Reserves are not needed Exchange rate is close to purchasing power (if capital movement is insignificant) Independent monetary policy	Short-term fluctuations are possible
Dirty Floating	Small reserves only are needed Exchange rate is close to purchasing power (if capital movement is insignificant) Extreme fluctuations are reduced Independent monetary policy (except in the short term)	Some reserves are needed Fluctuations are exaggerated by inaccurate forecasting
Adjustable Peg	Long periods of stability	Sudden dramatic changes (devaluation, revaluation) Substantial reserves are needed Exchange rate might diverge from purchasing power Speculation might occur Independent monetary policy is not possible
Creeping Peg	Short-term stability and long-term flexibility Small reserves only are needed Speculation is not possible Exchange rate is close to purchasing power (if capital movement is insignificant) Extreme fluctuations are avoided Independent monetary policy (except in the short term)	Some reserves are needed

The choice of exchange-rate policy is partly based on its likely economic effects and partly influenced by political considerations (including IMF rules and other pressures from other countries), and will also be constrained by the availability of reserves. The principal advantages and disadvantages of each of the principal types of exchange-rate system is summarised in Table 14. Policy measures (including tariffs, import quotas, export subsidies) that are designed to influence flows of international trade but which are not related to exchange rates are not discussed in this book. Since such policies can be applied to trade in individual products, they are usually considered to be part of microeconomics and not part of macroeconomics.

12

The *BP* line: Income, Interest Rates, and the Currency Market

The *IS–LM* diagram, which was discussed in Chapter 6, shows how the macroeconomic outcome is determined by the interaction of the equilibrium processes in the real market and in the money market. This mechanism will, however, be subject to constraints imposed by the international sector of the economy.

A high level of income (Y) will increase the demand for imports (Z) and therefore the demand for foreign currency, and *vice versa*, while a level of interest rates (r) which is high relative to the levels in other comparable countries will increase the flow of short-term capital into the country and thus increase the demand for domestic currency and *vice versa*. The balance of payments is, therefore, independent of neither the level of income nor the level of interest rates.

In addition, the macroeconomic outcome is not independent of the balance of payments, though the nature of the relationship depends on the type of exchange-rate policy that is in operation (see Chapter 11).

In a country with a floating exchange-rate system, a balance of payments deficit leads to a depreciation of the country's currency. This makes exports cheaper to foreign buyers and raises the prices of imports. The effects on aggregate demand (E_P) will depend on the elasticity of demand for imports and the elasticity of demand for exports. The *IS* line and the *AD* line might therefore move to the right (increasing Y and r) or to the left (reducing Y and r).

If the exchange rate is fixed, then a balance of payments deficit leads to a decrease in the money supply (M_S). This shifts the *LM* line to the left, causing an increase in r and a decrease in Y. If, however, the monetary effect of the balance of payments deficit is sterilised, then the money supply returns to its previous level and the *LM* line returns to its original position.

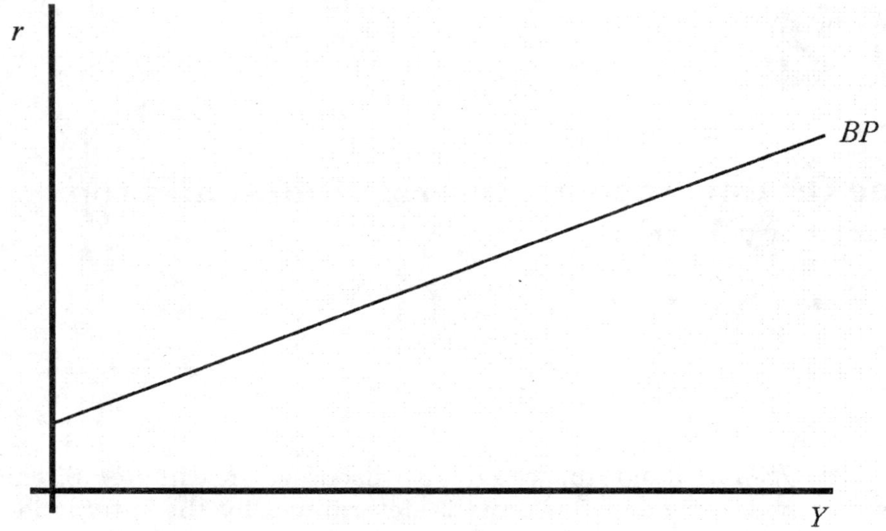

Figure 73. The *BP* Line.

The *BP* Line

Figure 73 describes the relationship between the levels of income (Y) and of interest rates (r) and the balance of payments. The *BP* line is the locus of points where the demand for a country's currency is equal to its supply. If F represents the net outflow of capital, the *BP* line shows those points where ($X - Z$) is equal to F. For the currency market to be in balance, the trade surplus (or deficit) must equal the net capital outflow (or inflow). This model ignores net flows of foreign property income and of foreign transfers, both of which are probably autonomous (which means that they are related in a consistent way neither to Y nor to r). Except in the case of clean floating exchange rates, when the economy spontaneously moves towards a zero balance of payments, this locus does not refer to equilibrium positions. Under a clean floating exchange-rate system, however, the exchange rate will change until the equilibrium point, at which the demand for the country's currency is equal to its supply, is reached; in this situation there is neither a deficit nor a surplus on the balance of payments.

The *BP* line is upward sloping; a zero balance of payments will occur when the effect of a high value of r (which causes an inflow of capital into India from other countries and therefore a demand for Indian rupees) is balanced by the effect of a high value of Y (which leads to a high level of demand for imports (Z) and therefore to a high level of demand for foreign currency), and *vice versa*. The gradient of the line depends on the responsiveness of Z to a change in Y, and on the responsiveness of capital flows to a change in r. The line will rotate to a new gradient following a change in either of these. The gradient falls as international capital mobility increases in response to a change in the level of domestic interest rates and as the sensitivity of imports (Z) to changes in income (Y) falls. A horizontal *BP* line indicates that international capital flows show an infinite response to changes in domestic interest rates or that the level of imports shows no response to a change in income. Since a change in Y almost always has an effect on Z, it may be assumed that a horizontal *BP* line indicates that international capital flows are infinitely mobile with respect to changes in r. In this situation, in order to avoid an infinite inflow or an infinite outflow of capital, the level of interest rates (r) will change until it is equal to the level of interest rates in other countries where the perceived risk is comparable (r_O). A vertical *BP* line indicates that changes in domestic interest rates have no effect on international movement of capital (or that such flows are not permitted) or that a change in income has an infinite effect on the level of imports.

A parallel shift of the *BP* line might be caused by events in other countries. For example, an increase in the level of interest rates in the United States will cause an outflow of short-term capital from India, and an increase in the level of Indian interest rates will be necessary to persuade it to return. This causes an upward shift of the *BP* line. Similarly, a reduction in the level of foreign interest rates will cause a downward shift of the *BP* line.

An increase in the demand for Indian exports (X), possibly as a result of an increased level of income in other countries, means that a zero balance of payments can be achieved with a smaller inflow of short-term capital, and therefore with a lower level of interest rates in India. It follows that increased demand for exports leads to a downward shift of the *BP* line and *vice versa*.

Figure 74 shows how the *BP* line is derived. Net international capital outflow (F) is shown as a negative function of the level of interest rates (r), and net exports ($X-Z$) is shown as a negative function of income (Y). It is assumed that the value of exports (X) and the level of other countries' interest rates (r_O) are autonomous (not related to changes in Y or in r). If the value of Y is Y_1 and the value of r is r_1 there will be a balance of payments surplus because ($X-Z$) is greater than F. In this situation, a zero balance of payments would result from a lower value of r, which would lead to a capital outflow (an increased value of F), and/or from a higher value of Y, which would lead to an increase in Z and so to a decreased value of $(X - Z)$. The *BP* line is the locus of the combinations of values of Y and r that lead to a zero balance of payments.

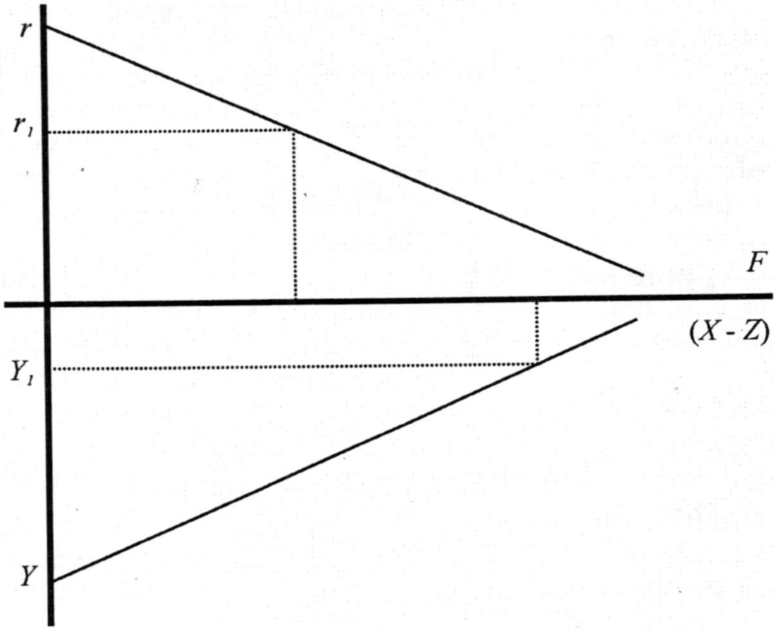

Net foreign property income is ignored

Figure 74. Equilibrium in the Currency Market.

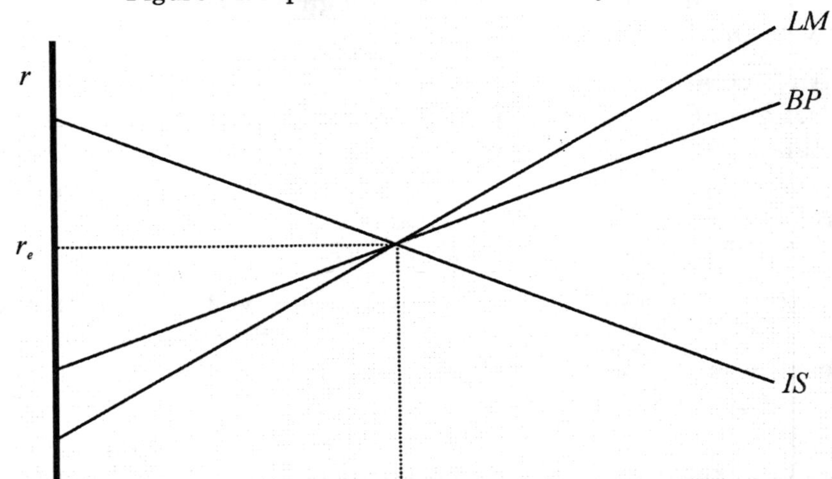

Figure 75. IS-*LM*-*BP*

The Balance of Payments Constraint

Superimposing the *IS–LM* and *BP* graphs enables the effect on the macroeconomic equilibrium of the balance of payments constraint to be analysed. If the three lines have a single intersection, as shown in Figure 75, the balance of payments has no effect on the outcome. The equilibrium is the combination of Y_e and r_e and, since this point is on the *BP* line, there is a zero balance of payments.

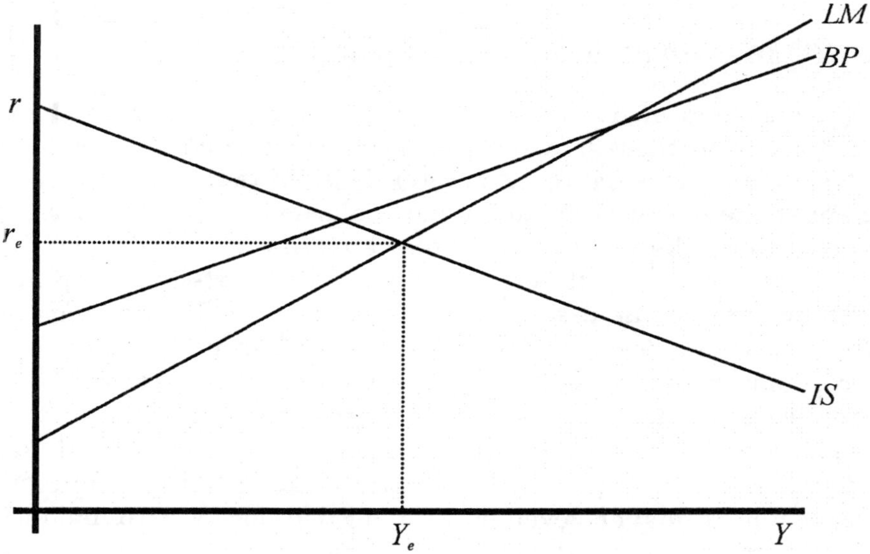

Figure 76. Balance of Payments Deficit.

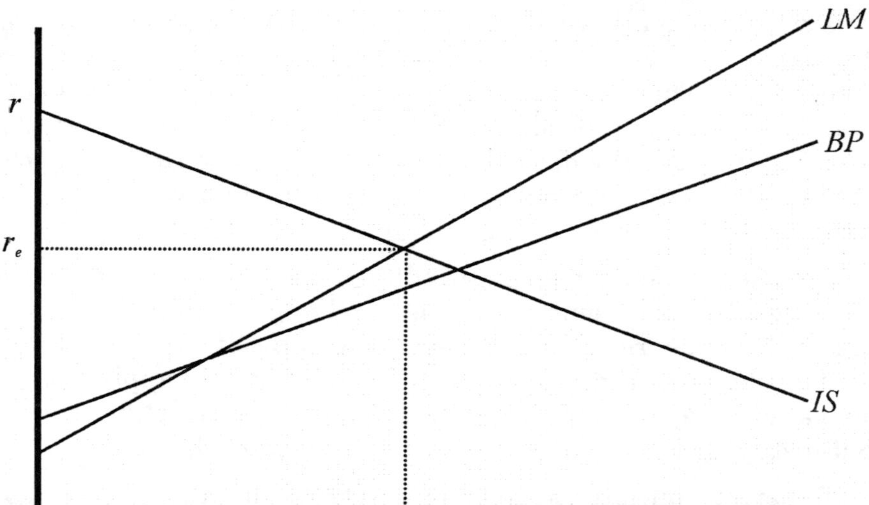

Figure 77. Balance of Payment Surplus.

It is, of course, possible that the balance of payments is in deficit or surplus when the equilibrium levels of *r* and *Y* have been reached. If it is in deficit, the *IS–LM* intersection will be below the *BP* line, as shown in Figure 76. This is because an increase in the level of interest rates (*r*) would be necessary to attract an inflow of short-term capital to produce a zero balance of payments. Similarly, the *BP* line will be below the *IS–LM* intersection, as shown in Figure 77, if the balance of payments is in surplus.

The *BP* Line and Floating Exchange Rates

In a system of floating exchange rates, the value of a currency will adjust until there is a zero balance of payments (where demand for the currency is equal to its supply). This shifts the *BP* line because it changes the incentive to hold a particular currency. If a currency is perceived to be likely to have a stable value in the longer term, then a depreciation will result in an inflow of short-term capital as wealth-holders buy an asset that they anticipate will appreciate. This shifts the *BP* line downwards because a sufficient inflow of capital for a zero balance of payments can be achieved with a lower level of interest rates (*r*) than previously. Similarly, the appreciation of such a currency will lead to an outflow of capital as wealth-holders sell an asset that is likely to fall in value. In this situation, the *BP* line moves upwards, as a higher level of *r* is needed for a zero balance of payments. Shifts of the *BP* line in the reverse direction will occur in the case of a country whose currency is thought likely to be unstable. In this situation, a depreciation causes a fear of a further depreciation and thus an outflow of capital, causing the *BP* line to move upwards, and *vice versa*. This phenomenon occurred following the rapid decline in value of the Indonesian rupiah, and of several other Asian currencies, in 1997. The direction of movement of the *BP* line following a change of parity (when the exchange rate is fixed) is similarly determined by the perceived stability of the currency.

The effect of the perceived stability of a currency on international capital flows, and hence on the exchange rate, following an appreciation or depreciation is an example of a self-justifying forecast. If people believe that there will be a further appreciation or depreciation, they will behave in a way that causes it. Other examples of self-justifying forecasts are explained in Chapter 9.

If there is infinite mobility of capital, and thus the *BP* line is horizontal, the *BP* line does not shift as a result of changes in the exchange rate. This is because, in this situation, the equilibrium level of interest rates (r) must be equal to the level of foreign interest rates (ro).

The effect on the value of imports (Z) and exports (X) of a depreciation or appreciation (under a floating exchange rate) is, like the effect of a devaluation or revaluation (under a fixed exchange rate), determined by how buyers respond to a change of prices. In particular, if the demand for imports is elastic then a depreciation leads to a reduction in the value of imports and a shift of the *IS* line to the right, and *vice versa* (see Chapter 11).

The movement of a floating exchange rate towards its equilibrium does not change the money supply, so an appreciation or depreciation does not shift the *LM* line. Similarly, the *LM* line does not shift following a devaluation or revaluation (under a fixed exchange rate).

The *BP* Line and Fixed Exchange Rates

In a system of fixed exchange rates (adjustable peg or creeping peg), a balance of payments surplus or deficit leads to government purchases or sales of its own currency, and this changes the money supply. This process continues until there is a zero balance of payments. This means that the *LM* line shifts to the left (balance of payments deficit) or to the right (surplus) until it reaches the *IS–BP* intersection. Under fixed exchange rates, therefore, a balance of payments deficit leads, as shown in Figure 76, to a decreased level of income and an increased level of interest rates. If the monetary effect is sterilised, the *LM* line returns to its previous position, and so do the equilibrium values of Y and r. The effect of a devaluation cannot be demonstrated on Figure 76 because a change in the exchange rate shifts both the *BP* line and the *IS* line, and the shift of the *IS* line might be in either direction.

The effects of monetary sterilisation are necessarily short term. A change in the money supply (Ms) causes a change in the level of interest rates (r). To an extent determined by the gradient of the *IS* line, this leads to a change in business investment (I) and, subsequently, to a multiplied change in the level of income (Y). Since the level of imports (Z) is a function of the level of income, and the level of interest rates influences capital flows, any change in the money supply has an effect on the balance of payments. The new equilibrium, following monetary sterilisation, will be at the position where the money supply was initially changed to bring the balance of payments into equilibrium. A system of fixed exchange rates means that the *LM* line will be moved, by changing the money supply, until it crosses the *IS–BP* intersection; monetary sterilisation moves it back to the position where such intervention became necessary, and where such intervention is therefore again needed if exchange rates are to remain fixed.

Equation of the *BP* Line

The *BP* line shows those points where the value of net exports $(X - Z)$ is equal to the net international capital outflow (F). Its equation can be derived by setting the behavioural equation for $(X - Z)$ equal to the behavioural equation for F.

As shown in Figure 74, the net international capital outflow is an inverse function of the domestic level of interest rates (r):

$$F = u - wr$$

In this equation, wr shows the effect on the net international capital outflow (F) of changes in the domestic level of interest rates. The autonomous term (u) shows the effects on F of changes in interest rates in other countries, of changes and predicted changes in exchange rates, of perceptions of the stability of the value of individual currencies, and of other types of capital flows (including personal payments, payments to international bodies, international aid). A linear relationship is probably reasonable for small changes in the level of interest rates.

Thus the equation for the *BP* line is:

$$X^* - (n + mY) = u - wr$$

$$r = \frac{u - X^* + n}{w} + \frac{mY}{w}$$

The possible determinants of upward (parallel) and clockwise shifts of the *BP* line are shown in Table 15. The directions of changes in the values of the parameters in the equation of the *BP* line are shown. Downward and anti-clockwise shifts are caused by changes of the same parameters in the opposite direction.

TABLE 15 Causes of *BP* shifts

Upward:	$u \uparrow$	$X^* \downarrow$	$n \uparrow$	$w \downarrow$
Clockwise:	$m \downarrow$	$w \uparrow$		

Effects of a Non-Zero Balance of Payments

The effect of a balance of payments surplus or deficit therefore depends on the exchange rate regime, the elasticity of demand for imports, the degree of capital mobility, and the perceived stability of the currency. The conclusions are summarised, in the case of a balance of payments deficit, in Table 16. In each case, the direction of movement of each of the *IS*, *LM* and *BP* lines is shown. Directions of shifts (and of capital flows and changes in exchange rates and money supply) would be reversed following a balance of payments surplus. Lines that do not shift in response to a balance of payments deficit or surplus are described as "stable". The elasticity of demand for imports is represented by *ez*.

TABLE 16 Effects of a Balance of Payments Deficit

<table>
<tr><td colspan="2" rowspan="2"></td><td rowspan="2">Fixed exchange rate [Ms decreases if $(X - Z - F) < 0$]</td><td colspan="2">Floating exchange rate [depreciation of the rupee if $(X - Z - F) < 0$]</td></tr>
<tr><td>$ez > 1$</td><td>$ez < 1$</td></tr>
<tr><td rowspan="2">Non-infinite capital mobility [non-horizontal BP]</td><td>Perceived stability [capital inflow follows depreciation]</td><td rowspan="3">IS stable
LM left
BP stable</td><td>IS right
LM stable
BP down</td><td>IS left
LM stable
BP down</td></tr>
<tr><td>Perceived instability [capital outflow follows depreciation]</td><td>IS right
LM stable
BP up</td><td>IS left
LM stable
BP up</td></tr>
<tr><td colspan="2">Infinite capital mobility [horizontal BP, $r = ro$]</td><td>IS right
LM stable
BP stable</td><td>IS left
LM stable
BP stable</td></tr>
</table>

It is assumed in Table 16 that the demand for exports is autonomous (in particular, the value of *X* does not change if there is a change in the exchange rate). The macroeconomic outcome might be different if the value of manufactured exports was influenced by changes in the exchange rate (and hence in their prices). Commodity exports are typically priced in foreign currency, so the foreign price is not affected by changes in the exchange rate. However, the subsequent change in the income (in local currency) of farmers (and of other commodity producers) is ignored.

It is also assumed in Table 16 that the Reserve Bank of India (the central bank) holds sufficient reserves so that a change of parity is not necessary as a result of a balance of payments deficit under a fixed exchange rate.

If capital mobility is infinite, the perceived stability of the currency following an appreciation or depreciation is not a relevant independent variable because the *BP* line does not shift (since, in equilibrium, the level of interest rates (r) will necessarily be equal to the level of other countries' interest rates (r_O)).

If there is a fixed exchange rate, unless a devaluation or revaluation occurs, neither the mobility of capital nor the elasticity of demand for imports affects the outcome. Under a fixed exchange rate, the perceived stability of the currency is not an independent variable (unless a devaluation or revaluation is predicted). If the exchange rate is fixed, the price of imports is not influenced by a balance of payments deficit or surplus, so the elasticity of demand for imports does not affect the outcome, and the mobility of capital (which affects the gradient of *BP*) does not affect the response (ΔM_S) to a balance of payments surplus or deficit.

One of the combinations shown in Table 16 is necessarily unstable, and another two might, depending on the relative gradients of the *BP* and *LM* lines, be unstable. If the demand for imports is inelastic (e_Z is equal to less than one), there is a floating exchange rate, and there is infinite capital mobility (and thus a horizontal *BP* line), then the shift of the *IS* line that follows a balance of payments deficit cannot lead to a single *IS–LM–BP* intersection. The leftward shift of the *IS* line moves it away from the *LM–BP* intersection.

If there is a floating exchange rate and perceived instability of the currency, the situation will be unstable if the demand for imports is inelastic (e_Z is equal to less than one) and the *LM* line is steeper than the *BP* line or if the demand for imports is elastic (e_Z is equal to greater than one) and the *BP* line is steeper than the *LM* line. In these two cases, both the *IS* line and the *BP* line move away from the intersection of the other two lines.

In these unstable situations, balance of payments deficits cause exchange-rate changes that lead to balance of payments deficits of increased size. This causes persistent currency depreciation causing persistent increases in import prices which, especially if there are no (or limited) substitutes for imports (the value of e_Z is less than one), causes hardship and decreased production through cost-push inflation (see Figure 61). In these situations, therefore, governments need to respond to a balance of payments deficit using measures, such as tariffs and import quotas, that are not shown in Table 16.

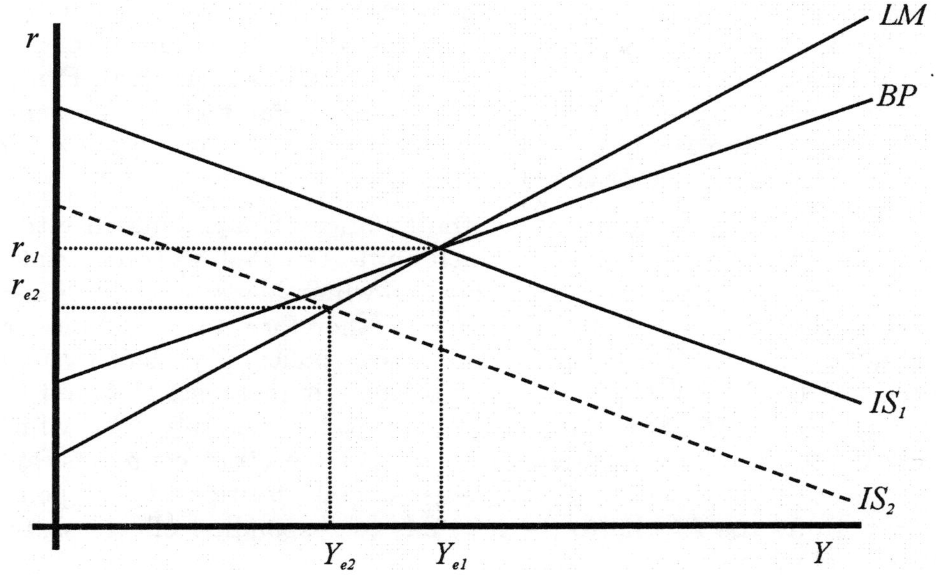

Figure 78. Tight Fiscal Policy.

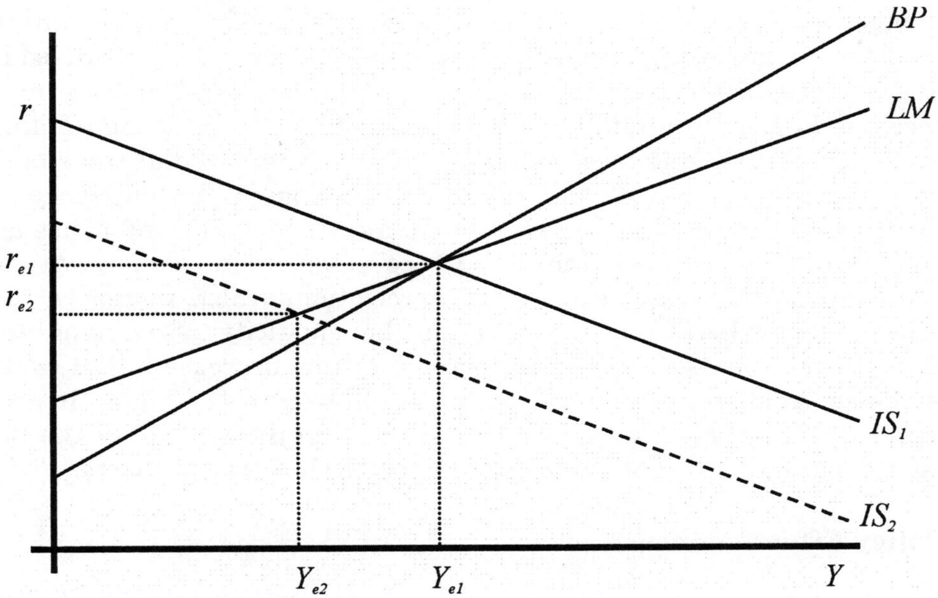

Figure 79. Tight Fiscal Policy.

The balance of payments constraint is relevant to all types of shifts of the *IS* and *LM* lines, though the precise nature of the effects depends on the relative gradients of the *BP* and *LM* lines. Figures 78 and 79 show the effects of an autonomous decrease in aggregate demand (for example, a tight fiscal policy) that shifts the *IS* line to the left. In both cases this causes decreased equilibrium values of both *Y* and *r*. If the *LM* line is steeper than the *BP* line, as shown in Figure 78, decreased aggregate demand leads to a balance of payments deficit, but if the *BP* line is steeper than the *LM* line, as shown in Figure 79, a balance of payments surplus will occur.

Fiscal policy can thus affect the balance of payments in either direction. A loose fiscal policy (which shifts the *IS* line to the right) leads to an increased level of income (*Y*) which leads to an increased level of demand for imports (*Z*) and therefore to a balance of payments deficit. However, a loose fiscal policy also leads to an increased level of interest rates (*r*) because it increases demand for money ($M_D{}^T + M_D{}^P$) (a function of the level of income (*Y*)), which encourages an inflow of short-term capital from other countries, and thus leads to a balance of payments surplus. A tight fiscal policy (which shifts the *IS* line to the left) has corresponding effects on the balance of payments.

A balance of payments surplus or deficit often leads to shifts both of the *AD* line and of the *AS* line, and therefore the direction of the changes in *Y* (and in *P* and other variables) might be difficult to predict. A balance of payments deficit with a fixed exchange rate leads to a reduction in M_S and therefore to an increase in *r*. This induces a decrease in *I*, and therefore of E_P, which causes a shift of the *AD* line to the left. In the long term, if equipment is not replaced at the end of its economic life, it will also cause a reduction in the efficiency of businesses which will increase production costs per unit and cause an upward shift of the *AS* line. A balance of payments deficit with a floating exchange rate leads to a depreciation, which increases the price of imports (*Z*). Depending on the elasticity of demand for imports (e_Z), this will lead to an increase or to a decrease in the value of *Z* and thus shifts the *AD* line to the left or to the right. It also increases firms' input costs and so leads to an upward shift of the *AS* line. A balance of payments surplus produces the reverse effects.

Policy Effectiveness

Attempts to influence the level of aggregate output (*Y*) using monetary policy will not be effective in a fixed exchange rate system because the government is committed to buying or selling its own currency in whatever amount is necessary to meet any excess demand or supply. A tight monetary policy shifts the *LM* line to the left. If there is initially neither a surplus nor a deficit on the balance of payments (as shown in Figure 75), the new equilibrium position, shown by the *IS–LM* intersection, is above the *BP* line, which indicates that there is a balance of payments surplus. In this situation, under fixed exchange rates, the government will sell its own currency to satisfy the excess demand for it. This increases the money supply, and therefore shifts the *LM* line to the right until it reaches its original position. The same process happens in reverse if a loose monetary policy is attempted with fixed exchange rates.

Monetary policy will, however, be effective under floating exchange rates. A tight monetary policy shifts the *LM* line to the left and, by reducing income (*Y*) and increasing interest rates (*r*), leads to a balance of payments surplus. This causes an appreciation of the currency, shown by a shift of the *BP* line to the left, which changes the price of imports and of exports. Depending on the elasticities of demand, the *IS* line will move to the right or to the left. The new equilibrium is reached when there is a single *IS–LM–BP* intersection. Whatever the direction of the *IS* shift, the final effect will be a reduction in the level of aggregate output, which was the intention of the tight monetary policy. The corresponding process occurs when a loose monetary policy is used with floating exchange rates.

In contrast, fiscal policy will probably be effective under fixed exchange rates and is likely to be ineffective under a system of floating exchange rates.

The conclusion of the discussion of Figures 78 and 79 was that fiscal policy can affect the balance of payments in either direction; the outcome depends on the relative gradients of the *LM* and *BP* lines. In recent years, with the relaxation of controls on the movement of funds between countries, there has been a marked increase in the mobility of capital in response to changes in interest rates. This causes a reduction in the gradient of the *BP* line, which is now likely to be less steep than the *LM* line. This means that a tight fiscal policy will lead to a balance of payments deficit, and, under floating exchange rates, a depreciation of the exchange rate, and *vice versa*. In this situation, imports become more expensive. If demand for imports is price-elastic, then demand for locally produced import-substitutes will rise, shifting the *IS* line to the right. This leads to an increase in income (*Y*), which is the reverse of the effect intended by the introduction of a tight fiscal policy. The corresponding conclusion follows if a loose fiscal policy is used.

If it is assumed that international capital flows are very sensitive to changes in interest rates, and that demand for imports is price-elastic, then it follows that fiscal policy will not be an effective instrument to influence the level of aggregate output if exchange rates are floating.

Under fixed exchange rates, however, fiscal policy will, to an extent that depends on the elasticity of demand for imports, be effective. If a tight fiscal policy causes a balance of payments deficit (as in Figure 78), it will lead to a contraction of the money supply (as the government responds to an excess supply of its currency). This moves the *LM* line to the left, until it reaches the *IS–BP* intersection. The result is an increase in the level of interest rates (r) and causes a further reduction in the level of income (Y). Since the exchange rate does not change, neither do import prices, and so the *IS* line does not move again.

If a tight fiscal policy leads to a balance of payments surplus (as shown in Figure 79), the government will increase the money supply, which shifts the *LM* line to the right until it intersects the *IS* line at the same point as the *BP* line. This decreases interest rates and leads to an increase in income. Although this decreases the impact of the fiscal policy, it does not destroy its effect altogether. It is not possible for the final level of Y to be greater than its initial level at the time of the introduction of the fiscal policy.

The extreme case of infinite mobility of capital across international boundaries is represented by a horizontal *BP* line. In this case, if there is a floating exchange rate, monetary policy has its maximum effect on the level of income (Y), and fiscal policy has no effect at all. Fiscal policy will have its maximum effect if the *BP* line is horizontal and the exchange rate is fixed.

The effects of a tight fiscal policy with infinite capital mobility and a floating exchange rate are shown in Figure 80. The policy shifts the *IS* line from IS_1 to IS_2, and the initial effect of this is to decrease the equilibrium level of Y from Y_e to Y_1 and the equilibrium level of r from r_0 to r_1 (at the *IS–LM* intersection). This is below the *BP* line and so the balance of payments is in deficit. This occurs because r_1 is below the level of other countries' interest rates (r_0) and there is an outflow of capital. The effect is that the exchange rate will depreciate and so the price of exports will fall and the price of imports will rise. With infinite mobility of capital, this capital outflow will continue, and the depreciation will continue, until the lower export prices and/or higher import prices have increased net exports ($X - Z$), and shifted the *IS* line to the right, by a sufficient amount to restore r to its original value (and thus to stop the capital outflow and the depreciation). At this point, Y will have returned to its original value. If there is infinite capital mobility and a floating exchange rate, therefore, fiscal policy (in either direction) is ineffective. This means that the value of the income multiplier (K) is zero.

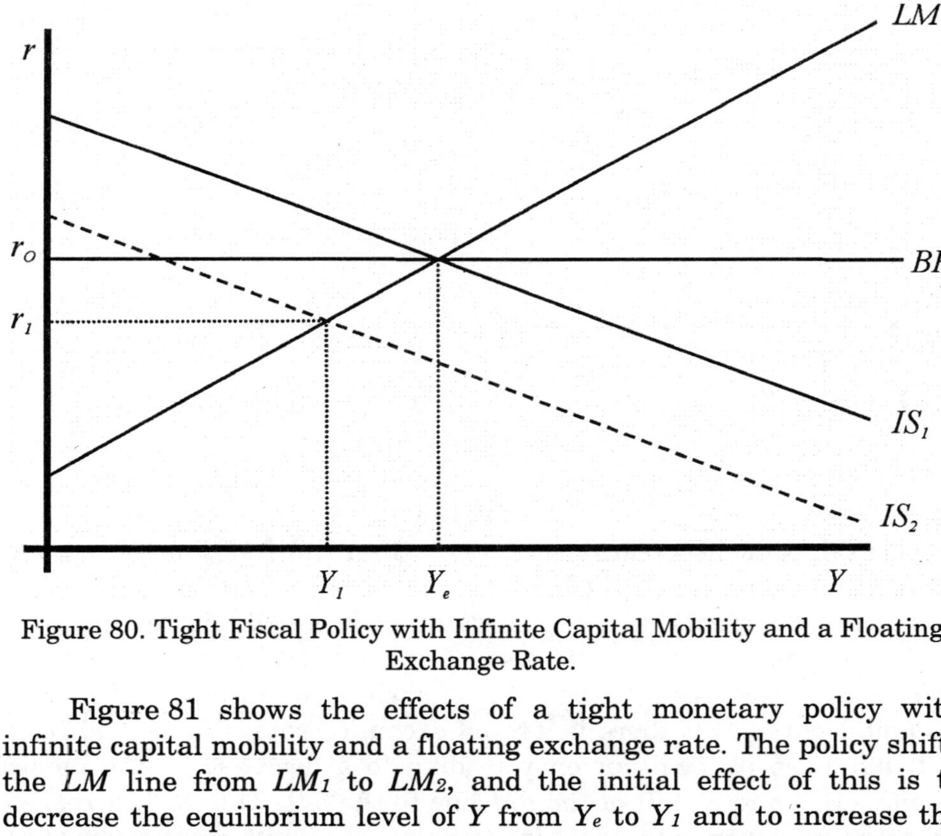

Figure 80. Tight Fiscal Policy with Infinite Capital Mobility and a Floating Exchange Rate.

Figure 81 shows the effects of a tight monetary policy with infinite capital mobility and a floating exchange rate. The policy shifts the *LM* line from LM_1 to LM_2, and the initial effect of this is to decrease the equilibrium level of Y from Y_e to Y_1 and to increase the equilibrium level of r from r_O to r_1 (at the *IS–LM* intersection). This is above the *BP* line and so there is a balance of payments surplus. The value of r is above r_O and will lead to a capital inflow and thus to an exchange-rate appreciation which decreases export prices and increases import prices. This will continue until the price changes have changed the demand for imports and/or the demand for exports by an amount that is sufficient to decrease net exports ($X - Z$), and shift the *IS* line to the left, by enough to make r equal to r_O again (and thus stop the inflow of capital and the appreciation). At this point, there has been a further reduction of Y (to Y_2) and the effect of the tight monetary policy has been enhanced. A loose monetary policy produces the same effects in reverse.

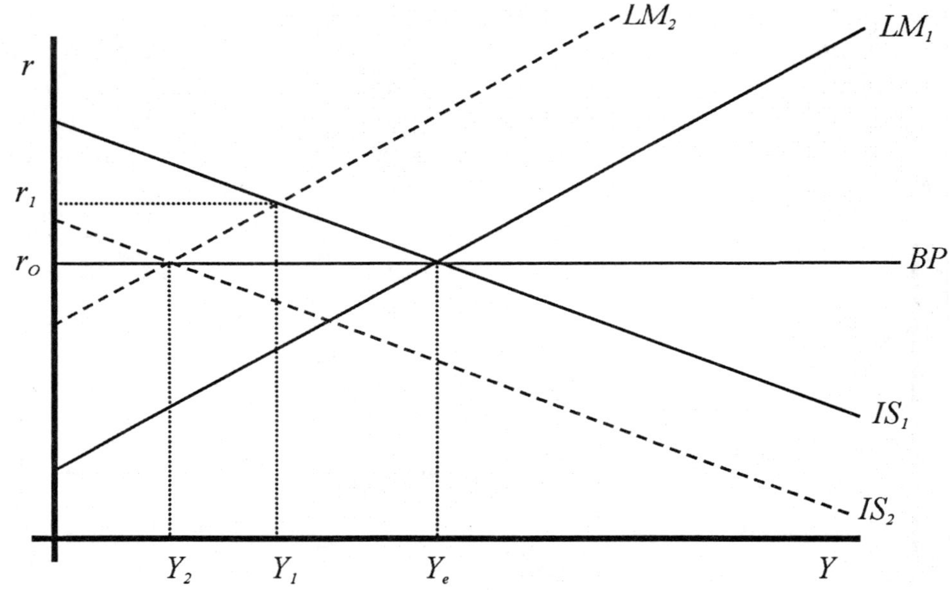

Figure 81. Tight Monetary Policy with Infinite Capital Mobility and a Floating Exchange Rate.

The effect of fiscal policy on the balance of payments depends on the relative gradients of the *LM* and *BP* lines. If the *BP* line is horizontal, it is necessarily less steep than the *LM* line, so a tight fiscal policy (causing the *IS* line to move to the left) will lead to a balance of payments deficit. The value of Y will be decreased (by a multiplied amount) and, because of the decreased money demand ($M_D{}^T + M_D{}^P$) that results, the value of r will also fall below r_O causing a capital outflow. If there is a fixed exchange rate, the central bank will purchase its own currency leading to a decrease in the money supply (M_S) and a shift of the *LM* line to the left. This will increase r to equal r_O again and the higher value of r will discourage some investment expenditure (I) and lead to a further multiplied decrease in Y, thus reinforcing the effect on Y of the tight fiscal policy. The corresponding process occurs if a loose fiscal policy is used with a fixed exchange rate and infinitely mobile capital.

Monetary policy is ineffective under a fixed exchange rate whatever the gradient of the *BP* line. Monetary policy shifts the *LM* line causing a balance of payments surplus or deficit. The operations of the central bank in its role of residual buyer or seller of its own currency changes the money supply (Ms) and moves the *LM* line back to its original position, this restoring *Y* and *r* to their original values.

TABLE 17 Effectiveness of Monetary and Fiscal Policy

	Fixed exchange rate [change in Ms if $(X - Z - F) \neq 0$] (*LM* shifts)		Floating exchange rate [change in exchange rate if $(X - Z - F) \neq 0$] (*BP* shifts if non-horizontal, *IS* shifts)	
	Non-infinite capital mobility [Sloped *BP*]	Infinite capital mobility [Horizontal *BP*]	Non-infinite capital mobility [Sloped *BP*]	Infinite capital mobility [Horizontal *BP*]
Monetary policy [change in Ms] (*LM* shifts)	No effect	No effect	Probably effective (depending on import and export demand elasticities, the *BP* gradient and the direction of *BP* shifts)	Effective
Fiscal policy [change in *G* and/or in *T*] (*IS* shifts)	Probably effective (depending on the gradient of *BP*)	Effective	Probably ineffective (depending on import and export demand elasticities, the *BP* gradient and the direction of *BP* shifts)	No effect

The effects of monetary policy and of fiscal policy (and of other comparable disturbances) when the *BP* line is horizontal may be summarised easily. Under a fixed exchange rate, the *LM* line will return to its original position following a shift, while a shift of the *IS* line will be followed by a shift of the *LM* line in the same direction. Under a floating exchange rate, the *IS* line will return to its original position following a shift, while a shift of the *LM* line will be followed by a shift of the *IS* line in the same direction. The extreme case of infinite mobility of capital across international boundaries is represented by a horizontal *BP* line. In this case, if there is a floating exchange rate, monetary policy has its maximum effect on the level of income (Y), and fiscal policy has no effect at all. Fiscal policy will have its maximum effect if the *BP* line is horizontal and the exchange rate is fixed.

Table 17 summarises the interaction between exchange-rate policy, capital mobility, and the effectiveness of fiscal and monetary policy. In each case, the conclusion is clear if there is infinite mobility of capital but, except in the case of monetary policy and a fixed exchange rate, more tentative otherwise.

13

The Complete Model

Macroeconomics is the study of the whole economy but, in order to make the theory manageable, it is presented as a series of separate models. In particular, there are three important equilibrium processes (determining the levels of income (Y), interest rates (r) and prices (P)) and two important constraints (the balance of payments and the government budget balance). None of the five of these is independent of any of the other four. The rate of exchange is determined by an equilibrium process if it is allowed to float (see Chapter 11). Figure 82, a summary of the complete model presented in this book, combines the *IS–LM* and *AD–AS* diagrams and shows their relationships with the government budget and the international sector. It also identifies the major interactions between macroeconomic variables that are analysed in this book. Arrows are used to show the direction of causation (but not the magnitude) of each effect.

Macroeconomic Equilibria and Constraints

For each of the three equilibrium processes, the immediate effect of adjustment is shown by a heavy arrow. If r is not at its equilibrium level, there will be an excess money demand (M_D is greater than M_S) or an excess money supply (M_D is less than M_S), and so people will sell or buy bonds, the price of bonds will fall or rise, and r will rise or fall. The diagram shows that the immediate effect is on money demand. Both for the Y equilibrium and for the P equilibrium, the adjustment has immediate effects on the value of Y and/or on the value of P. If the quantity of output (Y) produced by a firm is greater than the quantity that the customers wish to buy (E_P), the firm will have a strong incentive to decrease its production and/or to decrease its prices, and *vice versa*.

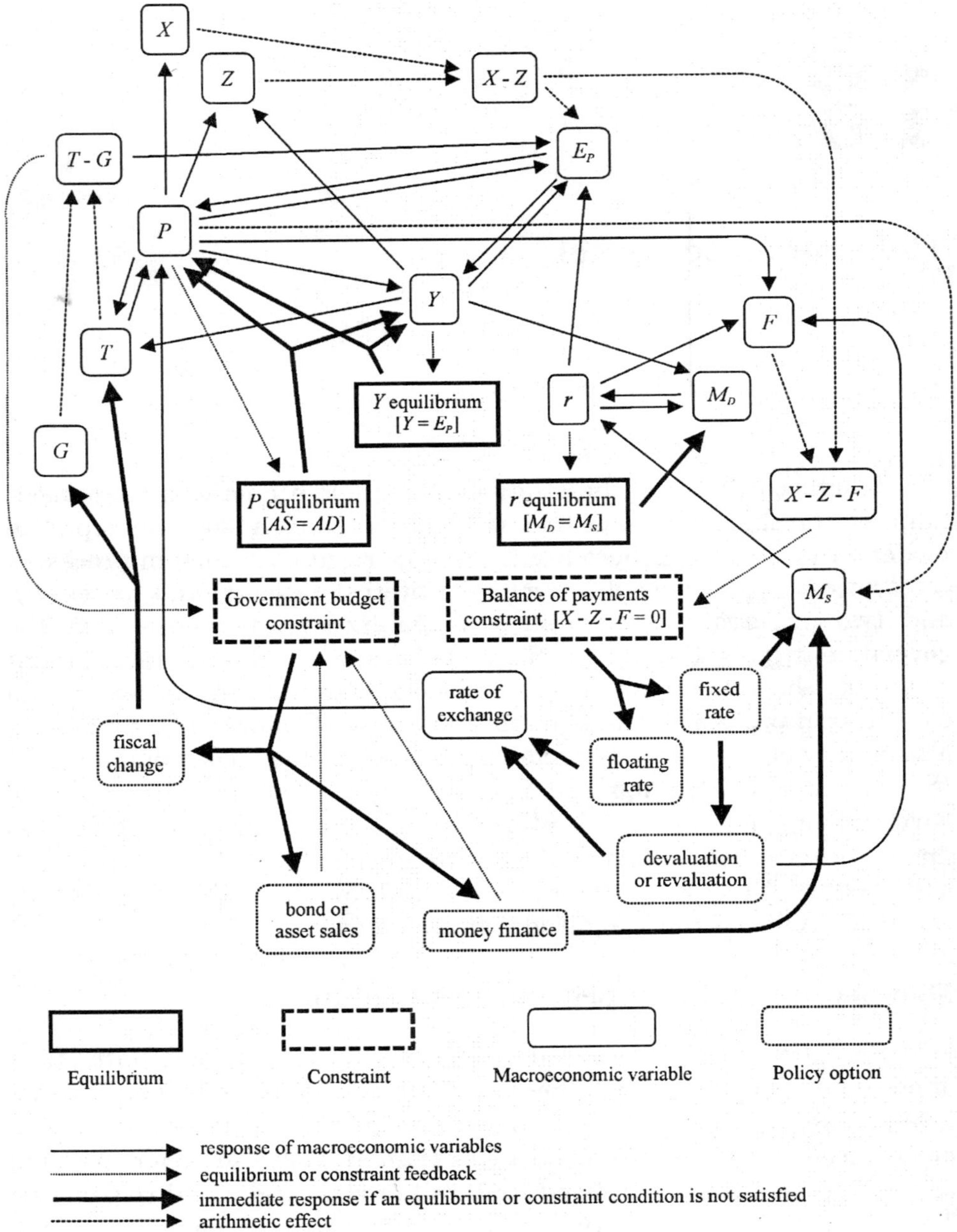

Fig. 82. The Complete Model.

For each of the two constraints, the immediate response, if the condition is not satisfied, is shown by a heavy arrow. If the government budget is not in balance, the government must choose some combination of three options: fiscal change (change in government spending (G) and/or in net taxation (T)), a sale or purchase of bonds (sometimes known as bond financing of the budget) or of real assets, or a change in the money supply (M_S) (sometimes known as money financing of the budget). If the balance of payments is not in balance, there are two options. If there is a fixed rate of exchange, there will be a change in M_S as a result of the residual buyer and seller functions of the country's central bank or, occasionally, there will be a devaluation or a revaluation. If, however, the exchange rate is floating, there will automatically be an appreciation or a depreciation of the currency. In this case, the balance of payments adjustment is an equilibrium process.

For each equilibrium and constraint, the feedback mechanism is shown with a dotted line. The adjustment process will continue until the feedback variable has an acceptable value. If there is a government budget deficit, for example, the government will continue selling assets or bonds, or issuing new money, until a sufficient amount of money has been received, or it will continue changing T and/or G until $(T - G)$ balances the government budget. Balance of payments adjustments (to M_S or to the exchange rate) will continue until $(X - Z - F)$ is equal to zero. Changes to P, to Y, and to r will continue until each of these variables has a value that satisfies its equilibrium condition and that will, therefore, remain stable if circumstances do not change.

Arrows with continuous lines represent the responses of macroeconomic variables. For example, an increase in Y causes an increase in imports (Z), and an increase in the level of interest rates (r) causes a decrease in investment expenditure (I) and therefore a decrease in aggregate demand (E_P). In some cases, Figure 82 shows an effect in both directions. For example, an increase in r causes a decrease in M_D (by causing the price of bonds to fall and encouraging people to buy them thus reducing $M_D{}^S$) and a decrease in M_D causes a decrease in r (by leading to an excess money supply and thus to an increased demand for bonds which raises their prices).

Arrows with broken lines indicate relationships that are arithmetically defined. For example, the value of net exports $(X - Z)$ can be calculated from the values of X and of Z. Similarly, an increase in the price level (P) leads to an inversely proportional effect on the real value of the money supply (M_S).

Figure 82 is a summary only and omits significant details of the interaction of the Y and r equilibrium processes (see Figures 42 and 43). It also does not refer explicitly to the use of fiscal policy, monetary policy, price controls, or other measures intended to influence the level of output or prices, although devaluation and revaluation, as options under a fixed exchange rate, are shown. It also does not refer to the nature of the Y and r equilibrium processes (see Figures 17 and 38) nor to the interaction of monetary policy and fiscal policy (see Table 10 and Figure 49). Also ignored are net property income and net transfer payments from other countries (see Chapter 1).

Because of the interdependence of the three equilibrium processes and two constraints, any autonomous disturbance affects all the variables shown on the diagram. This includes fiscal policy (autonomous changes in T and/or in G), monetary policy (autonomous changes in M_S) and price controls (autonomous shifts of the AS line affecting the P and the Y equilibrium processes). There are likely to be autonomous influences on all the variables shown with the exception of Y, r and P (which are purely determined by the equilibrium processes) and the three compound variables ($(X-Z)$ (balance of trade), $(T-G)$ (the difference between government expenditure and receipts from net taxation), and $(X-Z-F)$ (balance of payments)). These three are derived arithmetically by definition from other variables shown on the diagram. Other relationships that are purely arithmetic are the effects of $(X-Z)$ on E_P and the inversely proportional effect of changes in P on the real value of the money supply (M_S). The effect of $(T-G)$ on E_P is partly arithmetic. There is a purely arithmetic effect of G on aggregate demand (E_P), defined as $(C+I+G+(X-Z))$, but the arithmetic effect of T is not only on $(T-G)$ but also on disposable income (Y_d), defined as $(Y-T)$. This influences consumption expenditure (C) (see Figure 3) which has an arithmetic effect on E_P.

In addition to Y, r and P, an equilibrium process also determines the exchange rate if it is floating.

Aggregate Output, the Price Level, and Interest Rates

The diagram summarises the determinants and consequences of changes in aggregate output (Y). The level of Y will change if it and/or the price level (P) are not at their equilibrium levels. It will also respond to autonomous changes in the level of aggregate demand (E_P) and, as shown by the AS line (see Figure 56), to changes in P. Changes in Y affect money demand (by influencing the transactions and precautionary demand for money ($M_D^T + M_D^P$)) (see Figures 25 and 28), demand for imports (Z) (see Figure 8), and net tax revenue (T) (see Figure 4).

The determinants of changes in the price level (P) include the P and Y equilibrium processes. The price level will also respond to changes in E_P (shown in Figure 59 by shifts of the *AD* line) and in tax rates or in the exchange rate (shown in Figure 61 by a vertical shift of the *AS* line). Figure 82 does not show the effects of changes in the full-employment level of income (Y_{FE}), shown by a horizontal shift of the *AS* line in Figure 60. The precise effects on *P* of changes in tax rates and the exchange rate are not purely arithmetic, and will depend partly on the degree of competitive pressure; firms might decide not to change their prices by as much as the change in their input costs. The effects of a change in *P* include changes in E_P (see Figure 52) and, depending on the elasticities of demand, changes in expenditure on exports (*X*) and on imports (*Z*). When *P* changes there will be an inversely proportional effect on the real value of the money supply (M_S). There might also be some effects on international flows of short-term capital (*F*), though these might be moderated or increased by changes in the level of interest rates (*r*).

Changes in the price level (*P*) can have both direct and indirect effects on net tax revenue (*T*). These relationships vary depending on the nature of tax rules. If a tax is calculated on the physical quantity of a particular commodity (for example, tobacco), the effect on tax revenue will depend entirely on how customers react to the change in after-tax prices (which is measured by the elasticity of demand for the taxed product). The immediate effect on *T* of a change in *P* will be directly proportional for *ad valorem* taxes (for example, sales taxes) though the longer-term effect will depend on the extent to which the change in price (after tax) affects demand. There might be fiscal drag (see Chapter 9) if income tax rates are progressive. Changes in *P* are caused by shifts of the *AS* line and/or of the *AD* line, and so are likely to be combined with changes in *Y* which lead to changes in *T*.

The level of interest rates (*r*) is determined by the levels of money demand (M_D) and of money supply (M_S) (see Figures 31 and 32). By influencing investment expenditure (*I*), *r* affects E_P and thus *Y*, and, by affecting international capital flows (*F*), *r* directly affects the balance of payments. The value of *r* has indirect effects on the balance of payments through its effects on *Y* and *P* and thus on *X* and *Z*.

Government Budget Balance

Of the three possible responses to an unbalanced government budget, the fiscal-change option is of particular interest because changes in *T* and/or changes in *G* do not necessarily have the corresponding effects on $(T - G)$ (see Figure 24). Any change in $(T - G)$ affects E_P and therefore *Y* and therefore *T* and therefore changes the value of $(T - G)$ again. An increase in T causes an equal decrease in disposable income (Y_d) and leads to a decrease in consumption spending (C), which, like G, is one of the components of E_P. If there is an equal change in T and in G, the effect on $(T - G)$ will probably not be zero; this is the balanced budget multiplier theorem (see Figure 23). Changes in T also affect P and therefore have indirect effects on E_P and therefore on Y including through the effects on the demand for imports (Z) and for exports (X). A further effect of a change in P (which might be caused by a change in T) is that it causes an inversely proportional change in the real value of M_S and therefore a change in r (which influences E_P by affecting I and also influences F).

The money-finance response to a budget imbalance affects M_S and thus r and, ultimately, Y, P, F and other variables.

If the government balances its budget by borrowing or by selling assets, this does not change aggregate demand (so the *IS* line and the *AD* line do not move) nor does it change M_S (so the *LM* line does not move), and so no effect is shown in Figure 82. The consequences of adopting this policy option are long-term (see Chapter 6) and cannot be illustrated in short-term models such as the *IS–LM* and *AD–AS* diagrams.

Balance of Payments

A non-zero balance of payments will ultimately affect all the variables shown in Figure 82, though the sequence will depend on the exchange-rate regime. The frequent changes in M_S that occur under a fixed exchange rate affect the level of interest rates (r) and, subsequently, I, Y, P and other variables. If the exchange rate changes, either because it is floating or because a fixed parity is altered, the immediate effect is on the prices of imports and of exports. This affects P and then X, Z, Y and other variables. The effect on the level of aggregate demand (E_P) of a change in the exchange rate depends on the elasticities of demand for exports and for imports.

Figure 82 ignores the direct effect of the exchange rate (and of exchange-rate expectations) on net international capital flows (F), though this is incorporated in the effect of the price level (P) on F, which is shown. The speculative effect of a devaluation (or a revaluation) on F (see Chapter 11) is shown. Changes in P change the incentive to hold a country's currency and therefore affect F. There is both a direct effect, because changes in P have an inversely proportional effect on the real value of each rupee, and a less direct influence, via the effect of P on real M_S and hence on r. The exchange rate influences P through its effect on price of imports and therefore on the cost of running a business (which shifts the AS line).

Conclusions

The principal conclusions of Figure 82 are that there is no part of the macroeconomy that can be understood without also understanding each of the other parts, and that there are often so many responses of macroeconomic variables that the final net effect of a disturbance is likely to be difficult to predict. Even the direction of the effect on a particular variable might be indeterminate.

Multipliers

A further complication is that an autonomous change in a macroeconomic variable often produces a much greater effect than the size of the disturbance. The income multiplier (K) measures the effect on income (Y) of an autonomous change in expenditure (E_P) (see Chapter 2), the balanced budget multiplier measures the effect on Y of an equal change in government expenditure (G) and in net taxation (T) (see Chapter 3), and the money multiplier (MM) measures the effect on the money supply (M_S) of an additional deposit of cash at a bank or of the creation, by open market operations, of additional money by the Reserve Bank of India (the central bank) (see Chapter 4). Despite the definition of a multiplier, however, multiplier values might occasionally be equal to less than one (when the final effect is smaller than the initial disturbance) or even equal to zero (when an autonomous disturbance causes no change in the dependent variable).

The value of K depends partly on the extent to which changes in the level of interest rates (r) lead to changes in investment expenditure (I) and thus to changes in Y (see Chapter 6). The value of K will be zero if Y is at its full-employment level, so that the AS line is vertical and the output level cannot increase (see Figure 59). K will also be equal to zero if fiscal policy is used under a floating exchange rate with infinite mobility of capital (when the BP line is horizontal) (see Figure 80).

Numerical illustrations, such as Table 6, that demonstrate that a deposit of cash at a bank has a multiplied effect on the money supply imply that the money multiplier (MM) is equal to the reciprocal of the reserve ratio (RR) in the banking system. The money multiplier will, however, have a lower value than this if the banks' reserve ratio is greater than the banks' target reserve ratio (which occurs if the supply of loans exceeds the demand for loans) and/or if some or all of the money that is lent by the banks is not re-deposited. If the money multiplier is equal to one, its minimum value, monetary policy does not have a multiplied effect on the money supply (see Chapter 4).

There are two other important situations when a macroeconomic shock has no effect on *Y*. Both of these refer to changes in the money supply and are therefore relevant to an understanding of the effects of monetary policy decisions. During a severe depression, when aggregate demand (E_P) is substantially less than maximum output (Y_{FE}), loose monetary policy does not increase *Y* because the *IS–LM* intersection is on the horizontal part of the *LM* line and so *r*, which is at its minimum level, does not decrease when the money supply (M_S) increases (see Figure 64). Monetary policy, in either direction, is also ineffective when the exchange rate is fixed. Monetary policy shifts the *LM* line and changes *r* and *Y* and therefore affects the balance of payments. Under a fixed exchange rate policy, unless there is a devaluation or a revaluation, a balance of payments surplus or deficit will lead to a compensating change in M_S that returns the *LM* line to its previous position (see Chapter 12). In this case, a non-zero balance of payments changes M_S automatically and neutralises the effect of monetary policy.

14

Conclusions: Overview of Macroeconomic Theory

Both the content and the method of macroeconomics have features that make it significantly different to microeconomics and to other fields of study. The distinctive characteristics of macroeconomic analysis are summarised in Table 18.

TABLE 18 Macroeconomics Overview: Ten Critical Aspects

Three equilibrium processes: Y, r and P
Multiplier processes
Balance of payments constraint
Government budget constraint
Problems may be self-generating
Solving one problem probably makes others worse
Significant controversies
Measurement problems
Aggregation problem
Time dimension

Three Equilibrium Processes

There are three equilibrium processes in the macroeconomy that operate simultaneously and are of particular significance. In the real market, represented graphically by the *IS* line (which assumes a constant price level (P)), the level of aggregate output (Y) changes until it is equal to the level of aggregate demand (E_P). Firms change their output levels until they are producing the quantity of goods and services that their customers (including the foreign sector and the government) wish to buy. In the money market, represented by the *LM* line, the level of interest rates (r) changes until wealth holders are satisfied with the form of their wealth. If people want their wealth to have a greater degree of liquidity, they will sell some of their assets for money, which causes asset prices to fall and interest rates to rise, and *vice versa*. The equilibrium values of r and of Y are at the intersection of the *IS* line and the *LM* line. The third equilibrium process refers to the price level (P). If the demand for new output (E_P) is not equal to the quantity produced (Y) there will be some combination of changes in prices and changes in output until they are equal. The equilibrium values of P and of Y are at the intersection of the *AD* line and the *AS* line.

The rate of exchange is also determined by an equilibrium process if it is allowed to float. If the value of a currency is not imposed by a country's central bank, the rate of exchange will change until the demand for it is equal to the supply of it. This equilibrium will occur when the balance of payments ($X - Z - F$) is equal to zero.

The whole economy is in equilibrium when the real market, the money market, and the price level are in equilibrium simultaneously. However, each of the three equilibrium processes tends to disturb each of the other two. As the level of income (Y) moves towards its equilibrium, it changes the level of money demand ($M_D{}^T + M_D{}^P$) which changes the level of interest rates (r). It also changes the level of aggregate demand (E_P) which, if the *AS* line is not horizontal, will change the price level (P). As the level of interest rates moves towards its equilibrium, it changes the level of investment expenditure (I) (a component of aggregate demand (E_P)), which leads to a multiplied change in income (unless it is at its maximum level (Y_{FE})). This will also, if the *AS* line is not horizontal, lead to a change in the price level. As the price level moves towards its equilibrium, it influences E_P and so the level of income changes, and this influences money demand ($M_D{}^T + M_D{}^P$) and, hence, the level of interest rates (r). The outcome will also be determined by the balance of payments constraint and the government budget constraint.

Multiplier Processes

The effect of a disturbance might be much greater than the size of the initial shock. An autonomous increase in aggregate demand (E_P)

probably leads to a very much bigger increase in income (Y), and a deposit of cash at a bank probably leads to a multiplied increase in the volume of bank deposits, and *vice versa*. Influences on multiplier values are discussed in Chapter 13.

Balance of Payments Constraint

The macroeconomic outcome is subject to a balance of payments constraint. This is not always an equilibrium process; unless the government is following a policy of clean floating exchange rates, the system does not tend automatically towards a zero balance of payments. The balance of payments ($X - Z - F$) is related to Y (of which Z is a function) and to r (of which F is a function). The *BP* line is the locus of combinations of r and Y where the value of the balance of payments is equal to zero.

The balance of payments is an important constraint. Depending on the policy in use, a balance of payments surplus or deficit has effects on some combination of the money supply, the value of the reserves, the prices and volumes of imports and of exports, the level of interest rates, the level of income, flows of short-term capital, and, ultimately, the rate of inflation and the level of unemployment.

Government Budget Constraint

There will be macroeconomic effects if government expenditure (G) is not equal to net tax revenue (T), and these will vary depending on the government's response to a budget surplus or deficit. The *IS* line and the *AD* line will shift if there is a change in government spending or in net tax rates, the *LM* line will shift if the money supply changes, and neither the *IS* line nor the *AD* line nor the *LM* line will shift if the government sells or buys financial assets (borrows additional money or pays back some of its existing loans) or sells or buys real assets (including government-owned enterprises). The size of the budget imbalance, and the nature of the government's response to it, will therefore be a significant influence on the macroeconomic outcome.

Self-Generating Problems

Many macroeconomic problems tend to worsen spontaneously. Rising unemployment, for example, decreases the level of aggregate demand (because people who receive no wages have less money to spend than people who do receive wages) which leads to decreased output and therefore to increased unemployment. It also causes a decreased level of confidence, which decreases spending (by both households and firms) further, and therefore causes an even greater level of unemployment.

It is equally true that inflation, whether caused by demand-pull or cost-push factors, tends to cause even more inflation.

Problems are not Independent of Each Other

It is generally true that solving one macroeconomic problem makes another one worse. Examples are that reducing the rate of inflation usually causes increased unemployment and that stabilising the exchange rate (which might be a policy objective) is likely to decrease the value of the reserves (which are probably a scarce resource). The effect of this is that it is generally impossible for a government to solve all of its country's economic problems simultaneously (or even sequentially).

Major Controversies

There are numerous controversies in macroeconomics. The two main theoretical schools of thought, on which later analyses are based, are those of the Classical economists (see Chapter 7) and of John Maynard Keynes. The conclusions of each are very different. According to the Classical theory, unemployment cannot exist (except in the very short term), individual prices are flexible and a powerful incentive, and equilibrium is achieved by price changes, so government intervention in the macroeconomy is unnecessary. Keynes accepted none of these; he believed that unemployment is likely to occur, prices are often sticky and cannot be relied upon to change by a sufficient amount to achieve equilibrium, and government intervention is not only desirable but also probably necessary to achieve a satisfactory outcome. Keynes' and Classical views on the determination of the price level, the level of interest rates and other important macroeconomic variables also differ significantly. The views of Keynes and of the Classical economists are summarised in Table 19. The algebraic symbols are defined in the Notation appendix.

TABLE 19 Classical and Keynes' Macroeconomic Theory

	Classical	Keynes
Output (Y)	$Y = Y_{FE}$ [except in the short term] $E_P = Y$ [Say's Law] Supply influences demand	$Y >=< Y_{FE}$ $E_P = f(Y)$ Demand influences supply
Unemployment	Cannot occur [except in the short term]	Likely to be severe [unless the government intervenes]
Prices	Flexible Powerful incentive	Sticky May be a weak incentive
Demand for labour	Depends on the wage rate	Derived from aggregate demand
Investment (I)	$I = D_{LF} = f(r)$	$I = f(Y, r,$ confidence$)$
Savings (S)	$S = S_{LF} = f(r)$	$S = f(Y,$ confidence$)$
Consumption (C)	$C = f(r)$ [because $C \equiv Y - S$]	$C = f(Y,$ confidence$)$
Interest rates (r)	$r = f(D_{LF}, S_{LF})$	$r = f(M_D, M_S)$ $M_D \equiv M_D^T + M_D^P + M_D^S$ $M_D^T = f(Y, \text{FP})$ $M_D^P = f(Y,$ confidence$)$ $M_D^S = f(r)$ $M_S = f($government, banks, non-banks$)$
Price level (P)	$P = f(M_S)$ [proportional]	P increases if E_P is above (or near) Y_{FE}
Equilibrium	Achieved by price changes	Achieved principally by output changes
Money market and real market	Not linked [M_S affects P only]	Real variables affect money variables and *vice versa*
Velocity of circulation (V)	Constant	Not constant
Budget balance	Important policy target	Not an important policy target

Recent macroeconomic controversy has principally been between the monetarist view (which is a development of the Classical theory), and re-interpretations of Keynes' theory. There are, however, disagreements within each of these groups of academic economists. It is unhelpful to regard the Keynesian-monetarist controversy as a simple dichotomy. It is more of a spectrum from the extreme monetarists (whose positions are closest to the Classical theory) via the more moderate monetarists and the more moderate Keynesians to the extreme Keynesians (whose views are furthest from those of the Classical economists). This is not a continuum, however, as some economists may have relatively extreme views about particular aspects of macroeconomic theory and more moderate views about others. Further complications are that there exist other important schools of macroeconomic thought that are neither Keynesian nor monetarist, and that there are disagreements about the precise definition of monetarism. The principal differences between the monetarist and the Keynesian approaches to macroeconomic theory and policy are summarised in Table 20.

TABLE 20 Keynesian and Monetarist Approaches to Current Issues

	Keynesian	Monetarist
Main aim	Low unemployment	Stable price level
Main instruments	Fiscal policy Fixed exchange rate	Monetary policy Floating exchange rate
Main targets	Aggregate demand (E_p)	Money supply (M_s) Reduced intervention
Timing	Short term	Long term
Economic role of government	Large and frequent	Small
Prices (including wages)	Weak incentive	Strong incentive
Interest rates	Weak effect on investment [*IS* line is steep]	Strong effect on investment [*IS* line is not steep]
Money supply	Difficult to control	Easy to control

There are three types of macroeconomic controversy. First, there are differences of theory. These are disagreements about the determinants of aspects of economic behaviour. According to the monetarists, for example, reducing the rate of growth of the money supply is the most efficient way of reducing the rate of inflation; the Keynesian view is that this cannot be relied upon. Similarly, Keynesians tend to disagree with monetarist views on the significance of price incentives, including the effect on investment expenditure (I) of changes in the level of interest rates (r).

The second type of controversy refers to policy objectives. Monetarists regard the stabilisation of the price level as the highest priority, whereas Keynesians are more concerned about reducing the level of unemployment, especially in the short term.

The third type of controversy is about policy means. For example, Keynesians generally prefer the use of fiscal policy (and a fixed exchange rate), while monetarists usually concentrate their attention on monetary policy (and a floating exchange rate).

Many prominent economists and politicians are difficult to place in terms of the monetarist-Keynesian controversy. For example, many governments attempt to achieve a low level of unemployment, which is a Keynesian objective, but use policies such as import controls and farm subsidies which are regarded as being neither Keynesian nor monetarist. Other governments aim strenuously for a decreased rate of inflation, which is a monetarist policy stance, but use a prices and incomes policy that is regarded as neither a Keynesian nor a monetarist policy.

Measurement

There are two kinds of measurement problems in macro-economics. The first is that an appropriate operational definition for each variable must be chosen. This is frequently a difficult matter. There is not general agreement whether it is *M1* or *M4* (or some other selection of financial assets) that is the most appropriate definition of the money supply in India. Similarly, it is not clear whether it is Gross Domestic Product, Gross National Product, Net National Product, National Income, or some other aggregate that is the best measure of the amount of economic activity.

The second type of measurement problem concerns the accuracy of the data. It is often difficult to check the accuracy of statistical information provided by households and firms.

Aggregation

Macroeconomic data describe the whole economy, which is, of course, the summation of its parts. This has the drawback that fluctuations in one part of the economy might cancel with fluctuations in another, giving an average figure which is misleading because it conceals information about the distribution of the data around the mean.

Importance of the Time Dimension

There is likely to be a substantial delay before the adjustment by the macroeconomy to an autonomous disturbance is complete. The multiplier process is an important aspect of macroeconomic theory, though the time required varies and is difficult to predict. Additional disturbances will probably occur before the multiplied effects of a previous one are complete.

The time dimension of macroeconomics is also an important part of current controversies. Keynesians tend to concentrate on the short-term effects of policy measures, while monetarists are generally more interested in their long-term effects.

A Few Final Thoughts

Macroeconomic theory is a worthwhile subject for study because it helps in the understanding of recent economic experience, the attempts by governments to influence the economy, and the reasons for their frequent failures. The subject does, however, have numerous weaknesses. There are significant unresolved controversies both in theoretical and in applied macroeconomics, and there are also serious problems of measurement. Frequent autonomous changes, including political developments, also mean that relationships change in ways that are difficult to predict. On balance, however, it is better to increase understanding, however inefficiently, than not to.

Glossary

active balances The total of transactions balances ($M_D{}^T$) and precautionary balances ($M_D{}^P$).

adjustable-peg A type of exchange-rate policy in which each government specifies a peg for its currency although, if circumstances warrant, this value can be changed.

aggregate demand (E_P) The total value of goods and services produced in a particular country in a particular year that people wish to buy. Categories are consumption (C), investment (I), government spending (G), and net exports ($X - Z$).

aggregate demand schedule (AD) A graph showing the effect on the level of aggregate demand (E_P) of the price level (P)

aggregate supply (Y) Total output of goods and services in a particular country in a particular year.

aggregate supply schedule (AS) A graph showing the effect on the level of output (Y) of the price level (P)

appreciation An increase in the value of a currency unit for which a peg has not been specified.

asset Anything with a value that is under the control of an individual or firm. Assets may be physical (buildings, machinery, land, materials, etc) or they may be financial (bonds, shares, money, etc.). A loan is an asset to the lender (though a liability to the borrower). A bank deposit is an asset to the depositor.

automatic stabilisers Aspects of the budgetary system that tend to decrease the value of the multiplier; fiscal policy that comes into effect (by changing tax revenue and/or the value of government transfer payments) as soon as the level of income (Y) changes. Examples are social security payments, progressive income tax.

autonomous Caused other than by a change in the value of the independent variable which, in the Keynesian income-expenditure model, is the level of income (Y).

average propensity to consume (APC) (C/Y_d) The proportion of total disposable income (Y_d) that is spent on consumption (C).

balance of payments The difference between the demand for and the supply of a particular currency or the difference between net exports and the net outflow of capital $((X - Z) - F)$.

balance of trade The difference between exports (X) and imports (Z).

balanced budget Zero budget balance ($T - G = 0$).

balanced budget multiplier The ratio of a change in equilibrium income (Y_e) to the equal change in government spending (G) and in net taxation (T) that produced it.

bank deposits A liability of a bank that can be transferred to another customer by cheque (and other convenient methods). Bank deposits are regarded as money because they are widely accepted in payment.

***BP* line** The locus of combinations of levels of income (Y) and of interest rates (r) that lead to a zero balance of payments.

budget balance Budget surplus or deficit.

budget deficit Negative difference between net taxation (T) and government spending (G) $[(T - G) < 0]$.

budget surplus Positive difference between net taxation (T) and government spending (G) $[(T - G) > 0]$.

capital account International flows of short-term and long-term capital.

capital consumption Deterioration in value of the capital stock (buildings, machinery).

cash Notes and coins.

central bank The government body responsible for the issue of notes and coins, the administration of monetary policy, and the supervision of the monetary system. The Indian central bank is the Reserve Bank of India.

cheque	A written request to a bank by one of its depositors to transfer ownership of a bank deposit.
circular flow of income	The flow of money from firms to households (to pay for factors of production) and from households to firms (to pay for purchases of output).
Classical theory	Pre-Keynesian theory that emphasises the role of flexible prices in the achievement of equilibrium.
clean floating exchange rate	An exchange-rate policy in which the government does not attempt to influence the level of exchange rates by buying and selling its own currency.
confidence	The mood of households and firms. For example, when firms' confidence is low, they anticipate that profits will be low (so the level of investment spending (I) is low); when households' confidence is low, they anticipate that unemployment will be high (so the level of savings (S) is high).
consumption (C)	Expenditure from current disposable income (Y_d) on services and newly-produced goods for immediate use.
consumption function	A graph showing the effect of the level of disposable income (Y_d) on the level of consumption (C).
cost-push inflation	Inflation that occurs due to the pressure of business costs.
crawling peg	Creeping peg.
creeping inflation	Inflation that is slow enough not to cause significant disruption of the working of the economy.
creeping peg	An exchange-rate policy in which the government specifies a value for its currency unit but, if circumstances make this appropriate, changes this after a period of time (for example, one month) specified in advance.
current account	The balance of trade plus net foreign property income plus net foreign transfer payments.
demand for loanable funds (D_{LF})	The amount of money that people wish to borrow at the current level of interest rates (r). According to the Classical theory, this is one of the determinants of the level of interest rates.
demand-pull inflation	Inflation that occurs when aggregate demand (E_P) is greater than (or near to) the full-employment level of income (Y_{FE}).

depreciation A decrease in the value of a currency unit for which a peg has not been specified. This is the definition of depreciation when this word is used in connection with currency markets (see Chapter 11). It has a different but related meaning when it is used in accounting statements (see Chapter 1).

depression A situation in which the level of aggregate demand (E_P) is significantly less than the full-employment level of income (Y_{FE}); the quantity of goods and services that people (including the government) wish to buy is substantially less than could be produced.

devaluation A decrease in the value of a currency unit for which a peg has been specified this means that the peg itself is changed.

direct tax Tax levied on profits and on personal incomes.

dirty floating exchange rate An exchange-rate policy in which the government does not specify a peg but intervenes in the currency market to smooth extreme fluctuations in exchange rates.

discretionary measures Fiscal policy measures that require specific decisions on each occasion that they are used.

disposable income (Y_d) The difference between income (Y) and net taxation (T). Where taxation is negative (due to the payments of subsidies, social security payments, etc.) disposable income will be greater than income.

downturn Depression.

elasticity of demand (e) The ratio of the percentage change in demand for an item to the percentage change in its price. Demand is elastic if this ratio has a value greater than one, and inelastic if it has a value less than one. If the value of e is less than one, an increase in price leads to an increase in sales revenue, and *vice versa*. More information on elasticity of demand is in introductory textbooks of microeconomics.

elasticity of supply The ratio of the percentage change in supply for an item to the percentage change in its price. Supply is elastic if this ratio has a value greater than one, and inelastic if it has a value less than one. More information on elasticity of supply is in textbooks of microeconomics.

equilibrium	The point towards which the system is spontaneously moving, though it may not move there quickly or by the shortest route.
euro	The common currency that was introduced by eleven members of the European Union in 1999 and that has subsequently been adopted by other countries.
European Currency Unit	The point of reference of the European Monetary System consisted of a trade-weighted basket of its members' currencies.
European Monetary System (EMS)	Established in 1979, the exchange-rate arrangement in western Europe that replaced the Snake. The UK joined in 1990 and withdrew in 1992. Each member government undertakes to stabilise the value of its currency in terms of the European Currency Unit.
***ex-ante* expenditure** (E_P)	Planned expenditure, which does not include changes in the physical quantity of stocks that are due to inaccurate sales forecasts.
exports (X)	Purchases by people in other countries of goods and services produced in India.
***ex-post* expenditure**	Actual expenditure on output, measured after the event, which includes changes in the physical quantity of stocks that are due to inaccurate sales forecasts.
exchange rate	The price of a currency in terms of another currency.
factor cost	The price that would be paid for output if the government did not intervene though subsidies and indirect taxation.
final output	Output that is not used in the production of other goods and services.
fiscal drag	The faster rate of increase of tax revenue than of the price level in a progressive income tax system.
fiscal policy	Changes in net tax rules and/or the level of government spending that are intended to change the level of aggregate demand (E_P).
flexible prices	Prices that respond quickly to an imbalance between supply and demand and respond by a sufficient amount to make supply and demand equal to each other.
floating exchange rate	An exchange-rate policy in which the government does not specify a peg for its currency.

frictional unemployment	Short-term unemployment when employees have a short gap between leaving one job and starting the next. It may arise because of lack of information.
full employment	The maximum output level that is consistent with long-term efficiency.
full-employment budget surplus	The budget surplus or deficit that would occur if there was full employment.
galloping inflation	Hyper-inflation.
goods market	Real market.
government spending (G)	Payment by the government (both central and local) for the production of goods and services; this includes police, water supply, road maintenance, street lighting, etc., but does not include government transfers (including social security payments).
Gross Domestic Product (GDP)	The value of output produced with a country's boundaries.
Gross National Product (GNP)	Gross Domestic Product plus net property income from other countries.
hot money	Large sums of money that flow between countries in order to obtain the best return.
hyper-inflation	Inflation that is so rapid that the economy ceases to function.
idle balances	Speculative balances ($M_D{}^S$).
imports (Z)	Purchases by people in India of goods and services produced in another country.
income (Y)	The total sum received by producers of goods and services, and therefore a measure of the value of aggregate output.
income-expenditure multiplier (K)	The ratio of a change in equilibrium income (ΔY_e) to the change in autonomous expenditure (ΔA) that caused it.
indirect tax	Tax levied on expenditure on goods and services.
induced	Caused by a change in the value of the independent variable which, in the Keynesian income-expenditure model, is the level of income (Y).
inflation	Persistent increases in the general level of prices (P).
inflation expectations	The forecasts by households and firms of changes in the price level (P).

injections (J) — The part of expenditure that is not financed from current income. The categories are investment (I), government spending (G), and net exports ($X - Z$).

interest — The payment for holding money.

intermediate goods — Raw materials, components, fuel, machinery maintenance, other specialist services, etc. that are used in the production of other goods and services.

International Monetary Fund (IMF) — The international organisation, which was founded in 1944, that monitors exchange-rate developments, and provides a pool of international liquidity. Adoption of the adjustable-peg system was initially a condition of membership.

international reserves — Reserves.

international trade — Imports and exports.

investment (I) — Payment for work to be done that is for long-term benefit; expenditure that leads to an increase in the productive potential of the economy. Categories are fixed investment (new buildings and machinery), stocks (raw materials waiting to be used and finished goods waiting to be sold), and human investment (education and training).

invisible trade — Imports (Z) and exports (X) of services (not goods).

***IS* line** — The locus of combinations of levels of income (Y) and of interest rates (r) that lead to equilibrium output (Y_e).

Keynesian theory — Derived from the work of John Maynard Keynes, this approach is based on the critical role of the level of aggregate demand and on the belief that a satisfactory outcome in the macroeconomy is not automatic and may require substantial government intervention.

laissez-faire — The proposition, which is a part of the Classical theory, that the greatest economic welfare will result from non-intervention by the government so that the market is left to find its own equilibrium through the adjustment of prices.

legal tender — Any form of money which must, by law, be accepted in payment of a debt.

liability A claim on another firm or individual. A bank deposit is a liability to the bank (though an asset to the customer).

liquidity The ease with which an asset may be sold at a price known in advance.

liquidity preference The Keynesian theory of interest rates, in which bond prices (and, hence, interest rates) are determined by supply of and demand for bonds, which are determined by the form in which wealth-holders choose to hold their wealth.

liquidity trap A situation in which demand for money is infinite, because interest rates are at their minimum level. Since interest rates cannot fall and bond prices cannot rise, there is no incentive to hold bonds. In this situation, in which the money demand (M_D) function is horizontal, an increase in the money supply (M_S) does not decrease the level of interest rates (r), and *vice versa*.

***LM* line** The locus of combinations of levels of income (Y) and of interest rates (r) that lead to equilibrium interest rates (r_e).

long-term capital Flows of money between countries to pay for existing assets.

loose fiscal policy Fiscal policy that is intended to increase the level of aggregate demand (E_P).

loose monetary policy Monetary policy that is intended to increase the level of aggregate demand (E_P).

M1 In India, the value of notes and coins in circulation (outside the banks) plus the value of cheque accounts and other demand deposits at banks.

M4 In India, *M1* plus other deposits in banks and the post office.

macroeconomics The study of the behaviour of the whole of the economic system, rather than of its component parts.

managed floating exchange rate Dirty floating exchange rate.

marginal propensity to consume (MPC) ($\Delta C/\Delta Y_d$) The proportion of a change in disposable income (Y_d) that is spent on consumption (C).

marginal propensity to spend (MPE) $(\Delta E_P/\Delta Y)$	The proportion of a change in income (Y) that is spent (E_P).
marginal rate of tax $(\Delta T/\Delta Y)$	The proportion of a change in income (Y) that is paid in net tax (T).
market price	The price paid for goods and services at which demand is equal to supply.
microeconomics	The study of the behaviour of the component parts (households, firms, government, etc) of the economic system.
model	A simplified description of economic behaviour, usually expressed in a mathematical or diagrammatic form.
monetarism	The school of thought which believes that reducing the role of the government is likely to increase economic efficiency, that the most pressing economic problem is inflation, and that monetary policy is likely to be an effective anti-inflationary device.
monetarist	A supporter of monetarism
monetary policy	Government decisions that influence the money supply (M_S) by influencing the availability of loans.
monetary sterilisation	The returning (by open market operations) of the money supply to its level before intervention to maintain a fixed exchange rate.
money	Any commodity that is generally acceptable in settlement of debts.
money demand (M_D)	The quantity of money that people choose to hold. The categories are transactions balances ($M_D{}^T$), precautionary balances ($M_D{}^P$), and speculative balances ($M_D{}^S$).
money market	The demand for and supply of money and of financial assets.
money multiplier (MM)	The ratio of the value of additional bank deposits to the amount of an initial deposit of cash and, by inference, the ratio of an increase in the money supply to an increase in the amount of money created, by open market operations, by the Reserve Bank of India (the central bank).
money supply (M_S)	The quantity of money in the economic system, which may be defined as *M1* or *M4* or in some other way.

multiplier	The income-expenditure multiplier (*K*). A multiplier process occurs whenever the macroeconomic effect on a dependant variable differs from the size of the autonomous disturbance to another variable that caused it. Other important multipliers are the balanced budget multiplier and the money multiplier (MM).
National Income	Net National Product
natural rate of unemployment	The minimum amount of unemployment that monetarists believe will persist regardless of other circumstances.
net exports	The value of exports (*X*) minus the value of imports (*Z*).
Net National Product	Gross National Product minus capital consumption.
New Right	Monetarism.
nominal exchange rate (NER)	The value of a currency unit in terms of another currency or in terms of a weighted basket of currencies.
nominal GDP	Gross Domestic Product valued at current prices.
notes and coins	Tokens issued by the government for use as money.
open market operations	The buying or selling of securities by the government in order to change the money supply (M_S).
over-full employment	An output level that is above full employment, when employees are working very long hours each week, and may be doing work for which they are not adequately skilled. Machinery may also be over-worked.
overshooting	An excessive initial adjustment towards the equilibrium value of a variable that is subsequently corrected spontaneously.
parity	Peg.
peg	A fixed exchange rate that is specified by a government for its currency.
Phillips curve	A diagram showing the inverse relationship between the unemployment rate (as a percentage of the labour force) and the level of prices (*P*).
planned expenditure (E_P)	*Ex-ante* expenditure.

precautionary balances ($M_D{}^P$)	Money held to be spent if a disaster occurs.
price index	The ratio of the current price level to the price level in an earlier reference year.
price level (P)	A weighted average of prices of individual commodities.
prices and incomes policy	Direct controls on prices (including wage rates).
progressive income tax	Taxation of personal incomes such that the marginal rate of tax increases as the level of income increases.
quantity theory of money	The proposition, which is a part of the Classical theory, that the price level (P) is determined by the quantity of money (M_S) in circulation.
rate of exchange	Exchange rate.
rationing	Direct controls on the quantities of specified commodities that people are permitted to purchase.
real exchange rate (RER)	A measure of the international competitiveness of the output of a country.
real GDP	Gross Domestic Product valued at the prices that were current in an earlier reference year in order to enable comparisons to be made without being confused by the effects of inflation.
real market	The demand for and supply of goods and services.
real money supply	The nominal money supply divided by an index of the price level.
recession	Depression.
reserves	The stock of foreign money held by a government.
reserve ratio (RR)	The proportion of a bank's assets that is very liquid and not lent to customers. Banks' reserve assets include cash, discountable bills, and settlement accounts.
revaluation	An increase in the value of a currency unit for which a peg has been specified (the reverse of a devaluation).
savings (S)	The part of disposable income (Y_d) that is not spent on consumption (C). It is therefore the value of consumption that has been foregone in the current period in order to acquire resources for deferred spending. A negative value of savings implies that

	people are spending their accumulated wealth from previous periods' savings; this means that current consumption is greater than current disposable income.
Say's Law	The proposition, which is part of the Classical theory, that supply creates its own demand; production creates the means to buy output, so that whatever is produced will be purchased.
seasonal unemployment	Unemployment that occurs because of a seasonal pattern in the production process or in the level of demand.
short-term capital	Hot money.
slump	Depression.
Snake	An agreement between governments in western Europe, that lasted from 1972 to 1979, to stabilise the value of each of their currencies in terms of each of the other currencies within the group. The Snake was replaced by the exchange-rate mechanism of the European Monetary System.
speculation	The buying and selling of assets in the hope of making a gain.
speculative balances (M_D^S)	Money held in order to make a profit by avoiding the loss that would occur if an alternative asset, that was falling in price, was held.
sterilisation	Monetary sterilisation.
sticky prices	Prices that change infrequently and probably by an amount that is not sufficient to make supply and demand equal each other.
structural unemployment	Unemployment that arises because of changes in the structure of the economy, when labour is unable to adjust to new circumstances. People may have the wrong skills or be living in the wrong place.
supply of loanable funds (S_{ELF})	The amount of money that people wish to save from current income and lend at the current level of interest rates. According to the Classical theory, this is one of the determinants of the level of interest rates.
taxation (T)	Compulsory payments to the government that are not in return for the production of goods and services. Negative taxation comprises transfers by the government (including social security payments).

tight fiscal policy Fiscal policy that is intended to decrease the level of aggregate demand (E_P).

tight monetary policy Monetary policy that is intended to decrease the level of aggregate demand (E_P).

total final expenditure Aggregate demand (E_P); total expenditure on final output.

transactions balances (M_D^T) Money held in order to make payments.

transfer payments Payments that are not in return for the production of goods and services; examples are gifts, inheritances, gambling winnings, and sale of second-hand goods. Government transfers (negative taxation) include social security payments.

unemployment People who are not in paid work, who are both able and willing to work, and who are looking for employment.

value added The difference between the sum paid by a firm to other firms for services and materials and the sum received from its customers for output.

velocity of circulation (V) The average number of times per year that each rupee is used to make purchases.

visible trade Imports (Z) and exports (X) of goods (not services).

withdrawals (W) The part of (Y) that is not spent on consumption. The categories of withdrawals are net taxation (T) and savings (S), either or both of which may be negative.

yield The ratio of the annual income (interest or dividend) paid on a security to its market value.

Notation

This section lists the principal algebraic symbols that are used in this book.

Variables

C	Consumption expenditure
D_{LF}	Demand for loanable funds
E	Expenditure on current output $[C + I + G + (X - Z)]$
F	Net international capital outflow
G	Government expenditure on current output
I	Investment expenditure
J	Injections $[I + G + (X - Z)]$
M_D	Money demand $[M_D^P + M_D^S + M_D^T]$
M_S	Money supply
M_D^P	Demand for precautionary balances
M_D^S	Demand for speculative balances
M_D^T	Demand for transactions balances
P	Price level (weighted average)
r	Interest rate level (weighted average)
S	Savings
S_{LF}	Supply of loanable funds
T	Net tax revenue
V	Velocity of circulation of money

W	Withdrawals $[S + T]$
X	Expenditure on exports
Y	Income $[C + S + T]$
Y_d	Disposable income $[Y - T]$
Z	Expenditure on imports

With the exception of M_D, M_D^P, M_D^S, M_D^T, M_S, P, r, and V, the values of all the variables in the list are measured in money units per time period (for example, rupees per week, rupees per year). The values of M_D, M_D^P, M_D^S, M_D^T, and M_S are measured in money units at a moment in time. P and r are weighted averages, perhaps in index form, and V is measured per time period.

For some of the variables, the subscript e indicates the equilibrium level, the subscript P indicates the planned (*ex-ante*) level, an asterisk indicates the current level of a variable that is autonomously determined, the subscript O indicates a weighted average of relevant levels in other countries (and the absence of this subscript means that the variable refers to local data), and the subscript FE indicates the level corresponding to full employment. Examples are P_e, E_P, G^*, r_O, and Y_{FE}.

Parameters

a	Autonomous consumption expenditure (with respect to Y_d)
A	Autonomous expenditure $[(a - bv) + h + G^* + X^* - n]$ (with respect to Y)
b	Marginal propensity to consume (with respect to Y_d)
ez	Elasticity of demand for imports (with respect to prices)
f	Marginal propensity to invest (with respect to r)
g	Autonomous investment expenditure (with respect to Y and to r)
h	Autonomous investment expenditure (with respect to Y)
j	Marginal propensity to invest (with respect to Y)
K	Income-expenditure multiplier (with respect to A) $[\Delta Y_e/\Delta A]$
m	Marginal propensity to import (with respect to Y)
n	Autonomous expenditure on imports (with respect to Y)
p	Autonomous money demand (with respect to Y and to r)

q	Marginal propensity to demand money (with respect to Y)
s	Marginal propensity to demand money (with respect to r)
t	Marginal propensity to tax (with respect to Y)
u	Autonomous net international capital outflow (with respect to r)
v	Autonomous net tax revenue (with respect to Y)
w	Marginal propensity of net international outflow of capital (with respect to r)

Graphs (whose labels are not dependent variables such as C)

AD E_P as a function of P [the locus of *IS–LM* intersections]

AS Y as a function of P

BP Balance of payments constraint locus:

$$(X - Z) = F \quad \text{or} \quad ((X - Z) - F) = 0$$

IS Y equilibrium locus:

$$Y = E_P \quad \text{or} \quad W = \textit{ex-ante } J$$

LM r equilibrium locus:

$$M_D = M_S \quad \text{or} \quad (M_D{}^P + M_D{}^S + M_D{}^T) = M_S$$

Further Reading

Data

Important sources of Indian macroeconomic data include the Ministry of Statistics and Programme Implementation [www.mospi.gov.in] and the Reserve Bank of India [www.rbi.org.in]. In addition to extensive data, both of these sources provide detailed explanatory material.

World economic news is available at the internet site maintained by The Economist, London, UK [www.economist.com].

The International Monetary Fund [www.imf.org], Washington DC, USA, is probably the best source of macroeconomic data for each of the 189 nations and territories that are members of the IMF.

Theory and Recent Experience

There is, of course, a very large number of excellent books on theoretical and applied macroeconomics. This is not an attempt to list all of the important books in this area. The intention here is merely to list a small number of them which are of particular interest to the author and with which readers of this book might be unfamiliar. Each of the books listed contains numerous references to other books.

A good source on the Keynesian real-market (*IS*) and money-market (*LM*) models, the nature and importance of money, and the characteristics of macroeconomic data is:

David Rowan, *Output, Inflation and Growth* (Macmillan Press Ltd, London, UK, 1983).

The Keynesian revolution, and its effects and historical context, are described in:

Michael Stewart, *Keynes and After* (Penguin Books Ltd, Harmondsworth, UK, 1986).

The Keynesian-monetarist controversy is discussed in:

David Smith, *The Rise and Fall of Monetarism* (Penguin Books Ltd, Harmondsworth, UK, 1987).

Keith Cuthbertson, Macroeconomic Policy: The New Cambridge, Keynesian and Monetarist Controversies (Macmillan Press Ltd, London, UK, 1979).

The principal schools of macroeconomic thought are summarised in:

Steven Pressman, *Fifty Major Economists,* (Routledge, London, UK, 1999).

A thorough introduction to monetary economics is:

Keith Bain and Peter Howells, *Monetary Economics: Policy and its Theoretical Basis* (Palgrave Macmillan Ltd, Basingstoke, UK, 2003).

For a discussion of the strengths and weaknesses of prices and incomes policies, see:

Hugh Clegg, *How to Run an Incomes Policy (and why we made such a mess of the last one)* (Heinemann Educational Books Ltd, London, UK, 1971).

An explanation of galloping inflation is in:

Phillip Cagan, "The Theory of Hyperinflation" in Robert Ball and Peter Doyle (ed): *Inflation* (Penguin Books Ltd, Harmondsworth, UK, 1969).

An excellent source on exchange rates and related issues is:

Brian Tew, *The Evolution of the International Monetary System, 1945-85* (Hutchinson and Company (Publishers) Ltd, London, UK, 1985).

Recent issues concerning exchange-rate policy are discussed in:

Jerry Mushin, "Predicting Monetary Unions", *International Journal of Economic Research*, Vol 5, No 1, January 2008.

Jerry Mushin, "The Euro and its Antecedents", in Robert Whaples (ed), *Encyclopedia of Economic and Business History*, Miami University, USA, 2007. [www.eh.net/encyclopedia]

Jerry Mushin, "The Uncertain Prospect of Asian Monetary Integration", *International Economics and Finance Journal*, Vol 1, No 1, June 2006.

Jerry Mushin, "The Deceptive Resilience of Fixed Exchange Rates", *Journal of Economics, Business and Law*, Vol 6, No 1, March 2004.

Jerry Mushin, "Exchange-Rate Policy and the Efficacy of Aggregate Demand Management", *The Business Economist*, Vol 33, No 2, July 2002.

Jerry Mushin, "A Taxonomy of Fixed Exchange Rates", *Australian Stock Exchange Perspective*, Vol 7, No 2, January 2001.

Jerry Mushin, "Exchange-Rate Stability and the Euro", *New Zealand Banker*, Vol 11, No 4, June 1999.

Jerry Mushin, "Exchange-Rate Policy in the South Pacific", *Journal of Industrial Affairs*, Vol 4, No 2, December 1995.

Index